ASIAN DEFENCE REVIEW 2012

ASIAN DEFENCE REVIEW 2012

Edited by

Air Commodore
Jasjit Singh
AVSM, VrC, VM (Retd)

KNOWLEDGE WORLD
KW Publishers Pvt Ltd
New Delhi

in association with

Centre for Air Power Studies
New Delhi

2011 FPBA BEST PUBLISHERS AWARD (ENGLISH)

The Centre for Air Power Studies is an independent, non-profit, academic research institution established in 2002 under a registered Trust to undertake and promote policy-related research, study and discussion on the trends and developments in defence and military issues, especially air power and the aerospace arena, for civil and military purposes. Its publications seek to expand and deepen the understanding of defence, military power, air power and aerospace issues without necessarily reflecting the views of any institution or individuals except those of the authors.

Jasjit Singh
Director General
Centre for Air Power Studies
P-284, Arjan Path
Subroto Park
New Delhi 110010

Tele: (91-11) 25699131
E-mail: diroffice@aerospaceindia.org

Published in India by
Kalpana Shukla
KW Publishers Pvt Ltd
4676/21, First Floor, Ansari Road, Daryaganj, New Delhi 110002
T: +91.11.23263498 / 43528107 **E:** knowledgeworld@vsnl.net • www.kwpub.com

ISBN 978-93-81904-56-5

Printed and Bound in India

Contents

Contributors

Shri **Kanwal Sibal**, Former Ambassador and Foreign Secretary.

Dr **Manpreet Sethi**, Senior Fellow, Centre for Air Power Studies.

Air Marshal **TM Asthana** PVSM AVSM VM (retd), Former Commander-in-Chief, Strategic Forces Command & currently Distinguished Fellow, Centre for Air Power Studies.

Dr **Shalini Chawla**, Senior Fellow, Centre for Air Power Studies.

Dr **Sitakanta Mishra**, Research Fellow, Centre for Air Power Studies.

Air Marshal **PV Athawale** PVSM AVSM VSM (retd), Former Air Officer Commanding-in-Chief, Maintenance Command, IAF & currently Distinguished Fellow, Centre for Air Power Studies.

Group Captain **Manoj Kumar** VSM, Senior Fellow and Ms **Dhanasree Jayaram**, Associate Fellow at Centre for Air Power Studies.

Wing Commander **Nishant Gupta**, Research Fellow, Centre for Air Power Studies.

Ms **Debalina Chatterjee**, Associate Fellow, Centre for Air Power Studies.

Commodore **MR Khan** AVSM (retd), Senior Fellow, Centre for Air Power Studies.

Dr **Stuti Banerjee**, Associate Fellow, Centre for Air Power Studies.

1

India-China Relations: Problems And Prospects

Kanwal Sibal

China's extraordinarily rapid rise in the hierarchy of global power is raising concerns about its future policies. Opinion is divided on whether China will increasingly assert its power in disruptive ways or will act more responsibly as its own stakes in the international system grow. Arguments can be made for both views, though emerging signs suggest that China's self-assertion is becoming an unpleasant reality, whereas the expectation that it will work for, and within, a global consensus remains more a matter of hope.

A rising China presents both a threat and an opportunity. The dilemma for India, the US, Japan, the major European countries and others is how to find a balance between engaging China to build on the positives and constraining it to ward off the negatives.

China's economic and commercial expansion is making it a crucial country in global trade and financial flows. The opportunities provided by the huge and growing Chinese market cannot be ignored by governments and corporations. At the same time, with recession and unemployment in the Western countries, concerns about China's mercantilist approach, its Intellectual Property Rights (IPR) violations and resort to unfair competition are growing. The accumulation of huge foreign exchange reserves by China has led to demands by the West of financial rebalancing, revaluation of the Chinese currency and a shift in China's export led strategy towards stimulation of domestic demand. At the same time, with the Eurozone in crisis, China is being wooed to invest in European securities to alleviate the sovereign debt crisis there.

China's growing military strength is a natural fall-out of its phenomenal economic growth in the last thirty years. The weight of the People's Liberation Army (PLA) in decision-making in the country is causing muscle-flexing by China sooner than expected. The political fiction of China's peaceful rise is being exposed by its aggressive maritime claims in the South China Sea as well as stepped up claims on Indian territory, causing great anxiety in its neighbourhood.

India, with geographical contiguity with China since its occupation of Tibet in 1950, is directly affected by the various dimensions of China's rise. Its dilemmas are somewhat sharper than those of others because of this contiguity and the nature of the issues involved in the relationship.

India's China problem began with its failure to properly assess the security implications of the takeover of Tibet in 1950 by Maoist China. For the first time in history, a political and geographical buffer between China and India was being removed. In the absence of a formally demarcated border in the western sector in Jammu and Kashmir and China's position on the McMahon Line in the east, its occupation of Tibet should have warned us of the dangers ahead.

Within 12 years of its entry into Tibet, China imposed a border conflict on India, whereas without territorial contiguity, the two countries had no conflict between them for thousands of years. In fact, they interacted culturally very productively over centuries through the spread of Buddhism in China. The Indian and Chinese civilisations even marked the wider space between them without conflict or rivalry—the culture of Southeast Asia—and gave this region the name of Indo-China.

The 1962 border conflict came as a political shock to India as India had bent over backwards ever since its own independence and the Maoist revolution in China to reach out to the Communist regime and accommodate it bilaterally and regionally, whether by immediately recognising it, supporting its rightful entry into the United Nations, recognising Tibet as an autonomous region of China or holding China's hands at Bandung and helping to alleviate the fears of the Southeast Asian countries of the Communist take-over of this large country.

India made a crucial mistake in signing the 1954 Trade Agreement with the Tibet region of China that accepted, in effect, China's sovereignty over Tibet, without linking this vital concession to either a settlement of the boundary with Tibet or at least an agreement on the framework of a settlement. India should have anticipated that sooner or later, China would extend its physical control upto the geographical frontiers of Tibet as it perceived them or as they suited its strategic needs.

China's unilateral action in altering the ground situation by constructing the Aksai Chin road in Ladakh prompted India to hedge against further encroachments and *fait accomplis* by extending its presence and authority in remote areas hitherto left unoccupied. Its strategy failed with the Chinese decision to "teach India a lesson" in the 1962 border conflict which scarred India politically, militarily and psychologically.

The border issue is at the core of India's mistrust of China and the uncertainty about its future intentions. That two large rising countries should have an unsettled 3,000 km plus long border between them is a recipe for instability, tensions and even conflict. China is deliberately keeping the border issue unresolved so that it can continue to serve as a pressure point on India. It has kept changing its position on possible solutions, entailing India into interminable discussions of principles and guidelines that it interprets as suits its interests.

Any realistic solution to the border issue has to be based on the ground realities. As the long border is not permanently manned, each side has its own view of the border areas it actually controls and this generates periodic tensions. The understanding reached between the two sides some years ago to exchange maps of their respective perceptions of the Line of Actual Control (LAC) in order to identify the physical extent of the disputed areas was suddenly terminated by the Chinese side without explanation. During Prime Minister Vajpayee's visit to China in 2003, India proposed a "political solution" to the issue, to which end Special Representatives(SRs) of the two countries were nominated and given a mandate to establish a set of guidelines (which they have done) for proceeding towards resolution. The SRs have met **15** times without any real breakthrough. On the contrary, the Chinese have exploited the opening given to them to demand transfer of inhabited Indian territory—the Tawang tract—not actually under its control to China for "political" reasons. **China has, in effect, hollowed out the purpose of setting up the SR mechanism by expanding its agenda beyond the border dispute to the "strategic" relationship between the two countries. Meanwhile, in efforts to stabilise the relationship, the two sides have agreed to a hot line between the two leaders and a new mechanism at the Foreign Office level to contain any escalation of incidents at the border. India and China have also agreed to maritime cooperation in the Indian Ocean area with piracy in mind.**

In 1962, China withdrew from Tawang and the rest of Arunachal Pradesh largely to what is the McMahon Line, thereby *de facto* accepting its validity. In the western sector, it did not go back to the pre-1962 line and retained the fruits of its aggression. If it needed to hold Tawang for religious or security reasons or felt that its legal claim was rock solid, it would not have withdrawn; 50 years later, to demand the cession of Tawang exposes China's chicanery. China can, if it wants, solve the border issue on the same basis as it has done with Myanmar, Russia as well as with the Central Asian countries, with very nominal territorial adjustments.

The extent of Chinese cynicism is reflected in its specious claim on Tawang because of its Tibetan links and the fact that one of the earlier Dalai Lamas, an institution that it has tried to destroy politically, was born there. Its pretence that it raises the Tawang issue in deference to Tibetan sentiments flies in the face of the Dalai Lama's public position that Tawang belongs to India, as well as the 2008 Tibetan revolt against China's rule. The current incidents of self-immolation by Tibetan monks in the larger Tibetan region testify to the deep alienation of the Tibetan people with Chinese rule. Instead of seriously negotiating with the Dalai Lama to resolve the festering issue of denial of political and cultural rights of a distinctive people and the suppression of their separate identity, the Chinese are using Tibet as the platform to make territorial demands on India.

Unfortunately, India is unwilling to politically back the Dalai Lama out of concern for the repercussions of such a policy on India-China relations. There is no international pressure either on China to negotiate with the Dalai Lama. China can revile him as a "splittist", even when he has publicly reaffirmed on various occasions his acceptance of Chinese sovereignty and has limited his demand only to real autonomy. An honourable deal between China and the Dalai Lama is good for China, Tibet and India-China relations.

With China's unwillingness to settle the border issue and our incapacity to force the issue, India has tried to stabilise the situation on the border as much as possible through the Agreements on Maintaining Peace and Tranquillity and on Confidence Building Measures of the 1990s. These have contained but also frozen the border problem to India's disadvantage. The status quo favours the side not anxious for change. India wants peace on the border but also wants a border settlement. It suits China also to have peace as it defuses the border issue politically and militarily for the period China needs to consolidate its rise while giving it a free hand to settle Tibet internally.

If China raises territorial issues with India provocatively, it is because China has the confidence of a stronger hand. Militarily, China has advantage on the border because of the easier terrain on its side and vastly better infrastructure that now includes a railway line to Lhasa for easier and quicker movement of troops and war material. In the western sector, it holds a line beyond its own claims. In the eastern sector, it withdrew voluntarily in 1962 to its present position and now claims more territory as part of "meaningful" territorial adjustments. It plays the Tibet card against us without any complex, as all its claims on us are on Tibet's behalf. It is undeterred by the fact that its own position in Tibet is contested by the Dalai Lama and the Tibetan people.

Unlike Pakistan's position vis-a-vis us, India has not made the resolution of the border dispute a pre-condition for normalising bilateral ties with China. This gives China reduced incentive to reach a settlement. While we may see our approach as mature, constructive and contributing to peace, the Chinese could easily view it as yielding and conciliatory. China, thus, profits from our diffidence, believing that time is on its side. Its posture on the border keeps us off-balance, politically and militarily, while imposing economic costs on us, all of which retards our nation building effort.

Periodic reports of China making incursions into our territory raise jitters in India, recalling the trauma of 1962. To defuse the political fall-out, the government defensively claims that the incidents are confined to areas where the two sides have differing perceptions about the LAC. The rational approach of delineating the respective perceptions on the map, identifying the pockets of overlapping claims and then proceeding to find a solution have been rejected by the Chinese. The "political" approach proposed by India in 2003 has perversely allowed China to increase its appetite by claiming territory not under its control, with the result that the Special Representatives are not able to move forward. During his visit to India in December 2010, ostensibly to defuse mounting tensions, Premier Wen delivered the hard message that it may not be possible to ever resolve the boundary issue fully.

Rather than work to create a favourable political atmosphere for resolving boundary differences, China has poisoned it by asserting its claim over the whole of Arunachal Pradesh as a matter of principle and on Tawang in particular. The airing of this claim on the eve of President Hu Jintao's visit to India in 2006 showed China's scant regard for ground realities as well as Indian political sensitivities. China has upped the ante by broadening its bilateral differences over Arunachal Pradesh by raising them in a multilateral forum like the Asian Development Bank by objecting to the bank financing a small irrigation project there.

India's belated decision in the face of provocative Chinese territorial claims to improve the infrastructure in the border regions, activate airfields, position advanced aircraft as well as augment ground forces, have aroused reactions from Chinese analysts and newspapers. Even though it is claimed that opinion in China is no longer monolithic, such articles cannot appear in defiance of party or governmental thinking. Some condescending commentaries have appeared in the Chinese press warning of a repetition of 1962 if India continues to provoke China by asserting its sovereignty over Arunachal Pradesh. Even the break-up of India into several states has been advocated. Such writings have not appeared in China's state controlled press for years but some observers do not rule out China fomenting some border trouble, if only to deflect attention from its mounting internal problems. If India has increased its military capacity along the border compared to the past, it is essentially defensive in character and calculated to avoid a repetition of 1962.

The water issue between India and China looms as a major point of contention in the future given China's plans to build dams on the Brahmaputra in Tibet and divert its waters to the water deficit northern part of the country in what will be a colossal engineering feat. China's forays into the Indian Ocean, its efforts to establish port facilities in key strategic points there which later can be upgraded to naval facilities, its plans to obtain access to the sea through Myanmar and Pakistan in order to partially resolve its "Malacca dilemma", are all issues with a bearing on India's security.

Pakistan has been a willing pawn in China's hands to thwart India's ambitions and keep it boxed in South Asia. Without being seen as confronting India directly and generating an atmosphere of open hostility—which does not suit its strategy of presenting its rise as peaceful—it lets Pakistan do this. By making Pakistan nuclear and giving it weapon delivery capability, China has neutralised India strategically within South Asia itself. Pakistan has been given the means to continue its politics of confronting India without India being able to retaliate militarily even though it enjoys conventional military superiority.

By building up a countervailing military power in India's neighbourhood, China has used Pakistan to prevent India from exerting its leadership role even within South Asia. China opposed the India-US nuclear deal on the ground that it was discriminatory towards Pakistan. The depth of its strategic commitment to Pakistan is demonstrated by the fact that contrary to its Nuclear Suppliers Group (NSG) obligations, it has announced the decision to build two additional nuclear power plants in Pakistan. It wants to give Pakistan the benefit of international civilian nuclear cooperation without going through the NSG process and without imposition of non-proliferation conditions on it, even though that country has become the hot-bed of terrorism, Islamic extremism and clandestine nuclear proliferation. It is widely suspected that civilian nuclear cooperation with Pakistan is a convenient cover to continue assisting it in its strategic programmes.

While indirectly questioning India's sovereignty over Jammu and Kashmir by issuing stapled visas to residents of the state or those associated with it officially (a practice the Chinese state they will discontinue but the political point has already been made), China deals with Pakistan Occupied Kashmir(POK) and the Gilgit-Baltistan(GB) area as if Pakistan sovereignty there is undisputed and secure. It is getting involved in massive road building and hydel projects, disregarding Indian objections. India cannot but see the increased Chinese footprint in Pakistan Occupied Kashmir (POK), which includes the Northern Territories, as a threat of military encirclement in Jammu and Kashmir (J&K), especially as India and China are already in confrontation in the Aksai Chin area. Our Army Chief has publicly expressed concern about the presence of 3,000-4,000 Chinese, including PLA, troops, in POK.

With energy security and the unrest in Sinkiang in view, China has begun to look at this territory illegally occupied by Pakistan with even greater strategic interest than before. Uighur separatists can be kept under a watchful eye from there, while through

Gwadar, oil and gas from the Gulf can be transported to bordering Sinkiang. China can link up its interests in Afghanistan too through this contiguous area. China would, therefore, want Pakistan's hold over this region consolidated, economically and legally.

While massive infrastructure projects help achieve the former goal, questioning and contesting India's legal status in J&K serves the latter objective as it puts India on the defensive and erodes its *locus standi* in challenging Pakistan's illegal possession of POK and GB. With its new stakes in mind, China aims to become an inescapable factor in any India-Pakistan final settlement of the Kashmir issue, with the objective, in such an eventuality, of denying India any future role in Pakistani held territory.

Moreover, by entrenching itself in this region firmly, China would want to be able to protect its strategic investment in it, should the Pakistani state slide increasingly towards failure. China would not have made such large investments in POK if it did not intend to eventually protect them diplomatically and, if required, militarily. China protests if international institutions fund even minor development projects in Arunachal Pradesh on the ground that it is "disputed" territory, but does not apply its own logic to the development projects of magnitude that it is funding in POK.

With its increased political, economic and military weight, China is stepping up its presence in countries around India. In Afghanistan, China intends investing heavily in the mineral sector and a railway link. It is likely to accept an opening to the Taliban as an insurance for the stakes it is developing in Afghanistan within the framework of its strategic relations with Pakistan.

China has used a judicious mix of propaganda about Indian hegemony, the natural sense of insecurity of small countries under the shadow of a large one, religious and ethnic differences as well as economic and military assistance to add to pressures on India from within the region. In Nepal, it is becoming more assertive in demanding equal treatment with India in terms of our respective treaties with that country. With the Maoists now a powerful political force in Nepal, and given their ideological compulsion to be seen as drawing Nepal closer to China, coupled with their periodic statements calculated to inflame public opinion against India, the political terrain has become more favourable for China. This can only make India's task in handling Nepal more difficult.

China's position in Bangladesh is entrenched. Even Sheikh Hasina's friendly government would see it in its interest to maintain close ties with a rising China and the benefits that can bring, including giving India an incentive to woo Bangladesh more. China has earned the gratitude of the Sri Lankan government by supplying it arms that helped in defeating the Liberation Tigers of Tamil Eelam (LTTE). Sri Lanka, along with Myanmar, Bangladesh and Maldives, are targets for China's naval ambitions in the

Indian Ocean area to protect its vital lines of communication through these waters. The so-called "string of pearls" strategy, with commercial goals in view in the short term and military goals in the longer term, includes construction of new port facilties in select countries. To promote these objectives, China is bound to step up further its engagement with these countries, especially with increasing material means at its disposal, posing further challenges to India's interests in its neighbourhood.

China's penetration of Myanmar, its expanded presence in Iran and economic domination of Central Asian countries, all present a regional scenario for India that would limit India's future margin of manoeuvre, politically and economically.

China's policies and conduct tax the Indian government's effort to temper domestic reaction and maintain a friendly posture towards its northern neighbour. There is some disconnect between the government's positive, and even exonerating, discourse on China and the general public sentiment towards that country. The government may be right at one level to pursue an accommodating approach as India cannot afford to have tense borders with both China and Pakistan. If China needs peaceful borders for pursuing its development goals, India needs them even more. We have two inimical neighbours who are collaborating to contain India strategically. Tensions with at least one of them have to be reduced to the extent possible so that the military, political and economic burden on India is lightened. The government has allowed economic contacts to develop with China to the point that the country has become our largest trading partner in goods. China has exploited this Indian compulsion by pursuing a policy of containing India under cover of engagement, of touting a strategic partnership while gravely undermining us strategically, of inducing us to accept politically that it does not pose a threat to us and yet threatening our territorial integrity as well as our vital interests in our neighbourhood. If India's soft policies on China continue, China can conveniently treat India as a tactical piece in its larger design of deflecting concerns about its frenetic rise as a formidable power.

The settlement of the border issue would open doors wide for an across the board cooperation between the two countries, but China obviously does not see the need for combining our respective strengths to alter the global landscape to our advantage. China wants to keep India under pressure, give itself space to browbeat it when required and put it in a position where it has to appeal to Chinese goodwill for securing its international ambitions as was the case when India sought China's support in the NSG for international civilian nuclear cooperation and for its bid for permanent membership of the UN Security Council. China wants to slow down as much as possible India's rise to regional and global status.

Many arguments can be made in favour of not only normalisation of relations between India and China, but a strong entente between the two. Imagine the two most populous countries in the world, with two-fifths of humanity between them, growing energetically at close to double digit figures, integrating themselves rapidly with the global economy, with increasing claims on the world's resources to fuel their future growth, having a community of interest in tackling the problems at the forefront of international concern—environment, climate change, terrorism, religious extremism, pandemics, UN functioning, etc—working in tandem on the global stage. This would shift the global balance of power decisively towards Asia. But Sino-Indian differences have greater debilitating effect on India as compared to China as the gap in our respective national power has widened. China can offer economically more and it can intimidate more . It has a certain vision of its own preeminence and the romantic notion of two Asian giants working together to change the global landscape appeals little to the authoritarians in Beijing.

China's handling of its differences with India makes sense from the Chinese point of view. It has the upper hand on the border and its military infrastructure there is far superior. It already possesses large swathes of Indian territory. The economic gap between the two countries, already huge, is growing. China's economic integration with the world is far deeper than India's, giving others much greater stake in it as compared to us. It has successfully contained India by bolstering Pakistan against us with nuclear weapon and missile technology transfers. It has insidiously used other neighbours to prevent India from consolidating its leadership in South Asia. If it settles the border issue with India, it will release india from a two-front bind, supposedly expose Pakistan to increased Indian pressure at a time when it has become more vulnerable, lose leverage with other neighbours of India who will move into the Indian orbit more decisively and free India to pursue its regional and global ambitions more confidently. This would inevitably be at the cost of China's preeminence in Asia and at the global level. China may think it has more to gain than lose by a policy of thwarting India even as it engages it.

India too is engaging China but lacks the resolve to look for options for containing it. We cannot seek to contain China alone. We can, of course, build up our military strength, especially our strategic capability against China. This, in time, will help to "contain" Chinese ambitions. But we need to immediately join hands with others who too fear China's rise and the resurgence of nationalism in the country.

China reacted strongly to the attempt some years ago to build a qadrilateral arrangement among Asian democracies—India, Japan, Australia—along with the US, with Singapore thrown in. Australia retreated quickly, followed by Japan. President Obama has begun to talk of a better geo-political balance in Asia. India has to play a sophisiticated game of hedging its bets against China in a pragmatic manner. Apart from strengthening relations with Japan, South Korea and Vietnam, India has to reinforce its Look East policy as much as possible. Increased cooperation with the US Navy in the Indian Ocean would be part of containing the disruptive consequences of a rising China that is territorially expansionist and one that is at times accused of having a 19th century balance of power outlook.

Formulating a policy towards China that finds the right balance between engagement and resistance is not easy. We are obliged to engage with China as it is fast on the road to becoming the world's number two power. The balance of power in Asia has already shifted towards it in significant measure in the last couple of decades. Its inroads into the Gulf area, Africa and Latin America are now giving it a higher global profile. It has become the world's biggest exporting country; it has accumulated huge financial surpluses which it is using to secure access to raw materials across the globe, those that it needs to fuel its future needs. Its spectacular economic growth continues even as the advanced industrial countries are in the throes of a serious economic depression, tilting global financial power in its favour, especially as the US' financial health has become unduly dependent on China's investment of its surpluses in US securities. It is not surprising that China's position as a global manufacturing hub and its export over-drive have had a sizeable impact on neighbouring India too as China has become India's largest trading partner in goods.

As part of its engagement strategy, India holds a regular high level political dialogue at the bilateral level, including a bilateral strategic dialogue of sorts. India also engages with China in multilateral groupings such as the Russia-India-China dialogue and the Brazil-Russia-India-China-South Africa dialogue. The most recent Brazil, Russia, India, China and Singapore (BRICS) summit was held in New Delhi in March this year. At this summit, consensus could be reached by India, China and the other three countries on greater representation of emerging and developing countries in global governance, and concern was shared about the economic and financial policies of developed countries spilling over negatively into the emerging market economies. The slow pace of International Monetary Fund (IMF) quota reforms was criticised. The creation of a new development bank for infrastructure projects in BRICS and other developing economies was discussed and an agreement on extending credits in local currency under the BRICS Interbank Cooperation mechanism was reached. All these are initial steps to obtain a greater say in managing the global financial system and diluting the supremacy of the dollar, even as it is clear that progress on this will be slow and the biggest beneficiary will be China. Regrettably, Chinese reticence explains the absence of support from this group for India's (and Brazil's) candidature for permanent UN Security Council (UNSC) membership. This reflects the as yet unsettled political equations within the group that will detract from its global impact.

At the East Asia Summit and Association of Southeast Asian Nations (ASEAN) linked forums like ASEAN Regional Forum (ARF), India and China are working together without mutual grating. China now has observer status at the South Asian Association for Regional Cooperation (SAARC), notwithstanding our past paranoia about China's intrusions into our geographical space. Peace and tranquillity on the border are being maintained despite periodic testing of our nerves by the Chinese in "disputed" areas along the Line of Actual Control (LAC). Bilateral Confidence Building Measures (CBMs) now include limited joint military exercises. The two countries also cooperate on climate change and World Trade Organisation (WTO) negotiations.

China has become India's largest trading partner in goods, with bilateral trade reaching **over $70 billion in 2011** and expected to reach $100 billion by 2015. The economic dimension of the relationship has acquired a new dynamic with the institutionalising of a Strategic Economic Dialogue between the two countries—the second round of which will be held this year—and the setting up of a Chief Executive Officers (CEOs) Forum. China has become a powerful player in two vital sectors of the Indian economy—the power and telecommunications sectors—despite security concerns. India wants to have a manageable relationship with China.

India-China trade relations have expanded phenomenally in recent years, raising hopes that such increase in mutual stakes may help resolve outstanding political differences. This proposition has to be persuasively tested because the virtual economic and financial fusion of the US and Chinese economies has not ended serious political differences betwen the two, nor has the massive Japan-China economic relationship softened the undercurrents of Chinese hostility towards Japan.

In our case, although bilateral trade has reached an impressive figure, the ballooning trade deficit($20billion) with China imposes a limit on trade expansion unless the trade becomes more balanced, which would mean China giving more opportunities to Indian companies in its home market. Pro-China economic lobbies in India have, however, emerged. With an economic giant rising next to us, there are those in India who advocate an enlightened policy of taking maximum advantage of this development for sustaining our own growth rates, with the least amount of restrictions consistent with basic security.

In many areas of manufacturing, China can now provide world class equipment—in the power and telecommunication sectors, for instance—at much lower prices compared to Western equipment. But there are security concerns about sourcing telecommunication equipment from China, though the pro-China business lobby in India feels that such concerns are exaggerated. There is wariness about allowing Chinese companies to operate in "sensitive" areas, whether those close to our borders or near military centres and installations. China's practice of using its unskilled and semi-skilled labour to undertake projects abroad has run into problems in India. The mounting trade deficit with China is becoming unsustainable, more so as China restricts opportunities for our Information Technology (IT) and pharmaceutical companies in its domestic market. China's dumping practice is another source of irritation in relations. China's effort to corner a sizeable chunk of the Indian market through artificially low priced products is threatening competition and endangering domestic industry. China's interest in a Free Trade Agreement (FTA) with India is not looked at positively by us.

China's strategy of integrating its provincial economies with neighbouring regional economies, and creating the infrastructure to make this possible, presents problems for us. China can strengthen its market presence in our neighbourhood at our cost, besides becoming a magnet for our own border regions.

At the international level, it is easier to work out cooperative strategies in climate change or WTO negotiations, for instance, because there is no direct clash of interests. On the contrary, both countries can exert their joint weight to counter pressures from advanced industrial economies. But such cooperation in specific areas should not make us lose perspective on the total content of our relations.

China, as things are, is India's adversary, even if at the government level we avoid characterising our relations with our powerful neighbour in these terms. On the face of it, India has all the attributes to be in the same league as China, whether it is physical or demographic size, skills or civilisational depth. But China has outstripped India as a rising power, and the gap already existing between us will continue to grow in at least the decade and a half ahead. China is better organised, more puposeful in formulating policies and implementing them, and much less constrained by domestic public opinion.

Militarily, China has developed capacities that we will find difficult to match. China has rivalry with the US in mind, and the sinews it develops to pursue that will take care of any developing Indian challenge. No doubt, China does not currently have access to Western conventional defence technology because af an arms embargo imposed by the Western countries on it after the Tiananmen events. It is not able to secure from Russia the kind of platforms and weaponry that Russia readily supplies to us. But it has developed an indigenous defence production base that is impressive. In ballistic missile and nuclear weapon technologies, China has forged ahead of India decisively.

India has taken a substantial step forward in acquiring a credible nuclear deterrent capability against China with its recent successful Agni V test. The Indian press played up unnecessarily the China dimension of this missile, provoking Chinese press reactions to the effect that China was much ahead of India in missile capability and warning India not to be arrogant, apart from seeking to incite Western opinion against the Agni V by suggesting that India was downplaying the actual inter-continental range of the missile. The reaction of the Chinese government has been unusually sober, emphasising the cooperative nature of the India-China relationship and shared interests.

The Agni V should have in reality caused no surprise to the Chinese as India has been transparent about its Agni missile programme and the planned range of 5,000 km. India is also developing a sea-based long range missile for its nuclear powered submarine under development. China, in any case, possesses missiles with even longer range. Earlier, it was India that was vulnerable to Chinese missiles and now the reverse will be true, creating a better balance in deterrence.

The US' reaction to the Agni V reflects the new quality of India-US bilateral relations. In the 1990s and early 2000s, the US was pressing India to curb its missile programme because it was seen as destabilising. The thinking today is entirely different. While avoiding any specific disapproval of India's step, the US has lauded India's non-proliferation credentials and underlined its no-first use policy, which would suggest that India's missile advance is actually seen as serving US interests too in creating a better Sino-Indian strategic balance in the years ahead.

Even if China has a headstart over India, and in terms of "national power" is much more potent than us, India's steady economic rise, its human resource, the dynamism of its corporate sector and the size of its domestic market are elements playing in our favour. India too has weathered the current global slump well. Indeed, India and China are seen as two countries that the global economy counts on for easing the strains of the ongoing economic depression by their continued growth.

India is planning to spend huge amounts in the coming years on infrastructure development, an area in which it has been deficient so far. This will erode the advantage China has at present with its highly modern infrastructure. As labour costs in China go up, and other aspects of doing business in China begin to weigh more in the calculus of foreign investors such as absence of a well defined legal system, violation of IPR, lack of sufficient access to China's domestic market, etc. attention will move increasingly towards India, especially if India begins to address those physical and procedural deficiencies that discourage the inflow of foreign investment in large volumes. Countries like Japan, which are the biggest foreign investors in China are now looking at India.

China's export led growth model is considered unsustainable in the long run. The question is to what extent China can control the transition to a different model without serious internal disruptions. China's mercantilist approach does not endear it to other competing countries. The West has begun to see China's rise with mounting concern. These international sentiments play in India's favour. As a democratic country, with ways of doing business the West finds more congenial, and with financial and managerial experts ensconced in Western corporations, banks and financial institutions that can mediate business and investment between India and these countries, India's growth is seen with less trepidation. In certain sectors of the knowledge economy, we have a head start over China and this advantage we will enjoy for some time. Experts are generally agreed that by about 2025, as China's economic growth slows down and ours accelerates, the existing gap between the two economies will get very substantially reduced. At the same time, India's hunger for raw materials, especially energy resources, will pit it increasingly against Chinese competition in the years ahead. Our political leadership tries to minimise the prospects for such future rivalry by stating diplomatically that there is enough space for both India and China to grow without treading on each other's toes.

In China, a politically closed system works alongside an open economic system. Political dissent is smothered, but not economic enterprise. China accepts that the West can help in the modernisation of its economy, but must not ask for the modernisation of its politics. Its politics must cling to an outdated ideology, though its economics can be heartlessly pragmatic. How can this kind of contradiction endure in a country that is set to become the number two power in the world? When the rest of the world cedes so much space to China peacefully, it is not unreasonable for it to expect a reassuring change in how China governs itself and how it relates to its external environment.

Given China's size, its view of itself in historical terms, its claims on India, on Taiwan, in the South China Sea, its rancour against Japan, etc, its rise has wide regional and international implications. While a policy of containing China would be imprudent, it cannot be given a free hand in Asia. Other players in the region have to caution China about the political and other costs of seeking domination. Any initiative to that end serves India's interests even as its engagement with China continues. However, engagement does not mean acquiescence to Chinese hegemony in Asia.

China is manifestly a revisionist power that, to begin with, wants to change the status quo in its periphery where it has the capacity to make its power felt more immediately. It has begun to flex its muscles, most notably, in the South China Sea, over most of which it now claims sovereignty. It is locked up in maritime disputes with Japan, Vietnam, Malaysia and the Philippines over the Spratly and Paracel Islands. It has upped the political and security ante by unilaterally declaring the South China Sea as constituting its core national interest. Its claims are based on its own version of history and legality, which, of course, is contested by its other maritime neighbours.

In the South China Sea, China has larger strategic goals. It has so far been bottled up in these waters by the chain of islands ringing it in the east: Japan, Taiwan and the Phillipines. It cannot be a major naval power if it remains so confined. The blue water navy that it is developing needs unhindered access to the Pacific as well as the Indian Ocean, both to protect its vital trade and energy life-lines as well as to challenge the sway the US Navy enjoys over these oceans, the Pacific in particular. China has plans to operate a number of aircraft carriers, the first of which has begun sea-trials. It is expanding its conventional and nuclear submarine fleet and modernising its destroyer and frigate fleet.

China must be able, initially, to deny the US the level of domination it has so far exercised in the South China Sea. The assertion of its claims in the South China Sea is a foretaste of its larger naval ambitions. As its military power grows, the balance with the US and its allies in the region will change automatically, making its neighbours more vulnerable to Chinese pressure and emboldening China to become more demanding. Already, the US is concerned about the capability China is developing to target American aircraft carriers with anti-ship ballistic missiles, as that will make it more difficult for the US to deploy its assets close to the Chinese mainland. Consequently, the deterrence balance in the Strait of Taiwan will change.

Most recently, India has had a taste of China's claims in the South China Sea when its naval ship moving along the Vietnamese coast was warned by radio to stay away from Chinese waters. More seriously, China has objected to Indian oil exploration projects in two Vietnamese blocks by calling countries to refrain from oil exploration in maritime areas offered by Vietnam in the South China Sea on the ground of its "indisputable sovereignty" there. India has rebuffed these objections by stating that its cooperation with Vietnam or with any other country is always as per international laws, norms and conventions. India has also reiterated its position that it "supports freedom of navigation in the South China Sea and hopes that all parties to the dispute would abide by the 2002 declaration of conduct" pertaining to it. At the recent East Asia Summit, India has joined others in expressing concern about China's claims in the South China Sea interfering with the freedom of navigation. The Indian Prime Minister, in his talks with the Chinese Premier, has also stood his ground on our right to pursue our commercial interests jointly with Vietnam in the area of oil exploration. **Our Foreign Minister has again reiterated that the South China Sea is not the property of any one nation and is an international waterway, inviting criticism by the Chinese spokesman.**

China's position on India's cooperation with Vietnam in the so-called disputed areas contradicts flagrantly its policies in that part of the Indian state of Jammu and Kashmir (J&K) under illegal Pakistani occupation, exposing the often unprincipled and bullying nature of its postures. In J&K, in an area which has seen actual military conflict, where a ceasefire is holding even though Pakistani-backed efforts to infiltrate terrorists continue, China has already undertaken strategic projects and is now believed to have signed up for a variety of infrastructure projects totalling US $10 billion. China has argued that these projects do not pre-judge the status of the territory which has to be resolved between India and Pakistan.

During his visit to India in 2010, President Obama had exhorted India not only to Look East but also to Engage East, in line with the wishes of Asian countries to see India playing a more active role in the region. Now the call is for India to Act East. India is cautiously responsive to US calls because it wants to avoid the risk of sharpening misunderstandings with China that developing joint strategies with the US may produce, only to find the US and China reaching bilateral understandings over India's head as situations evolve.

The US relationship with China is far more developed and mutually dependent than the India-US relationship, though the conflictual elements in the US-China relationship are much more present than in US relations with India, whether now or in the future. The US continues to hope that China will evolve and the potential clash of interests can be avoided. There is a counter-intuitive willingness to accept that China's responsible behaviour, the legitimacy to some extent of its paranoia and the development of its military power are to protect its globally spreading economic interests. American China watchers, thus, send mixed signals about the implications of China's rise.

India queries the relaxed view the US takes of the China-Pakistan nuclear cooperation. The US has chosen not to oppose expanded China-Pakistan nuclear trade in violation of China's NSG obligations. Some US specialists explain that the US did not want to throw the gauntlet at China on this issue as it wants China's cooperation in dealing with the nuclear challenge from Iran and North Korea. US experts, in fact, claim that China and India are responsible nuclear powers unlike Pakistan and North Korea. This is offensive to Indian ears as India considers China's transfers of nuclear and missile technology to Pakistan as the greatest threat to its security, transfers that the US has deliberately kept below its radar screen.

The US wants India to focus on the China threat in East Asia by prodding India to Act East, whereas for India, the more immediate and pressing Chinese threat is in South Asia. The US, however, remains either silent on this threat or actually distorts reality by projecting China as a responsible player in South Asia with which the US could work to promote regional peace and stability. If India had concluded that the Bush Administration's endorsement of this position and that of the Obama Administration earlier in its tenure had been repudiated, it was mistaken as Adm Willard, the US CINCPAC Chief has spoken the same language again, even as he has referred to the reality of China's developing capacity to target moving US aircraft carriers upto 2,000 miles away with anti-ship ballistic missiles.

India and the US are far from developing any shared view on China's stepped up claims on Arunachal Pradesh, the expansion of its military infrastructure in Tibet, its river water diversion plans there, its strategic moves in Myanmar and Pakistan to gain access to the Indian Ocean, the future of the institution of the Dalai Lama, etc. India's territorial integrity is under threat from China and Pakistan combined, but, unlike in the case of China where the US endorses the principle of China's territorial integrity, there is no similar expression of support for the territorial integrity of India.

While China's rise is a threat that has to be addressed constructively, it also has to be considered that China too has its options curtailed because of the export dependence of its economy. It needs world markets for maintaining its growth rates as well as internal political stability in view of the social fractures caused by grossly unequal distribution of wealth between the urban and rural areas that has accompanied the phenomenal expansion of its economy in the last decade in particular. To achieve their goal of modernising the Chinese economy and achieve middle-income status, the Chinese leaders claim they need a couple of decades more of peace. During this period, however, while maintaining the fiction of its peaceful rise or development, China can build up its military power steadily. With every passing year, the options available to others to restrain China would become fewer and *fait accomplis* being established under their very noses would have to be accepted. Western democracies, unlike China's closed door political system, have electoral cycles, public expectations and, most importantly, the bottom-lines of their corporations that make them more disposed to make concessions to China under the convenient garb of investing in peace and stability.

China presents the biggest strategic challenge to India in the years ahead. In Asia, India and China are the biggest countries, geographically and demographically. On the face of it, rivalry and competition between the two seem inevitable. The two countries are rising at the same time, although China's rise began more than a decade before India's and it has been faster. There is now a considerable gap in the economic and military strength of the two countries, and this gives China more options on the international stage and an upper hand for the time being in its dealings with India.

With such large economies registering sustained high growth rates, with India growing at high single digit figures and China enjoying double digit growth, access to resources has become important, and this importance will increase in the years ahead. China has moved ahead very fast in tying up international resources while India has lagged behind. There is no collision yet with China but this could occur as India steps up its efforts.

As India catches up with China in rates of economic growth, as many studies show it will in a decade or so when Chinese growth levels are expected to go down, China's sense of rivalry with India is likely to become sharper. For the time being, China considers the US as its principal rival for power, undoubtedly in the Asian region, if not beyond. This implies that China is taking for granted its leadership of Asia. In such a scenario, China will resist any effort by India to contest its primacy. China's current disregard of India as a serious challenger is an indicator of its regional outlook. When India is seen as becoming one, China's thinking and intentions in relation to India will be stress-tested.

Notwithstanding globalisation and interdependence that call for cooperation rather than confrontation and a search for win-win situations rather than zero-sum games, rivalry for power is unavoidable between states. China is particularly problematic on this score because it is nursing historical grievances and is territorially expansionist. Lack of democracy in China makes the situation more difficult for other countries in the region and beyond as the Chinese decision-making process remains opaque and public sentiment about policies pursued by the government is difficult to assess.

China's spectacular economic growth cannot but be accompanied by growing military strength. China can well argue that its expanding international interests require it to develop the means to protect these interests by deterring interference by others, as otherwise it will always remain vulnerable to external pressures. Under cover of this rational argument, China can expand its military strength, as it is in the course of doing. It has powerful nuclear and missile capability, with more potent missiles being tested. It seems on course to build a blue water naval capability for force projection and to be able to protect its long lines of communication stretching across the Indian Ocean. It has now ample financial resources for expanding its military budget. Its growing military power has already begun to cause concern.

As part of its hedging strategy, India holds regular naval exercises with the US in the Indian Ocean as a joint affort to protect the sea lanes of communication. Combined naval exercises are held with the US and Japanese Navies too, the strategic import of which could not be lost on the Chinese. We now have a strategic dialogue with Japan. India has agreed to a India-US-Japan trilateral political dialogue. We are stepping up our relationship with Vietnam.

China's rise is a reality India and others have to deal with. The challenge has to be met without confrontation or appeasement. India must create space for itself to target China's sensitive spots, even as we engage the country, the strategy that China follows towards India. The ultimate answer for India's China challenge, of course, is to develop its own economic and military sinews as rapidly as possible, as well as strategies of cooperation with the US and others concerned about China's muscle-flexing in the future, while, at the same time, maintaining its independence of action.

For all the reasons outlined earlier, our dilemmas in dealing with China are particularly acute. As modern nations, India and China have different conceptions about their international role. The two countries have marked differences in temperament and outlook, and these have a bearing on the future. Unlike the Chinese, we are not a competitive people, we do not think in grandiose terms, we are not power conscious, we are tolerant of dissent, we are less dominated by the state, and we are not as regimented and disciplined. Our dilemmas with China, apart from stemming from power equations, reside also in differences of mentality.

2

Regulating Human Activities in Outer Space: Is Code of Conduct the Answer?

Manpreet Sethi

The fact that outer space is an integral part of terrestrial life today is hardly a secret. Activities related to global information availability, weather forecasting, education, financial services, transportation, communication, agriculture, natural resource mapping and management, disaster management and emergency response and relief are only a few of those that are dependent on assets deployed in space. The reliance of the military too on space enabled services such as intelligence, surveillance, reconnaissance, navigation, early warning and even arms control verification is immense and rapidly growing. It is self-evident, therefore, that any disturbance to these assets would have significant consequences for the mere mortals on Earth. The disruption could occur as a result of a deliberate act of malintent to interfere with the functioning of the satellites, or as an inadvertent act of disruption caused by a natural collision with other objects or debris in space. The chances of the former grow as military capabilities in space expand and trust deficits between nations on Earth grow. But the chances of the latter are not inconsequential either owing to the increasing presence of more players, as well as more man-made debris in outer space.

Common sense would point to an easy solution to this problem. Just as man has crafted rules and laws to regulate behaviour on Earth – whether on road, air, sea, or in social contact at the individual and national levels – so should some rules of responsible behaviour be put in place for human activities in space too. But this appears easier said than done considering that outer space is a global common like no other. A common heritage of this nature and significance must be handled with the sensitivity and sanity that it demands.

At present, there is no universally accepted, holistic system of governance of human activities in outer space. The five formulations of space law currently in force: Outer Space Treaty – 1967; Rescue Agreement – 1968; Liability Convention –

1972; Registration Convention – 1975; and Moon Treaty – 1979, deal with specific issues and are ill-equipped for handling the rapid influx of new technologies and new players into this domain. The last legal instrument to be negotiated on outer space was 35 years ago, in 1979. The three and a half decades since then have seen such an exponential growth and yet, or perhaps because of it, there are no new legal measures in sight. As someone said, "Science soars like an eagle while law drags on like a turtle".[1]

It is surprising that for a realm as critical as this, so little attention has been paid to keeping space law apace with the changing times. In fact, in the last couple of decades, as the profile of usage of space has changed drastically, efforts at formulating new legal regimes to prevent, or at least regulate, some kinds of activities have had little traction in the international fora. The issue of Prevention of Arms Race in Outer Space (PAROS) was set free by China in 2003 when it relented that the relevant Ad Hoc Committee could meet for talks aimed at *discussions*, not for negotiating a new space treaty. But it has been unable to make any headway in the Conference on Disarmament (CD), which has been now stalemated for the last decade or so on the Fissile Material Cut-off Treaty (FMCT).

Meanwhile, at least four unusual developments in the last five years have brought episodic attention to the issue of space security. The first of these was the conduct of an Anti-Satellite Test (ASAT) by China in 2007 at a height of 864 km, which highlighted two kinds of threats: one, the risks to space-based assets from deliberate national actions that use kinetic kill to destroy satellites. The last such test had been undertaken by the USA in 1985 and the lull since then was perceived as having set in place a norm against ASATs. China's action reopened the issue of legitimacy of ASATs; second, it highlighted the dangers from the huge amount of debris, thus, created that endangers satellites of other nations for years to come.[2] Then, in February 2008, the USA found it prudent to kill one of its allegedly ailing, hydrazine packed satellites in space. While the US justified this as an act necessary to neutralise a threat and claimed to have taken the precaution of causing the explosion in a low orbital altitude to minimise debris, it nevertheless demonstrated the utility of such a capability. One year later, in 2009, there was an inadvertent collision between an American and a Russian satellite, the Iridium 33 and Cosmos 2251, which drew attention to the issue of space traffic management, especially as some orbits of outer space become congested. A fourth unprecedented incident occurred in 2010 when a private communications satellite launched by Intelsat, the Galaxy 15, went out of control and the owners could not maintain its ascribed position nor turn off its communications payload. As the satellite drifted, it posed dangers to other satellites not just of physical collusion but also of interference with their signals. Precautionary measures had to be taken by other satellites and while no major mishap took place, the risks were starkly evident.

Despite these wake-up calls, or perhaps because of the capability that the first two demonstrated, there is no international consensus yet on how to regulate human activities in space. As far as the US is concerned, it has little appetite for any new legal instrument that binds its hands in outer space. China and Russia, in contrast, are more in favour of a treaty that they tabled in the CD in 2008 which proscribes space weapons, but does not define the term. In fact, it does not include in its scope capabilities that could be used from Earth to interfere with space-based assets. Meanwhile, the European Union (EU) has proposed a Space Code of Conduct as an interim compromise between the two positions.

A draft International Code of Conduct for Outer Space Activities (CoC) was first prepared and introduced into the international discourse by the EU in 2008. This was revised in 2010 and yet again in 2012. It contains a set of voluntary and non-binding best practices to regulate the behaviour of states in outer space and to inject transparency and mutual trust and confidence into their activities. In May 2012, the EU Council officially launched a multilateral diplomatic process envisaging up to three meetings of multilateral experts to discuss and negotiate the CoC for wider acceptance and endorsement. It also put the United Nations Institute for Disarmament Research (UNIDIR) in charge of the outreach programme to build a consensus on the Code. The first meeting of UNIDIR experts, open to participation of all UN members, was scheduled for October 2012 with a view to finalising the Code by 2013. But, the deliberations have not started on schedule.

Meanwhile, in India, the CoC has received little serious attention from the strategic community and its participation in the group of experts is also unclear at the time of this writing. This is not behaviour that behoves a country that has been engaged in utilisation of space for many decades, and has ambitious plans to use space for socio-economic and military support functions. As a major space-faring nation, India has a substantive stake in the security and sustainability of space for safe operations and, therefore, must give due thought to the issues relating to the CoC and beyond.

This paper is an attempt to explore the issue from an Indian perspective. It is broadly divided into four sections. The first one identifies the current state of affairs in outer space by fleshing out the nature of some of the new players and new technologies in this domain. The second section presents the rationale for, and content of, the CoC. The third section flags the limitations of the CoC and the last one then examines the options for India.

The Current State of Affairs in Outer Space

Outer space remained a preserve primarily of the two superpowers from 1957 to the end of the Cold War. During this period, 95 per cent of the activities in space were conducted by the USA and USSR. It is only now, over the last couple of decades, that the presence of many more players has become much more pronounced and visible. Over 80 actors – state and private commercial entities – are active in space today. Many more access and use space services and products. There are over 1,300 satellites presently operational in space. The year 2011 saw the largest number of launches to place satellites in orbit in a decade, as also a significant increase in government spending on space activities, which is indicative of the kind of priority that nations are currently attaching to national space programmes.[3]

Meanwhile, there is a boom in the private players in space too, a trend that started tentatively in the late 1990s.[4] By 2004, state run programmes no longer held monopoly over space flights. The launch of SpaceShipOne in that year opened outer space to private venture. In 2005, Virgin Galactic became the first private company to offer commercial flights into space. In fact, the owner of Virgin Galactic, Richard Branson, has also invested along with some other billionaires in the enterprise Golden Spike to undertake a lunar mission in 2020.[5] Bigelow Aerospace is engaged in private construction of prototype orbital space stations. More recently, there has been the entry of private players for cargo transportation[6] as demonstrated by the launch of the vehicle DragonX by Space Exploration Technologies (SpaceX) to provision the International Space Station (ISS). In its maiden flight in June 2012, the unmanned capsule carried 500 kg of supplies and equipment for the ISS and returned with 650 kg of retired material and scientific samples. Besides, the commercial sector today holds a huge chunk of the space launch, communications, imagery and manufacturing services, with estimated annual revenues of $200 billion.[7] Many of these services are being used by states as also by individual users. Even more significantly, a new company, Planetary Resources Inc. has announced in 2012 its plan to mine asteroids as they zip close to the Earth.[8] While the idea may seem far-fetched today, it could become a reality in the future and it will raise issues of ownership of resources in an area designated as the common heritage of mankind.

Two facts are evident from the above. One, that *outer space is fast becoming congested.* The increasing traffic, in turn, poses twin challenges – of increasing space debris; and of space traffic management. Most space missions create debris as rocket booster stages are expended. However, serious fragmentations caused by explosions of the kind that China undertook in 2007 are activities that create maximum debris. That one act added 3,000 new pieces of large sized (over 10 cm in diameter) fragments and several thousands of smaller ones, increasing the debris by 14 percent. According to the Space Security Index 2012, the US Department of Defence is using the Space Surveillance Network to catalogue about 17,000 objects of 10 cm or more in diameter, while there are more than 300,000 objects with a diameter larger than one cm and millions of pieces of smaller sizes. That even the smallest piece of debris, travelling as it is at a speed of around 8 km/s, can destroy or disable a spacecraft is a sobering thought, even more so for nations that have planned manned missions. Meanwhile, the accidental collision of an active US satellite with a defunct Russian satellite in 2009 highlighted the problem of traffic. Unless nations are aware of other satellites and their orbits, especially when unexpected manoeuvres are undertaken, the crowding of space could cause more such inadvertent accidents. These could also have repercussions on terrestrial inter-state relations, especially if the satellites involved are those of countries that do not share high trust levels and have reason to believe that the collision could have been engineered on purpose. Congestion of space, therefore, in a situation where there are no accepted rules of the road, presents the first set of challenges to space security.

The second obvious contemporary reality is that *outer space is getting crowded with all kinds of players – national, private and consortia*. Different players have different priorities and security concerns. For instance, national progammes often include military objectives, which make them less open to calls of transparency on numbers or types of spacecraft or even the manoeuvres they carry out. But, the private players who are primarily driven by commercial/profit considerations are more amenable to accepting rules on transparency but less on undertaking steps on debris mitigation activities that entail a financial cost such as moving defunct satellites into higher parking orbits or de-orbiting them to burn up in the atmosphere. Therefore, the disparate nature of the actors and their interests in outer space carries the potential for a conflict of interest.

To further add to the complexity, there are newer military technologies that are constantly making their presence felt. While space is now an established domain for military support functions, placement of instruments that could lend themselves to defensive and offensive uses remains a possibility. The link between ballistic missile defence and weaponisation of space is fast evolving. In August 2012, the US gave further evidence of this when a Ballistic Missile Defence (BMD) test involved its Space Tracking and Surveillance System to detect and track mid-course reentry vehicles and pass the information to the fire control elements of the Aegis BMD to launch interceptors.[9] With this, the BMD moved up into the space layer for sensors. Interceptors in space could be next. US efforts at building a space-based infrared system to undertake boost-phase interception are technological capabilities that are pushing the envelope of military use of space. Hedging against such technologies, Russia and China are engaged in Research and Development (R&D) on their repertoire of space weapons too. For instance, in May 2012, Russia announced that it was developing a sea-based space defence system that will be able to engage targets in Low Earth Orbit (LEO). China demonstrated the capability to blind/jam satellites through lasers in 2006 and then the ASAT in 2007. At the moment, the idea of deploying space weapons is not popular, but that is certainly not stopping any of the major players from keeping themselves ready for any eventuality.

In sum then, the current reality of the domain of space points to a newness in the manner of its utilisation, the nature and numbers of the players involved, and also the scope of that use. And, at the moment, it largely seems to be a case of free for all, except for the limited stipulations placed by the five treaties enacted in the 1960s and 1970s when the state of affairs in outer space was quite different from what it is today.

Rationale and Content of CoC

It is to remedy this situation that a need has been felt for a conscious effort to regulate human activities in a way that minimises risks and maximises the safe and sustainable use of the domain. The idea of the CoC arises from this rationale. It has been framed as a voluntary set of best practices, especially on two particular aspects of space security -- debris control and mitigation[10], and traffic management. The main emphasis of the CoC is on building transparency and confidence among space-faring nations. The proponents of CoC emphasise the value of norms for distinguishing responsible from irresponsible behaviour, for facilitating appropriate responses for the latter and for providing a foundation for graduating eventually to more legally binding agreements. As Michael Krepon, a strong advocate of the CoC, argues, it would at least establish norms "upon which sanctions or other penalties can be imposed" since "without rules, there are no rule breakers". [11] He strongly supports the CoC for its 'doability' compared to getting nations to negotiate and conclude a legal treaty to this effect.

The stated purpose of the CoC is to "enhance the security, safety and sustainability of all outer space activities"[12]. It seeks to do so by, firstly, encouraging all states to comply with the treaties, conventions and commitments relating to outer space activities, and secondly, by recommending responsible state behaviour through the acceptance of uniform practices on space launches, operations, and debris mitigation. It envisages achievement of these objectives by improving transparency on national space programmes by urging nations to register their launches and space objects, and sharing information on national space policies and strategies, including for defence related activities, as well as collisions/ break-ups in orbit, reentry events, etc. In order to minimise the possibility of accidents in space, collisions between space objects or any form of harmful interference with other states' right to use of space, the CoC not only enjoins upon states to refrain from such activities that may directly or indirectly damage the space objects of other nations, but also to execute manoeuvres of their spacecraft only after providing advance notification, or details on proposed manoeuvres, etc. With every country providing information on its objects in space and own operations, as well as on the general environment of space around its objects, it is believed that it would result in a network of radars, telescopes and other instruments to track space traffic and debris and, thus, help avert inadvertent accidents or collisions through better Space Situational Awareness (SSA). Meanwhile, the CoC seeks to mitigate the production of new debris by calling upon states to commit to refraining from intentional destruction of any operational space object or from other actions that may generate long-lived space debris, as also the adoption and implementation of the United Nations General Assembly (UNGA) Resolution 62/217 that lays down Space Debris Mitigation Guidelines.

The CoC also provides for a consultation mechanism in case of conduct of activities by a state that are believed to be "contrary to the core purposes of the Code". In such instance, the complainant could "request consultations with a view to achieving mutually acceptable solutions" which will be through "diplomatic channels" and would involve "working jointly and cooperatively in a timeframe sufficiently urgent to mitigate or eliminate the identified risk initially triggering the consultations". The CoC is envisaged as a dynamic entity subject to biennial review and updating through decisions taken by consensus of the subscribing states.

Apparently, from the rationale and the content of the proposed CoC, there seems to be every reason to support the initiative since it does appear to enhance space security. Where then, do the problems lie? Why are nations not overly enthusiastic about the initiative? The following section examines some of the specific limitations of the CoC as well as the broader concerns on space security.

Limitations of a Code of Conduct

The CoC essentially promotes compliance with already existing legal instruments relating to outer space activities or seeks to formalise practices that are already expected to be followed by responsible space-faring nations. UN approved space debris mitigation guidelines, a convention on registration of objects launched to outer space, pre-notification on manoeuvres, etc, are practices that have been existence for some time now. However, not all nations diligently follow the requirements. Will the CoC, a set of voluntary, legally non-binding rules, be able to ensure any better compliance?

Ajay Lele, a scholar on the subject in India, is sceptical. He opines that the CoC would serve "no purpose beyond offering a feel good notion" and he questions the use of "forming so-called rules of behaviour, principles, values and standards when there is no authority to punish". He argues that such a Code would end up being based on "optimism that states are essentially ethical actors and that they understand their responsibilities and duties and are keen to bind themselves into following a mutually agreed upon set of rules."[13]

This argument is not without merit. An example of how little attention nations pay to such voluntary, political commitments is evident from the treatment meted out to the existing guidelines on debris mitigation. The Inter-Agency Space Debris Coordination Committee, an international forum of governmental bodies for coordination activities related to man-made and natural debris, had adopted the IADC Space Debris Mitigation Guidelines in 2002. These explicitly lay down requirements for states to prevent on-orbit break-ups, removal of spacecraft and orbital stages that have reached the end of mission, depletion of residual propellants, disposal of Geo-stationary Earth Orbit (GEO) satellites in graveyard orbits 235 km above the GEO and removal of dead spacecraft from Low Earth Orbit (LEO) within 25 years. The guidelines also obviously implicitly encourage nations to desist from activities that can produce more debris. These guidelines were in existence when China conducted the ASAT in 2007, paying scant regard to the debris it would cause and thereby endanger the environment, and its safe use for years to come.[14] However, since the guidelines had no enforcement procedure for violation, no action could be taken against China. Similarly, a CoC would have little power to hold back a nation from an activity that it considers imperative for national interest.

In fact, with no authority to enforce compliance, even in case of a conflict between nations, the CoC only envisages a consultative process with the consent of states that may request consultations and the subscribing states that receive the request. The nations that are obviously going to be having low mutual trust given that they are in such a state, are then expected to "work jointly and cooperatively" to find a solution "through diplomatic channels" and "in a timeframe sufficiently urgent". This does appear to take an overly optimistic view of state behaviour when perceptions of national interests are involved.

Meanwhile, some of the practices that states don't currently follow such as providing information on defence related activities are unlikely to be followed despite the CoC calling upon states to do so. In fact, increasing geo-political rivalries and military hedging strategies are likely to further clam up the states.

It is certainly not coincidental that China's conduct of an ASAT in January 2007 that marked a "troubling display of non-transparency and insensitivity to the space environment"[15] provided the trigger for the EU proposal of a draft CoC. The timing revealed the urgency to put in place a set of acceptable norms of behaviour to prevent future repetitions. This is interesting since the idea of "rules of the road" had been doing the rounds in the USA from the early 2000s. Given the scepticism of the Administration of President Bush, Jr., towards formal treaties, and his propensity towards coalition of the willing arrangements, some Washington-based, think-tanks such as the Henry L Stimson Centre had proposed establishing rules of the road for space as a "way station until states could agree on how to move ahead with more formal controls".[16] The Centre for Defence Information too expressed support for a voluntary international norm of enhanced cooperation among major international space actors.[17] But the US (read Pentagon) remained averse to the idea of space restraint and in 2005, also voted (along with Israel) against the otherwise unanimous UN resolution calling upon states to refrain from using space for weapons purposes and urging the CD to take up the issue of a new treaty at its earliest convenience. It repeated its nay vote yet again on the UNGA resolution on PAROS in 2011.

Obviously, the US is not open to the idea of PAROS or any other legal instrument that could bind its hands on the kind of capabilities it could place in outer space. It has only agreed to go along with the idea of the CoC primarily because it addresses one of its major concerns of space debris and because such cooperation could help assist its efforts in building space situational awareness through inputs received from other nations. But, it is averse to any provisions in the CoC that could constrain its freedom to build and test offensive or defensive systems since its documents on its space ambitions routinely talk of control and dominance. As opined by one analyst, the US wants to reserve options "to inflict reversible space effects on others' space systems to convince another nation to behave as a good global citizen".[18]

Seen from this perspective, the value and intent of the CoC come under a cloud. It appears to seek to address the concerns of space security in a very limited envelope of debris control and mitigation and encouraging transparency to ease traffic management. While this is desirable, it is not enough. The CoC does not address the military dimension of space related usage. Rather, it accepts that states have "legitimate defence interests" and steers clear of related issues. So, it neither proscribes any technology, nor makes any mention of ASATs. It only calls upon states to "take all the appropriate measures and cooperate in good faith to prevent harmful interference in outer space activities".[19] Therefore, the CoC has no role in preventing either an arms race in outer space or the prospect of weaponisation of space. This is likely to tempt major space-faring nations to follow hedging strategies.

At the same time, the CoC is also seriously lacking in anticipating future challenges such as the prospect of countries becoming capable of harvesting resources from the Moon, Mars or asteroids in the coming two-three decades. China, for instance, has announced that it wants to establish a lunar base by 2024. The National Aeronautical and Space Agency (NASA) is working on a new space vehicles, the Orion, to fly to the Moon by 2021, to deploy a permanent base there. Russia plans a lunar base in 2015 with the help of a new reusable spacecraft, the Kliper. All are eyeing the huge amounts of Helium 3 that could be accessed from the Moon as an energy source. The Moon is currently designated a global common and, therefore, the exploitation of resources through individual national efforts will bring up challenges of legitimacy of rights. The CoC makes no reference to such issues which will confront mankind sooner rather than later.

Going by historical experience, international legal instruments succeed when there is concurrence of interests among major powers, largely owing to a shared sense of vulnerability, and they can get others to bandwagon with them to make the instrument as universally acceptable as possible. The nuclear Non-Proliferation Treaty (NPT) emerged like this. But, given that there are so many wrinkles in the relationship not only amongst the USA, Russia and China, the three most important stakeholders in space, but also among the other significant space-faring nations, the possibility of being able to craft an acceptable instrument remains low. In fact, the contemporary international climate is in complete contrast to the unidimensional state of the Cold War where nations accepted bloc positions and considerations. In contrast, the permutations and combinations of nations in today's international environment are more complex. And, the major powers have less leverage over nations to force them into accepting instruments that they do not want to. In this context, different national interests – directly related to outer space or not – are likely to shape the debate and pace of movement towards a CoC. In fact, many of the space-faring nations are likely to use this opportunity to manoeuvre the leverages they have to maximise national gains.

India's Options

There is no doubt that India has an interest in avoiding anarchy in outer space. As its footprint in space grows in size and the impact on terrestrial activity gets magnified, so will India's vulnerabilities, a progression that is inevitable and is being experienced by other countries too. In such a situation, a CoC that regulates human activities on the basis of some best practices that minimise the risks of both the advertent and inadvertent variety should be of as much value to India as to other space-faring nations. However, one of the issues of concern for India is that in the absence of any verification, there would be no way of ascertaining whether other countries are attaching the same amount of sanctity and rigour to the implementation of the Code. An apprehension of non-compliance, especially by a country with which India has a disputed relationship and which is demonstrably ahead in capability, is likely to keep its threat perceptions alive. So, while the CoC might ease India's fears of an inadvertent collision with a piece of debris or another satellite, it would do little to reassure it against the possibility of a deliberate attack on its satellite by a nation.

Is the CoC setting the bar too low by premising itself on the assumption that the major powers do not have an appetite for anything stronger at the moment? While many in India would answer this in the affirmative, the reality of the moment demands that keeping national interest and international security in view, India must approach the CoC from the following understanding:

- India must **participate in rule formulation rather than remaining outside** the process. Given its current standing in the international order and ambitions in space, India must not abjure its right and responsibility to be a part of the exercise. Instead of being piqued that the country was not invited when the initial initiative was taken by the EU to draft the Code, New Delhi must now participate in the forthcoming meetings of the multilateral group of experts which is open to all UN members. The CoC is still work in progress and India must use its participation to protect its national interests.
- India must see the CoC for what it is – **beneficial, yet of limited value** as far as addressing threats to space security are concerned. The CoC can address concerns arising from crowding in space given that Indian civilian investments alone in space are valued at $37 billion, including ground-based infrastructure and value added services.[20] Therefore, the risks from space debris and lack of situational awareness are not inconsequential. And in this regard, the CoC can be of help.
- India must accept that the **CoC does not address the possibility of weaponisation of space**. Countries promoting the CoC are interested in treading safe ground and steering clear of difficult issues such as PAROS or space weaponisation. With the US not open to any constraints in this regard, neither Russia nor China is likely to rein in its military oriented space ambitions. Therefore, India should not even expect that the CoC would redress its security concerns from the growing military capabilities of China in space. China has demonstrated its ability to kill a satellite, to use lasers and jammers for interfering or destroying satellites and no politically binding guidelines have been able to restrain the development and demonstration of these capabilities. The CoC does not infringe on any of these technologies either. But

that also means that India too has the same options for itself. The draft CoC presently allows "due consideration for the legitimate defence interests of states", with the issue of legitimacy of those interests subject to national discretion. So, while the CoC does not bring any major advantages from the military point of view, it does not take away anything either.

- India must continue to press the point that the **CoC can only be an interim measure, and that the best space security lies in establishing a legal regime that more clearly confronts the issue of weaponisation of space**. This will, of course, require treading carefully since many space relevant technologies and military systems have dual uses. For example, better radars and optical systems for improved SSA and verification capabilities also allow better tracking and targeting options, including for boost phase interception of enemy missiles. Similarly, the development of micro- or nano-satellites can be seen as stabilising if used to enhance redundancy but these could also be used as 'space mines'[21] to disrupt and disable enemy spacecraft. Moreover, unlike in other domains of war-fighting, an attack on a space-based asset would have ramifications beyond the immediate target, a situation that spreads vulnerabilities. Therefore, for the sake of safe and sustainable use of space, it is necessary that nations be ready to subsume narrow national interests for the greater good of international security. One such precedence exists from the Cold War period. When the use of space first opened up in the 1960s, the two superpowers raced to exploit the environment for military gains, including the conduct of nuclear tests in space. By the end of the 1970s, technologies in both nations were headed towards weaponising space with magnetic rail guns, lasers and advanced kinetic kill vehicles and even space-based MIRVed (Multiple Independently Targetable Reentry Vehicle) nuclear weapons. But both sides desisted from turning this into reality owing to the understanding that such abuse of space would mar its future use for all, including themselves. Greater merit was seen in maintaining the sanctity of space for civilian, commercial and military support functions. A similar realisation and reaffirmation is yet again necessary, and this time from a much wider set of nations, to allow for the continued safe use of space by all. For the time being, the CoC is being touted as the only doable proposition and while India can afford to go along with it for whatever limited benefits it may bring, New Delhi cannot afford to become complacent or allow the rest to rest either. In fact, just as in the case of nuclear weapons, India perceives its long-term interest in universal nuclear disarmament, so in outer space too, its long-term interest lies in getting a more binding agreement.

- Lastly, India must make all efforts to **deal with trust deficits in such a way as to avoid getting embroiled in an arms race**. In the present times, it is evident that the military doctrines of a growing number of states increasingly emphasise the use of space for military purposes and even dominance. This has the potential to create mutual suspicions and mistrust leading to an arms race as countries seek to develop offensive and defensive measures to protect their interests in space and on Earth. This is of particular relevance to India because the centre of gravity in space ambitions has shifted to Asia. China, India, South Korea and Japan are all expanding their space programmes. Iran, Indonesia, Singapore, Thailand and Vietnam as also Sri Lanka are keen to use space more proactively. Many of the mutual relations between these powers are prisoners of mistrust, unresolved territorial conflicts, etc which have the potential to acquire a new dimension as a result of the space capabilities' bearing on terrestrial conduct of relations and operations. Regional transparency and Confidence Building Measures (CBMs) in space appear very difficult at this moment and, therefore, the issue of space sustainability has to be dealt with at the multilateral level.

Conclusion

It is obvious that creation of a safe space environment is in the interest of all. While the capabilities in space might be nationally owned and exploited, vulnerabilities in space are shared. In that sense, it is a truly strategic resource because the impact of any mishap – intentional or unintentional – has widespread ramifications. Therefore, it becomes useful to ensure maintenance of long-term sustainability, safety, stability and security of space through the creation of some rules of governance for its responsible use.

For more than five decades now, space has progressively been used by new players with new technologies. Five treaties and some customary practices have largely governed the behaviour of space-faring nations. In that sense, outer space is not, as graphically put by an analyst, "the Wild West, a lawless area of chaos and risk"[22]. Yet, there obviously is scope for improvement given that risks will grow as the domain becomes more congested, and, therefore, contested.

To preempt such an eventuality, a CoC amongst space-faring and using nations and entities could be useful to the extent that nations follow it diligently and consider it in their interest to do so. As has been proven time and again, even laws and treaties cannot stop nations from disingenuous behaviour if they are set upon it. The CoC will only be a set of voluntary political commitments with no legal obligations. Therefore, while it can bring a sense of predictability and security in orbital behaviour of spacecraft, it cannot bring about a sense of reassurance on threats to national security.

That can be better obtained through efforts to **reinforce and build collective deterrence**. Cooperation in space through joint ownership, operation and data sharing could enforce collective deterrence by spreading the risk. Collaborative endeavours in space programmes, such as the International Space Station, or space exploration can be an effective way of enforcing collective deterrence. In fact, international cooperation can promote space security by enhancing transparency of the nature and purpose of the programmes and by raising inter-state trust levels through sharing of expertise and technology with emerging nations in space. Additionally, the growth of the private commercial space industry also has the potential to positively impact space security since the services provided would increase the number of actors that access or use space or space-based applications, thus, creating a wider pool of stake holders who have a vested interest in maintaining space security. Creating interdependence and mutual vulnerabilities can be an effective way of building collective deterrence in space.

In the ultimate analysis, the CoC is a good idea but it is not sufficient to address some of the more difficult challenges of space security such as weaponisation of space. It does not address the significant security implications of many dual use space capabilities, or the terrestrial capabilities that can produce weapon effects in space. Despite these weaknesses, there is no reason for India to shun the CoC, even if it perceives only limited merit in its present form. New Delhi should participate in the negotiations to try to mould the CoC as best as possible to accommodate its interests, but, nevertheless, realise that it need not be burdened in the first go with every stipulation that India finds necessary. A more pragmatic approach would be to share in the process and accept whatever benefits, however limited, that can be realised while keeping an eye on the larger goal of more comprehensive space security as and when that might be possible. For the moment, it is essential for India to remain engaged in rule formulation on space. In fact, the Code may be compared to some of the ad hoc regimes crafted to regulate weapons of mass destruction such as the Australia Group, Wassennar or the Nuclear Suppliers Group.[23] These exist as cooperative, voluntary groups of member states sharing the common objective to counter the spread of technologies and materials that pose a threat to international security. They have served a purpose in preventing proliferation, even though their efficacy has been highly contingent on national compliance. Nevertheless, for the member-states, the groups have provided the advantage of having a voice and vote in decision-making. Similarly, India's 'membership' of the CoC will bring certain advantages that it will not have if it were to stay out of the process.

Meanwhile, for real space security concerns to be adequately addressed, the international community will have to invest much more energy and ideas, including accepting constraints on national ambitions of space dominance. The CoC can only hope to provide a partial answer to the critical concerns facing mankind today and it should be seen as such – desirable for the limited benefits it brings, but inadequate for guaranteeing real space security.

Notes

1. As cited in Kaza Lalitendra, *Militarisation of Space* (New Delhi: Knowledge World, 2010).
2. According to physicist Joel L. Primack, "Debris in orbits higher than about 880 km above the Earth's surface will be up there for decades, above 1,000 km for centuries, and above 1,500 km effectively forever," as cited in James Clay Moltz, *The Politics of Space Security: Strategic Restraint and the Pursuit of National Interests* (Stanford: Stanford University Press, 2008), p. 52. It may be mentioned that China undertook the ASAT at a height of 864 km.
3. For more on this, see Cesar Jaramillo, ed., *Space Security Index 2012* (Ontario: University of Waterloo, 2012), as available at http://www.spacesecurity.org
4. The idea of private space ventures for human spaceflight began to capture public attention in the mid-1990s when a small group of entrepreneurs and flight enthusiasts formed the X Prize foundation to raise funds for the purpose. This effort resulted in the successful launch of *SpaceShipOne* in September 2004. For details, see Moltz, n.2, pp. 284-285.
5. "Branson Keen on Moonwalk in 2020", *The Times of India*, December 4, 2012.
6. NASA contract worth $1.6 billion to SpaceX to run 12 cargo missions. Saswato R. Das, "A New Era Blasts Off", *The Times of India*, June 27, 2012.
7. Jaramillo, ed., n.3. p. 17
8. Kenneth Chang, "In Pursuit of Riches in the Asteroid Belt", *Indian Express*, April 29, 2012.
9. "Northrop Grumman Built STSS Demonstration Satellites Participate in Test of Next Generation Aegis BMD Weapon System", http://www.nasdaq.com, accessed on September 4, 2012.
10. It may also be mentioned that technological R & D is also being undertaken to address this problem. For instance, Switzerland is building a $11 million satellite called CleanSpace One as a space janitor. Planned for 2015, it would be designed to pick up orbiting debris to bring it back to the Earth's atmosphere where it could burn on reentry. "Space Janitor: Satellite to Get Rid of Orbiting Debris", *The Times of India*, February 16, 2012.
11. For more on this, see Michael Krepon, "Space Code of Conduct: Inadequate Mechanism – A Response", in Ajay Lele, ed., *Decoding the International Code of Conduct for Outer Space Activities* (New Delhi: Pentagon Security International, 2012), pp 9-12.
12. Text of the International Code of Conduct for Outer Space Activities, 2010, as released by the Council of the European Union and reproduced in Ibid., Appendix 1.
13. Ibid., p. 6
14. Of the debris created as a result of the Chinese test, only about 6 percent is estimated to reenter the Earth's atmosphere by 2017, as against 79 percent that will continue to be in LEO till 2018. Brian Weedon, "2007 Chinese ASAT: Fact Sheet", *Secure World Foundation*, November 23, 2010, available at http://wwwswfound.org. Pieces of debris have significantly multiplied to about 21,000 of 10 cm or more, out of which nearly 6,000 have been added in just the last five years and 1,500 by a collision between US-Russian communication satellites in February 2009.
15. Jana Robinson, "Europe's' Space Diplomacy Initiative: The International Code of Conduct", in Lele, ed, n.11, p. 27.
16. Michael Krepon and Christopher Clary, *Space Assurance or Space Dominance? The Case Against Weaponising Space* (Washington DC: Stimson Centre, 2003).

17. Theresa Hitchens, *Future Security in Space: Charting a Cooperative Course* (Washington DC: Centre for Defence Information, September 2004).
18. Thomas D. Taverney, "Working Towards a Space Code of Conduct", *Space Review*, April 16, 2012, http://www.spacereview.com
19. Point 2.3 of the Section "Purpose, Scope and Core Principles" of the EU Draft Code of Conduct, reproduced as Appendix 1 in Lele, ed., n.11, pp 163 - 170.
20. Rajeswari Pillai Rajagopalan, "The Space Code of Conduct: A View from Delhi", *Strategic Studies Quarterly*, Spring 2012, pp. 137-148.
21. G.S. Sachdeva, *Outer Space: Security and Legal Challenges* (New Delhi: Knowledge World, 2010), pp. 187-206.
22. Eric Sterner, "Not Lost in Space: Managing the Domain", *World Politics Review*, April 16, 2011.
23. The author is grateful to Air Cmde Jasjit Singh, Director General, Centre for Air Power Studies, for bringing out this point during a private conversation on the subject.

3

Ballistic Missile Defence

T. M. Asthana

Introduction

There are 77 nations in the world today that have cruise missiles, 40 nations have Short Range Ballistic Missiles (SRBMs) (less than 1,000 km range), 11 nations have Medium Range Ballistic Missiles (MRBMs) i.e. 1,000-2,500 km and/or Intermediate Range Ballistic Missiles (IRBMs) i.e. 2,500-6,000 km range, and 5 nations have Inter-Continental Ballistic Missiles (ICBMs) i.e. above 6,000 km range.

Ballistic missile defence is a system, weapon, or technology involved in the detection, tracking, interception and destruction of attacking missiles. Originally conceived as defence against nuclear-armed ICBMs, its application has broadened to include shorter-ranged, non-nuclear tactical and theatre missiles. The interception technology used has varied over time. In the 1960s, missile defence against ICBMs emphasised nuclear warheads for the Kinetic Kill Vehicle (KKV). In recent decades, non-nuclear, kinetic warheads have been used. Directed-energy weapons such as lasers have been investigated and deployed on a limited basis.

The United States, Russia, France, India and Israel have all developed such air defence systems. In the United States, missile defence was originally the responsibility of the army. The US Missile Defence Agency has developed maritime systems and command and control that will eventually be transferred to the navy and air force for operation and sustainment.

The best defensive strategy against all stand-off missiles, be they ballistic or cruise missile class weapons, is to preemptively attack and destroy the launch platform. This was true in 1944 when the first V-1 and V-2 weapons were deployed, and remains true today – 'killing the archer rather than the arrow.' This is unfortunately easier said than done, and counter-force air strikes against mobile missile launchers have been bedevilled with targeting problems since 1944 – the US Air Force effort against Saddam's Scud force in 1991 represents the most recent example. With ballistic and cruise missiles more recently deployed on submarines and surface warships, the problem gains a further dimension. Ground-based mobile launchers, however, represent the greatest difficulty, as these are highly mobile and easily concealed. Users favour the 'shoot and scoot' strategy, and tracking weapons post launch leaves a very narrow time window to locate and kill the launcher before it departs. Interception of both cruise and ballistic missiles in flight is challenging, and it is an open question as to which is the more difficult target. Ballistic missiles are characteristically easy to detect and track once launched, but their hypersonic terminal phase velocity represents a real problem for defensive weapon systems. The problem is often described as 'hitting a bullet with another bullet', and the problem increases in difficulty as the range of the missile and its terminal velocity increase. Killing a Scud B is easier than killing an IRBM, and killing an IRBM, in turn, is easier than killing an ICBM.

Missile Defence Terminologies

Ballistic missiles and cruise missiles are the most rapidly growing category of offensive weapons in Asia, in response to which we are seeing increased planning for investment in defensive measures. The recent announcement that Japan and Australia were likely to participate in a feasibility study on ballistic missile defence, and Japan's overt pursuit of the F-22A Raptor fighter for cruise missile defence, are both indicators of a developing trend.

Fig 1: India's Advanced Air Defence (AAD) Endo-Atmospheric Anti-Ballistic Missile

Missile defence can be divided into categories based on various characteristics: type/range of missile intercepted, the trajectory phase where the intercept occurs, and whether intercepted inside or outside the earth's atmosphere.

Type/Range of Missile Intercepted

The types/ranges are strategic, theatre and tactical. Each entails unique requirements for intercept, and a defensive system capable of intercepting one missile type frequently cannot intercept others; however, there is sometimes overlap in capability.

Strategic Missile Defence: Targets long-range ICBMs, which travel at about 7 km/s (15,700 mph). Examples of currently active systems: Russian A-135 system which defends Moscow, and the US Ground-Based Mid-course Defence (GMD) system that defends the United States from missiles launched from Asia. Geographic range of strategic defence can be regional (Russian system) or national (US system).

Theatre Missile Defence: Targets medium-range missiles, which travel at about 3 km/s (6,700 mph) or less. In this context, the term "theatre" means the entire localised region for military operations, typically, a radius of several hundred kilometres. Defence range of theatre defensive systems is usually on this order. Examples of deployed or soon-to-be deployed theatre missile defences: Israeli Arrow (missile), American Theatre High Altitude Area Defence (THAAD) and Russian S-400 Triumf.

Tactical Missile Defence: Targets short-range tactical ballistic missiles, which usually travel at less than 1.5 km/s (3,400 mph). Tactical Anti-Ballistic Missiles (ABMs) have short ranges, typically 20–80 km (12–50 miles). Examples of currently deployed tactical ABMs: American MIM-104 Patriot and Russian S-300V.

Trajectory Phase

Ballistic missiles can be intercepted in four regions of their trajectory: boost phase, after burn out, mid-course phase and/or terminal phase.

Boost Phase: Intercepting the missile while its rocket motors are firing, usually over the launch territory [example: American aircraft-mounted laser weapon, Boeing YAL-1 (under development)].

Advantages:

- Bright, hot rocket exhaust makes detection, discrimination and targeting easier.
- Decoys cannot be used during boost phase.

Disadvantages:

- Difficult to geographically position interceptors to intercept missiles in boost phase (not always possible without flying over hostile territory).
- Short time for intercept (typically about 180 seconds).

Boost phase intercept is the easiest from a detection, tracking and kinematic perspective. The exhaust plume can be seen from orbit, and hundreds of kilometres away in the air. The missile is climbing at a supersonic speed, and early in the boost phase, will have all of its stages attached, presenting a large radar target. The difficulty with boost phase intercept is that the defending aircraft, be it equipped with an interceptor missile or Directed Energy Weapon (DEW), must be near enough to the launcher to effect a timely shot. Where the missile user has good 'anti-access' capability, via Surface-to-Air-Missiles (SAMs) and fighter aircraft, this becomes a challenging problem. Much of the justification for the design of the stealthy Northrop B-2A Spirit bomber was the hunting of highly mobile Soviet ICBM launchers. Fighters equipped with interceptor missiles are presented with a high risk environment in which they must orbit for many hours awaiting unpredictable ballistic missile launches, either to affect a boost phase shot, or to kill the launcher.

Mid-Course Phase: Intercepting the missile in space after the rocket burns out (example: American Ground-Based Mid-course Defence (GMD)).

Advantages:

- Extended decision/intercept time (the coast period through space before reentering the atmosphere can be several minutes, up to 20 minutes for an ICBM).
- Very large geographic defensive coverage; potentially continental.

Disadvantages:

- Requires large/heavy anti-ballistic missiles and sophisticated powerful radar which must often be augmented by space-based sensors.
- Must handle potential space-based decoys.

Mid-course phase intercepts are arguably the most challenging from a detection and tracking perspective, as the missile is at the peak of its trajectory, and having shed booster stages, is a small and cool radar target. Kinematically, mid-course phase intercepts are demanding in terms of altitude, even if the missile's speed is modest as it flies across the top of the ballistic arc.

Terminal Phase: Intercepting the missile after it reenters the atmosphere (examples: American Aegis ballistic missile defence system, American Sprint, Russian ABM-3 Gazelle).

Advantages:

- Smaller/lighter anti-ballistic missile required.
- Balloon decoys do not work during reentry.
- Smaller, less sophisticated radar required.

Disadvantages:

- Very short intercept time, possibly less than 30 seconds.

- Less defended geographic coverage.
- Possible blanketing of target area with hazardous materials in the case of detonation of nuclear warhead(s).

Terminal phase intercepts see the delivery vehicle produce a prominent ionisation trail and heat signature, as ablative coatings evaporate during reentry. The ionisation plume provides a radar signature much larger than the vehicle itself, permitting a tracking system to cue precisely to the position of the warhead. The principal tracking challenge is discrimination between the reentry vehicle and debris or counter-measures reentering concurrently. The latter proved a major issue for Patriot intercepts of the Scud in 1991. Kinematics then become the primary challenge for a defender's missiles.

Cruise missile defence is conceptually simpler, but technically no less difficult. This is because cruise missiles are low signature targets, with small radar cross-sections in most bands and cool exhausts mostly – only supersonic cruise missiles have an appreciable heat signature. Flying low altitude terrain following profiles, cruise missiles are often routed to take advantage of terrain to further effect terrain masking, and hide the missile in the radar shadow of valleys and hills. Radars with high power aperture performance, usually in the X-band, are the sensors of choice for hunting cruise missiles. While in principle any air-to-air or surface-to-air missile can be used for this purpose, in practice, fusing and seeker modifications are typically required to provide a high kill probability.

Intercept Location Relative to the Atmosphere

Missile defence can take place either inside (endo-atmospheric) or outside (exo-atmospheric) the earth's atmosphere. The trajectory of most ballistic missiles takes them inside and outside the earth's atmosphere, and they can be intercepted in either place. There are advantages and disadvantages to either intercept technique.

Some missiles such as THAAD can intercept both inside and outside the earth's atmosphere, giving two intercept opportunities.

Endo-atmospheric

Endo-atmospheric anti-ballistic missiles are usually shorter ranged (example: American MIM-104 Patriot).

Advantages:

- Physically smaller/lighter.
- Easier to move and deploy.
- Endo-atmospheric intercept means balloon-type decoys won't work.

Disadvantages:

- Limited range and defended area.
- Limited decision and tracking time for the incoming warhead.

Exo-atmospheric

Exo-atmospheric anti-ballistic missiles are usually longer ranged (example: American ground-based mid-course defence).

Advantages:

- More decision and tracking time.
- Fewer missiles required for defence of a larger area.

Disadvantages:

- Larger/heavier missiles required.
- More difficult to transport and emplace than smaller missiles.
- Must handle decoys.

Fig 2

A NORAD Distant Early Warning (DEW) Line station in western Greenland is visible in the distance beyond the snow-drifted equipment pallets in the foreground of the photograph (Fig 2). The DEW Line was designed to track in-bound ballistic missiles.

History of Missile Defence in USA

In the 1950s and 1960s, the term ballistic missile defence meant defence against strategic (usually nuclear-armed) missiles. The technology mostly centred around detecting offensive launch events and tracking in-bound ballistic missiles, but with limited ability to actually defend against the missile. The Soviet Union achieved the first non-nuclear intercept of a ballistic missile warhead by a missile at the Sary Shagan anti-ballistic missile defence test range on March 4, 1961.

Throughout the 1950s and 1960s, the United States Project Nike air defence programme focussed initially on bombers, then ballistic missiles. In the 1950s, the first United States anti-ballistic missile system was the Nike Hercules, which had a limited ability to intercept incoming ballistic missiles, although not ICBMs. This was followed by the Nike Zeus, which, using a nuclear warhead, could intercept ICBMs. However, the Nike Zeus had other limitations which prevented it being deployed. In any case, by the early 1960s, the Nike Zeus was the first anti-ballistic missile to achieve hit-to-kill (physically colliding with the incoming warhead).

The Zeus missile was enhanced, and the shorter range Sprint missile was added to the Nike defence system, then called Nike-X. The system included large powerful radars and a computer complex.

Eventually, the Nike-X programme was realigned and renamed Sentinel. This programme's goal was to protect major US cities from a limited ICBM attack, especially focussing on China. This, in turn, reduced tensions with the Soviet Union, which retained the offensive capability to overwhelm any US defence.

The Soviet Union deployed the A-35 anti-ballistic missile system around Moscow in 1966, which also defended nearby ICBM sites. That system has been upgraded several times and is still operational. The United States announced an Anti-Ballistic Missile (ABM) programme to protect twelve ICBM sites in 1967.

In 1967, then-Secretary of Defence Robert McNamara stated: *"Let me emphasize -- and I cannot do so too strongly -- that our decision to go ahead with a limited ABM deployment in no way indicates that we feel an agreement with the Soviet Union on the limitation of strategic nuclear offensive and defensive forces is in any way less urgent or desirable."*

The SALT I talks began in 1969, and led to the Anti-Ballistic Missile (ABM) Treaty in 1972. The ABM Treaty was a bilateral treaty between the US and Soviet Union which initially permitted two ABM sites with not more than 100 missiles per site. This was probably, one, for the capital and the other for the protection of one missile launching site. Ultimately, the treaty limited the US and USSR to one defensive missile site each, with no more than 100 missiles per site. The US unilaterally abandoned the ABM Treaty in 2002.

As a result of the treaty and the technical limitations, along with public opposition to nearby nuclear-armed defensive missiles, the US Sentinel programme was redesignated the Safeguard programme, with the new goal of defending US ICBM sites, not cities. The US Safeguard system was deployed to defend the LGM-30 Minuteman ICBMs near Grand Forks, North Dakota. It was deactivated in 1976 after being operational for less than four months due to a changing political climate, plus concern over limited effectiveness, low strategic value, and high operational cost.

In the early 1980s, technology had matured to consider space-based missile defence options. Precision hit-to-kill systems more reliable than the early Nike Zeus were thought possible. With these improvements, the Reagan Administration promoted the Strategic Defence Initiative (SDI), an ambitious plan to provide comprehensive defence against an all-out ICBM attack. Reagan established the Strategic Defence Initiative Organisation (SDIO), which was later changed to the Ballistic Missile Defence Organisation (BMDO). In 2002, BMDO's name was changed to its current title, the Missile Defence Agency (MDA). In the early 1990s, missile defence expanded to include tactical missile defence, as seen in the first Gulf War. Although not designed from the outset to intercept tactical missiles, upgrades gave the Patriot system a limited missile defence capability. In the late 1990s, and early 2000s, the issue of defence against cruise missiles became more prominent with the new Bush Administration. In 2002, President George W. Bush withdrew the US from the Anti-Ballistic Missile Treaty, allowing further development and testing of ABMs under the Missile Defence Agency, and allowing for deployment of interceptor vehicles beyond the single site allowed under the treaty.

There are still technological hurdles to an effective defence against ballistic missile attacks. The United States National Ballistic Missile Defence System has come under scrutiny about its technological feasibility. Intercepting mid-course (rather than launch or reentry stage) ballistic missiles travelling at several miles per second with a "kinetic kill vehicle" has been characterised as trying to hit a bullet with a bullet. Despite this difficulty, there have been several successful test intercepts and the system was made operational in 2006, while the tests and system upgrades continue. Moreover, the warheads or payloads of ballistic missiles can be concealed by a number of different types of decoys. Sensors that track and target warheads aboard the kinetic kill vehicle may have trouble distinguishing the "real" warhead from the decoys, but several tests that have included decoys were successful.

As of February 2007, the US missile defence system consisted of 13 ground-based interceptors at Fort Greely in Alaska, plus two interceptors at Vandenberg AFB, California. The US planned to have 21 interceptor missiles by the end of 2007. The system was initially called National Missile Defence (NMD), but in 2003 the ground-based component was renamed Ground-Based Mid-course Defence (GMD).

Defending against cruise missiles is similar to defending against hostile, low-flying manned aircraft. As with aircraft defence, counter-measures such as chaff, flares, and low altitude can complicate targeting and missile interception. High-flying radar aircraft such as the Airborne Warning and Control System (AWACS) can often identify low flying threats by using the doppler radar. Another possible method is using specialised satellites to track these targets. By coupling a target's kinetic inputs with infrared and radar signatures, it may be possible to overcome the counter-measures.

In March 2008, the US Congress convened hearings to reexamine the status of missile defence in the US military strategy. Upon taking office, President Obama directed a comprehensive review of the ballistic missile defence policy and programmes. The review's findings related to Europe were announced on September 17, 2009. The full Ballistic Missile Defence Review (BMDR) Report was published in February 2010.

As of 2012, there is no pressing need for an American missile defence system. Those countries that do have nuclear armed missiles that can reach the United States are all either American allies, or are, in the case of Russia and China, in a stable deterrence posture with the United States.

NATO and its Missile Defence Future

Mechanisms

The Conference of National Armaments Directors (CNAD) is the senior North Atlantic Treaty Organisation (NATO) committee which acts as the tasking authority for the Theatre Missile Defence Programme. The Active Layered Theatre Ballistic Missile Defence (ALTBMD) Programme Management Organisation, which comprises a Steering Committee and a Programme Office hosted by the NATO C3 Agency, directs the programme and reports to the CNAD. The focal point for consultation on full-scale missile defence is the Reinforced Executive Working Group. The CNAD is responsible for conducting technical studies and reporting the outcome to the group. The NRC Ad hoc Working Group on TMD is the steering body for NATO-Russia cooperation on theatre missile defence.

Missile Defence

By early 2010, NATO has an initial capability to protect Alliance forces against missile threats and is examining options for protecting territory and populations. This is in response to the proliferation of weapons of mass destruction and their delivery systems, including missiles of all ranges. The Alliance is conducting three missile defence related activities.

Active Layered Theatre Ballistic Missile Defence System Capability

Active Layered Theatre Ballistic Missile Defence System is "ALTBMD" for short. By early 2010, the Alliance will have an interim capability to protect troops in a specific area against short-range and medium-range ballistic missiles (up to 3,000 km). The end system will consist of a multi-layered system of systems comprising low and high-altitude defences (also called lower and upper layer defences), including Battle Management Command, Control, Communications and Intelligence (BMC3I), early warning sensors, radar, and various interceptors. NATO member countries will provide the sensors and weapon systems, while NATO will develop the BMC3I segment and facilitate the integration of all these elements.

Missile Defence for the Protection of NATO Territory

A Missile Defence Feasibility Study was launched after the 2002 Prague Summit. The NATO Consultation, Command and Control Agency (NC3A) and NATO's Conference of National Armaments Directors (CNAD) were also involved in negotiations. The study concluded that missile defence is technically feasible, and it provided a technical basis for ongoing political and military discussions regarding the desirability of a NATO missile defence system.

During the 2008 Bucharest Summit, the Alliance discussed the technical details as well as the political and military implications of the proposed elements of the US missile defence system in Europe. Allied leaders recognised that the planned deployment of European-based US missile defence assets would help protect North American Allies, and agreed that this capability should be an integral part of any future NATO-wide missile defence architecture. However, these opinions are in the process of being reconstructed given the Obama Administration's decision in 2009 to replace the long range interceptor project in Poland with a short/medium range interceptor.

Theatre Missile Defence Cooperation with Russia

Under the auspices of the NATO-Russia Council, a study was launched in 2003 to assess possible levels of interoperability among in-theatre missile defence systems of NATO Allies and Russia.

Together with the interoperability study, several computer-assisted exercises have been held to provide the basis for future improvements to interoperability and to develop mechanisms and procedures for joint operations in the area of in-theatre missile defence.

Aegis-Based System

In order to accelerate the deployment of a missile shield over Europe, Barack Obama sent ships with the Aegis ballistic missile defence system to European waters, including the Black Sea as needed.

In 2012, the system will achieve an "interim capability" that will for the first time offer American forces in Europe some protection against an IRBM attack.

Defence Systems and Initiatives

Missile defence systems of various nations:

- Akash missile surface-to-air missile defence system.
- Arrow missile.
- HQ-9 regional air defence/anti-ballistic missile.
- Indian ballistic missile defence programme.
- Iron Dome.
- KS-1 regional air defence missile.
- Medium Extended Air Defence System (MEADS).
- MIM-104 Patriot Surface-to-Air Missile (SAM) system
- Hawk medium range SAM system.
- RIM-161 Standard missile 3.
- Russian A-135 anti-ballistic missile system.
- S-400 Triumf.
- Strategic Defence Initiative ("Star Wars").
- Terminal High Altitude Area Defence (THAAD)
- Vigilant Eagle airport surface-to-air missile protection system.
- SAMP/T Italian-French missile air defence system.

Regional Theatre Ballistic Missile Capabilities

The biggest user of ballistic missiles in Asia is China, followed by North Korea, India, and Pakistan. The most numerous weapons are theatre oriented, either Tactical Ballistic Missiles (TBMs) or Intermediate Range Ballistic Missiles (IRBMs), along with Inter-Continental Ballistic Missiles (ICBMs) operated by China and being developed by India and North Korea. China operates a wide range of weapons. Legacy weapons include the DF-3/DF-3A (2,800 km), DF-4 (4,750 km), and DF-5/DF-5A (13,000 km). TBMs include the M-7 (160 km), DF-11/M-11 (300 km), DF-15/M-9 (500 km). The primary IRBM and SLBM is the DF-21/JL-1 series (1,800 km), supplemented by the DF-25 (1,800 km). Modern ICBMs include the developmental DF-31 and DF-41 series. There are claims that China is adapting the DF-21 with terminal guidance as an anti-shipping weapon.

India's capabilities are modest in comparison, and include the Prithvi TBM in three variants, with ranges between 150 and 350 km, and the navalised Dhanush with 250 km class range, recently tested. IRBM capability is provided by the Agni I (900 km) and Agni II (1,800 km). The Agni III is a developmental ICBM derivative (2,500-3,000 km). India has also tested the Agni IV (5,000 km).

Pakistan has been very active in developing TBMs and IRBMs, mostly based on Chinese and North Korean technology. The indigenous Hatf 1 and 2 span ranges between 100 and 280 km, the M-11 Shaheen, M-9 Shaheen I and the M-18 Shaheen II are Chinese technology, and the Ghauri I is an IRBM based on the Korean No Dong.

The Democratic People's Republic of Korea (DPRK) has been very active in developing IRBM and ICBM technology, as part of its long running strategy of extracting concessions by WMD blackmail of regional powers. The regime has also been a primary supplier to Iran, and partly to Pakistan. The DPRK has three families of missiles, based on the R-11/SS-1 Scud, the R-21/SS-N-5 Sark, and the R-27/SS-N-6 Serb. The Hwa-Song 5 and 6 are stretched Scud B/C/D TBMs, the No Dong A IRBM is a derivative of the Soviet R-21, and the No Dong B of the Soviet R-27. The Taepo Dong 1 and 2 are three-stage ICBM growth variants of the No Dong series, with the capability to reach the US or Australia.

Ballistic Missile Defence Systems

At this point in time, a number of systems are deployed or in the development stage to effect engagements against ballistic missiles.

USAF YAL-1A Airborne Laser System

The technologically most advanced system at this time is the cancelled Boeing/USAF YAL-1A Airborne Laser (ABL) system, a 2 megawatt Chemical Oxygen Iodine Laser (COIL) DEW carried by a modified Boeing 747-400F airframe. The weapon was being developed to effect boost phase engagements against TBMs, IRBMs and ICBMs from ranges of up to 400 km. The US aim was to deploy a small fleet of these aircraft to patrol the borders of rogue states, like the DPRK or Iran, and destroy any ballistic missiles which might be launched, resulting in their WMD payloads falling back on the territory of origin. The ABL was a challenging programme with ambitious goals, as the turbulent and particle laden atmosphere is a difficult propagation environment for the 1.315 micron laser beam to penetrate over a distance. The ABL uses a pilot beam laser to illuminate the target, and a Hartmann-Shack wavefront sensor to generate beam wavefront distortions, intended to compensate for atmospheric effects. Problems encountered to date include the 'firefly' effect, where atmospheric dust particles floating in the beam are partly vapourised, producing superheated gas plumes and further disturbing the propagation environment. The programme was in the development phase, with funding for production systems contingent on the success of the development article, when funding was cut in 2010, and the programme cancelled in late 2011, as the US defence budget collapsed.

Almaz-Antey S-300PMU1/PMU2/S-400 Gargoyle/Growler

Russia is currently marketing two families of the ABM system, based on the S-300PMU/S-400 Grumble/Gargoyle system, and the S-300V/VM Giant/Gladiator system. While both had shared their early origins during the 1970s, they are unique missile systems with different radars, missiles and guidance systems. The S-300PMU-1/PMU-2 provides some ABM capability akin to that in the early Patriot PAC-1 series, with variants of the 48N6 missile guided by the L-band 64N6E Big Bird acquisition radar and the X-band 30N6E Flap Lid engagement radar, the latter an analogue to the US MPQ-53 Patriot radar. With the transition to the newer S-400 variant, the 9M96E/E2 interceptor missiles were introduced, and radar enhancements added, to provide an ABM capability similar to the PAC-3. All weapons use Track Via Missile (TVM) guidance similar to the Patriot series. The system has been actively marketed in the ABM role.

Almaz-Antey S-300V Gladiator and Antey 2500/S-300VM

The alternative is the Antey 2500 or S-300VM, an enhanced PVO-SV S-300V system, armed with the hypersonic 9M82 and 9M83 missiles, guided by the 9S19M Imbir / High Screen acquistion radar and the 9S32M Grill Pan engagement radar. The missiles use semi-active continuous wave homing, with illuminators on each Transporter Erector Launcher (TEL). Unlike the S-300PMU/S-400 series which evolved from killing aircraft to an ABM, the S-300V was designed from the outset as an ABM, to the extent that the specialised High Screen ABM radar is used. Both the S-300V and the S-300PMU-2/S-400 are highly mobile weapon systems, equipped with radio datalinks to connect battery elements.

Raytheon MIM-104 Patriot PAC-1/2/3

The US competitor to the S-300PMU/S-400 and S-300VM is the MIM-104 Patriot supported by the MPQ-53 family of acquistion and engagement radars. The Patriot MIM-104B PAC-1, with limited ABM capability via warhead and fusing modifications was introduced during the late 1980s, and used during the 1991 Gulf War with widely disputed success. The further improved MIM-104C PAC-3 was also deployed during the 1991 conflict. It was followed in 1994 by the MIM-104D PAC-2/GEM (Guidance Enhanced Missile) system, since to be replaced with the enhanced MIM-104E GEM+ system, with further missile modifications. The most recent variant is the PAC-3 variant, in three consecutive configurations, the latest of which includes the revised MPQ-65 radar and the Lockheed Martin ERINT (Extended Range Interceptor) missile. The ERINT is a US analogue to the Russian 9M96 series, a compact and agile missile with Ka-band active seeker and thrusters.

Theatre High Altitude Area Defence System

The THAAD employs the Raytheon Systems AN/TPY-2 X-band Ground-Based Radar (GBR), a 9.2m² phased array with 25,344 solid-state X-band transmit and receive modules and a cited range of up to 1,000 km. The THAAD missile is a two-stage design using a Kinetic Kill Vehicle (KKV), equipped with a liquid fuelled manoeuvring system and imaging thermal seeker. A typical battery uses 9 M1075 Oshkosh Truck Corporation Heavy Expanded Mobility Tactical Truck with Load Handling System (HEMTT-LHS) as TELs and a single towed AN/TPY-2 radar.

Fig 3: The Aegis Ballistic Missile Defence System.

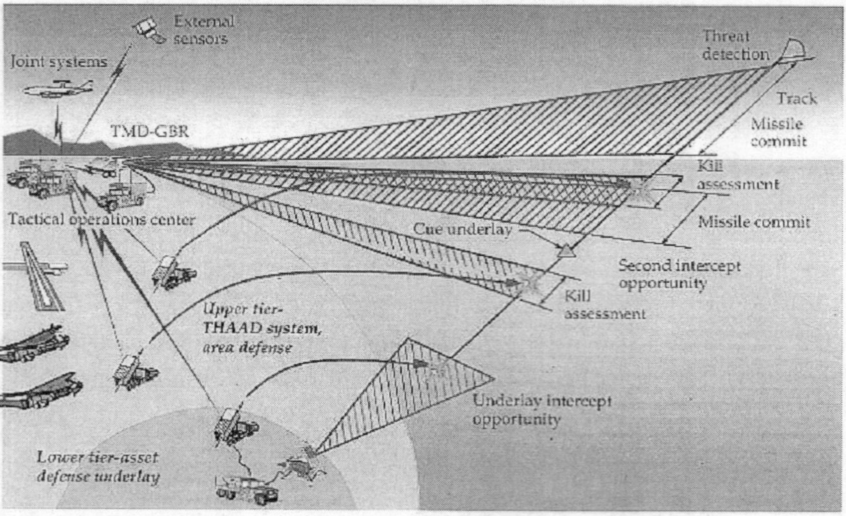

Fig 4: A RIM-161 Standard Missile 3 Anti-Ballistic Missile is Launched from the USS *Shiloh*, a US Navy Ticonderoga-Class Cruiser.

IAI Green Pine / Arrow System

The Israeli competitor to the THAAD is the Green Pine / Arrow system. The Elta EL/M-2090 Green Pine is a phased array acquisition and engagement radar, which guides the two stage IAI Arrow 2 ABM. The hypersonic missile is equipped with an active radar and infrared seeker.

Raytheon RIM-161 Standard SM-3

The US Navy is the final big player in this market with a planned two layered system built around the SPY-1 Aegis radar, and two variants of the Standard series missile. The NTW-TBMD (Navy Theatre-Wide - Theatre Ballistic Missile Defence) was to use the RIM-156 Standard SM-2ER Block IV missile for lower altitude engagements, and the Raytheon RIM-161 Standard SM-3 for high altitude engagements. With the cancellation of the RIM-156 capability, the system is now centred on the RIM-161, which uses a new booster, and a LEAP (Lightweight Exo-Atmospheric Projectile) infrared guided terminal vehicle.

Fig 5: Aegis BMD SM-3 Evolution Plan

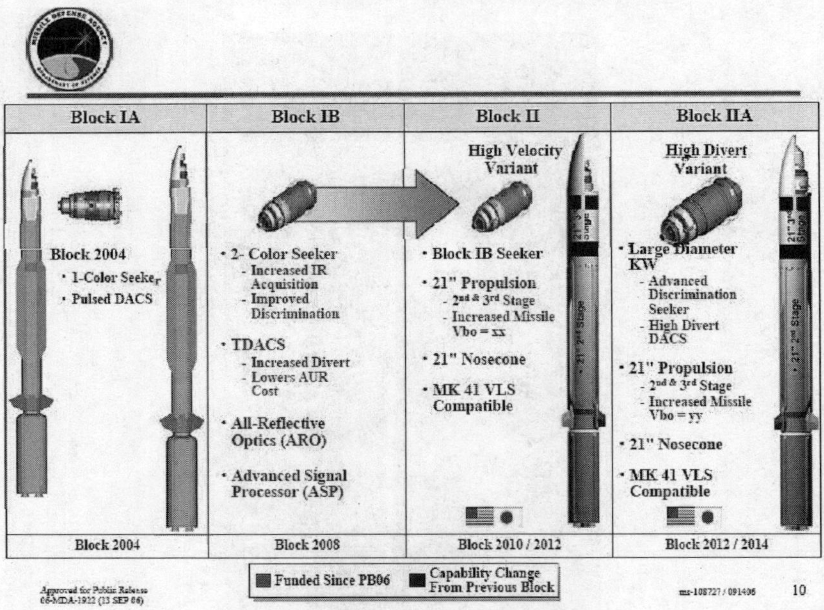

Fig 6: RIM-161/SM-3 LEAP Infrared Seeker Module (US DoD)

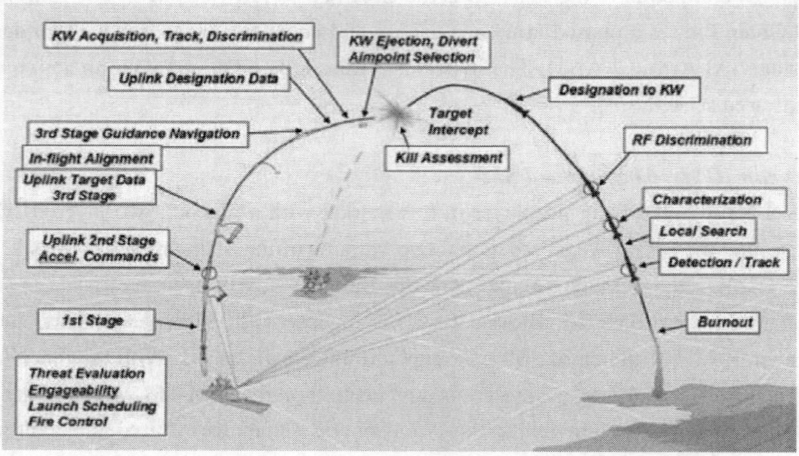

Fig 7: Launch of Advanced Air Defence (AAD) Missile

From Wikipedia, the free encyclopaedia

- Launching of Advanced Air Defence (AAD) Missile
- The Indian ballistic missile defence programme is an initiative to develop and deploy a multi-layered ballistic missile defence system to protect India from ballistic missile attacks.
- Introduced in the light of the ballistic missile threat from Pakistan, it is a double-tiered system consisting of two interceptor missiles, namely the Prithvi Air Defence (PAD) missile for high altitude interception, and the Advanced Air Defence (AAD) missile for lower altitude interception. The two-tiered shield should be able to intercept any incoming missile launched 5,000 km away.
- The PAD was tested in November 2006, followed by the AAD in December 2007. With the test of the PAD missile, India became the fourth country to have successfully developed an anti-ballistic missile system, after the United States, Russia and Israel. On March 6, 2009, India again successfully tested its missile defence shield, during which an incoming "enemy" missile was intercepted at an altitude of 75 km.

Background

Since the early 1990s, India has faced the threat of ballistic missile attacks from Pakistan against which it has fought multiple wars in the past, and also from China. With the heightening of tensions in the region, and in response to Pakistan's deployment of M-11 missiles bought from China, in August 1995, the Indian government procured six batteries of Russian S-300 surface-to-air missiles to protect New Delhi and other cities. In May 1998, India, for the second time (since its first test in 1974), tested nuclear weapons (Pokhran-II), followed by Pakistan (Chagai-I) with its first ever nuclear test. With Pakistan's testing of nuclear weapons and missile delivery systems, this threat intensified. India has also developed and tested missile delivery systems. In 1999, the Kargil War between India and Pakistan became the first direct conflict between two declared nuclear powers. As the war progressed, the first hint of the possible use of a nuclear weapon was on May 31, when Pakistani Foreign Secretary Shamshad Ahmad made a statement warning that an escalation of the limited conflict could lead Pakistan to use "any weapon" in its arsenal. This was immediately interpreted as an obvious threat of nuclear retaliation by Pakistan in the event of an extended war. The leader of Pakistan's Senate noted that "the purpose of developing weapons becomes meaningless if they are not used when they are needed." Some experts believe that following the nuclear tests in 1998, the Pakistani military was emboldened by its nuclear deterrent cover to markedly increase coercion against India.

Development of an anti-ballistic missile system began in late 1999, suggesting that India initiated the programme in the light of Pakistan following a nuclear first use policy and heightened tensions during the Kargil War, including a possibility of full scale nuclear war.

Development

Phase 1

Development of the anti-ballistic missile system began in 1999. Around 40 public and private companies were involved in the development of the systems. They include Bharat Electronics Ltd and Bharat Dynamics Ltd, Astra Microwave, Advanced System Laboratory (ASL), Larsen & Toubro, Vem Technologies Private Limited and KelTech. Development of the LRTR (Long Range Tracking Radar) and MFCR (Multi-Function Fire Control Radar) was led by the Electronics and Radar Development Establishment (LRDE).

The Defence Research and Development Laboratory (DRDL) developed the mission control software for the AAD missile. The Research Centre, Imarat (RCI), developed navigation, electromechanical actuation systems and the active radar seeker. The Advanced System Laboratory (ASL) provided the motors, jet vanes and structures for the AAD and PAD and the High Energy Materials Research Laboratory (HEMRL) supplied the propellants for the missile.

Description

The two-tiered BMD system consists of the PAD, which will intercept missiles at exo-atmospheric altitudes of 50–80 km (31–50 mi) and the AAD missile for interception at endo-atmospheric altitudes of up to 30 km (19 mi). The deployed system would consist of many launch vehicles, radars, Launch Control Centres (LCC) and the Mission Control Centre (MCC). All these are geographically distributed and connected by a secure communication network.

The MCC is the software intensive system of the ballistic missile defence system. It receives information from various sources such as radars and satellites which is then processed by ten computers which run simultaneously. The MCC is connected to all other elements of defence through a Wide Area Network (WAN). The MCC performs target classification, target assignment and kill assessment. It also acts as a decision support system for the commander. It can also decide the number of interceptors required for the target for an assured kill probability. After performing all these functions, the MCC assigns the target to the LCC of a launch battery. The LCC starts computing the time to launch the interceptor based upon information received from a radar based on the speed, altitude and flight path of the target. The LCC prepares the missile for launch in real-time and carries out ground guidance computation.

After the interceptor is launched, it is provided target information from the radar through a datalink. When the interceptors close onto the target missile, it activates the radar seeker to search for the target missile and guides itself to intercept the target. Multiple PAD and AAD interceptors can be launched against a target for high kill probability.

Fig 8: Prithvi Air Defence (PAD) / Pradyumna Ballistic Missile Interceptor

Prithvi Air Defence (PAD) 	
Type	Exo-atmospheric anti-ballistic missile
Place of origin	India
Service history	
In service	Under development
Production history	
Manufacturer	DRDO
Produced	November 26, 2006
Specifications	
Detonation mechanism	Proximity
Engine	Two-stage
Propellant	Liquid fuel propelled first stage with two propellants and oxidizers, solid fuel propelled second stage with gas thrusters.
Flight altitude	80 km[13]
Speed	>Mach 5
Guidance system	Inertial Navigation System Ground-based mid-course correction Active radar homing (Terminal phase)
Launch platform	8 x 8 Tatra TEL (Transporter Erector Launcher)

The **Prithvi Air Defence (PAD)** is an anti-ballistic missile developed to intercept incoming ballistic missiles outside the atmosphere (exo-atmospheric). Based on the

Prithvi missile, PAD is a two-stage missile with a maximum interception altitude of 80 km (50 mi). The first stage is a solid fuelled motor while the second stage is liquid fuelled. It has manoeuvre thrusters which can generate a lateral acceleration of more than 5 gs at 50 km (31 mi) altitude. Guidance is provided by an inertial navigation system with mid-course updates from the Long Range Tracking Radar (LRTR) and active radar homing in the terminal phase. The PAD has capability to engage the 300 to 2,000 km (190 to 1,200 mi) class of ballistic missiles at a speed of Mach 5.

The LRTR is the target acquisition and fire control radar for the PAD missile. It is an active phased array radar having capability to track 200 targets at a range of 600 km (370 mi). The PAD missile has also been called Pradyumna.

Further development led to the improvement of the interception range to 80 to 50 km (50 to 31 mi) . The improved missile will utilise a gimballed directional warhead, a technology that until now has only been used by the US and Russia. This technology allows for a smaller warhead to destroy the target missile.

Prithvi Air Defence Exercise

The PADE (Prithvi Air Defence Exercise) was conducted in November 2006 in which a PAD missile successfully intercepted a modified Prithvi-II missile at an altitude of 50 km (31 mi). The Prithvi-II ballistic missile was modified successfully to mimic the trajectory of M-11 missiles.

The Defence Research and Development Organisation (DRDO) plans to test the anti-ballistic shield against missiles with a range of 1,500 km (930 mi). The test will be conducted with a modified Prithvi missile launched from a naval ship and the anti-ballistic missile launched from Wheeler Island. The interception of the target missile will take place at approximately 80 km (50 mi) altitude.

On March 6, 2009, DRDO carried out a second successful test of the PAD interceptor missile. The target used was a ship launched Dhanush missile which followed the trajectory of a missile with range of a 1,500 km (930 mi). The target was tracked by the Swordfish (LRTR) radar and destroyed by the PAD at 75 km (47 mi) altitude.

On March 6, 2011, DRDO successfully test-fired an interceptor missile from the Advanced Air Defence (AAD) missiles which destroyed a 'hostile' target ballistic missile, a modified Prithvi, at an altitude of 16 km over the Bay of Bengal. The AAD missile positioned at Wheeler Island, about 70 km across sea from Chandipur, received signals from tracking radars installed along the coastline and travelled through the sky at a speed of 4.5 Mach to destroy it.

Fig 9: Advanced Air Defence (AAD)/Ashwin Ballistic Missile Interceptor

Advanced Air Defence (AAD)	

Advanced Air Defence (AAD) missile being launched during Electronic Target Trials on December 2, 2007 from Wheeler's Island Test Range in Orissa.	
Type	Endo-atmospheric anti-ballistic missile
Place of origin	India
Service history	
In service	Under development
Production history	
Manufacturer	DRDO
Produced	December 6, 2007
Specifications	
Weight	1,200 kg
Length	7.5 m
Diameter	<0.5 m
Detonation mechanism	Kinetic Kill (Hit-to-Kill)
Engine	Single stage
Propellant	Solid fuel
Flight ceiling	30 km
	SAM operational range = 150-200 km
Speed	Mach 4.5
Guidance system	Inertial Navigation System mid-course update active radar homing (terminal phase)
Launch platform	8 x 8 Tatra TEL (Transporter Erector Launcher)

The AAD is an anti-ballistic missile designed to intercept incoming ballistic missiles in the endo-atmosphere at an altitude of 30 km (19 mi). The AAD is a single stage, solid fuelled missile. Guidance is similar to that of the PAD: it has an inertial navigation system, mid-course updates from ground-based radar and active radar homing in the terminal phase. It is 7.5 m (25 ft) tall, weighs around 1.2 t (1.2 long tons; 1.3 short tons) and has a diameter of less than 0.5 m (1 ft 8 in).

On December 6, 2007, the AAD successfully intercepted a modified Prithvi-II missile acting as an incoming ballistic missile enemy target. The endo-atmospheric interception was carried out at an altitude of 15 km (9.3 mi). The interceptor and all the elements performed in copy book fashion, validating the endo-atmospheric layer of the defence system. The launch was also shown through a video link at a control room of DRDO at Delhi.

The sequence of events of the test was as follows. At 11 am, the Prithvi missile lifted off from Launch Complex III at the Integrated Test Range (ITR) at Chandipur, Orissa. Radars at Konark, Paradip, detected the missile and were continuously tracking it. The target information was sent to the MCC for further processing. The MCC classified the target, calculated the trajectory of the missile and assigned the target to an AAD battery located on Wheeler Island, 70 km (43 mi) across the sea from Chandipur.The AAD was launched when the Prithvi reached an apogee of 110 km (68 mi). The AAD, with the help of mid-course updates and its terminal seeker, manoeuvres itself towards the target. The AAD makes a direct hit at an altitude of 15 km (9.3 mi) and at a speed of Mach 4. Radars detected formation of a large number of tracks, signifying that the target had broken into multiple pieces. The thermal cameras located on Wheeler Island also picked up the direct hit through thermal images.

Due to two successful interceptor missile tests carried out by India, scientists have said that the AAD missile could be modified into a new extended range (up to 150 km (93 mi)) surface-to-air missile that could be possibly named 'Ashvin'.

On March 15, 2010, the AAD interceptor missile test from the Orissa coast was aborted, as the target missile deviated from its path and plunged into the sea. The AAD missile was to intercept the target at an altitude of 15 to 20 km over the sea. The target, a Prithvi missile, fired at 10:02 am from a mobile launcher from the Integrated Test Range Complex-3 at Chandipur-on-Sea, 15 km away, deviated from its trajectory after travelling about 11 km and fell into the sea.

On July 26, 2010, the AAD was successfully test-fired from the Integrated Test Range (ITR) at Wheeler Island off Orissa's east coast.

On March 6, 2011, India launched its indigenously developed interceptor missile from the Orissa coast. India successfully test-fired its interceptor missile which destroyed a 'hostile' target ballistic missile, a modified Prithvi, at an altitude of 16 km over the

Bay of Bengal. The interceptor, an AAD missile positioned at Wheeler Island, about 70 km across sea from Chandipur, received signals from tracking radars installed along the coastline and travelled through the sky at a speed of 4.5 Mach to destroy it. As the trial was aimed at achieving the desired result with precision, the interceptor missile had its own mobile launcher, secure datalink for interception, independent tracking and homing capabilities and sophisticated radars. "It was a fantastic launch. The trial, conducted from two launch sites of ITR off the Orissa coast for developing a full-fledged multi-layer Ballistic Missile Defence (BMD) system, was fully successful."

On February 10, 2012, the AAD was again successfully test-fired from Wheeler Island off the state coast near Dhamra in Bhadrak district, about 170 km from Bhubhaneswar.

Swordfish Long Range Tracking RADAR

The Swordfish is the target acquisition and fire control radar for the BMD system. The LRTR currently has a range of 600 km (370 mi) to 800 km (500 mi) and can spot objects as small as a cricket ball. The DRDO plans to upgrade the capacity of the Swordfish to 1,500 km by 2011.

Phase 2

Two new anti-ballistic missiles that can intercept IRBMs are being developed. These high speed missiles (AD-1 and AD-2) are being developed to intercept ballistic missiles with a range of around 5,000 km (3,100 mi). The test trials of these two systems are expected to take place in 2013. The new missile will be similar to the THAAD missile deployed by the USA. These missiles will travel at hypersonic speeds and will require radars with scan capability of over 1,500 km (930 mi) to successfully intercept the target. On May 6, 2012, Dr. V. K. Saraswat, while confirming the completion of Phase-I, added that Phase-II would be completed by 2016 to protect against missiles having a range up to 5,000 km.

India is also planning to develop a laser-based weapon system as part of its defence to intercept and destroy missiles soon after they are launched towards the country. DRDO's Air Defence Programme Director V. K. Saraswat says it is ideal to destroy a ballistic missile carrying nuclear or conventional warheads in its boost phase. Saraswat further added that it will take another 10–15 years for the premier defence research institute to make it usable on the ground.

PDV

In 2009, reports emerged of a new missile named the PDV. The PDV is said to be a two solid stage hypersonic anti-ballistic missile similar in class to the THAAD. The PDV is intended to replace the existing PAD in the PAD/AAD combination. It will have an Infinite Impulse Response (IIR) seeker for its kill vehicle as well. The PDV will replace the PAD with a far more capable missile and will complete the Phase 1 of the BMD system, allowing it to be operational by 2013. Whereupon Phase 2 development will take over for protection against missiles of the 5,000 km (3,100 mi) range class. The first test flight of the missile is expected in 2010. The PDV is designed to take out the target missile at altitudes above 150 km (93 mi).

Deployment

According to scientist V. K. Saraswat of DRDO, the missiles will work in tandem to ensure a hit probability of 99.8 percent. On May 6, 2012, Dr. V. K. Saraswat confirmed that Phase-I is complete and can be deployed to protect two Indian cities at a short notice. He also added that Phase-I is comparable to the PAC-3 system. New Delhi, the national capital, and Mumbai, have been selected for the ballistic missile defence shield. After successful implementation in Delhi and Mumbai, the system will be used to cover other major cities in the country. This shield can destroy incoming ballistic missiles launched from as far as 2,500 km away. When Phase II is completed and PDV is developed, the two anti-ballistic missiles can intercept targets up to 5,000 km in both exo- and endo-atmospheric (inside the atmosphere) regions. The missiles will work in tandem to ensure a hit probability of 99.8 per cent.

Cooperation Offered by United States

According to US Deputy Defence Secretary Ashton Carter, there is potential for cooperation with India to develop a BMD shield. "That is an important potential area for our future cooperation," Carter said while on his visit to India in July 2012.

References

1. PRC Theatre Missile Systems - http://www.fas.org/nuke/guide/china/theater/index.html
2. Indian Missile Programs - http://www.fas.org/nuke/guide/india/missile/index.html
3. Pakistan Missile Programs - http://www.fas.org/nuke/guide/pakistan/missile/index.html
4. DPRK Missile Programs - http://www.fas.org/nuke/guide/dprk/missile/index.html
5. Imagery Sources: US DoD, Author, PLA, Others.

4

Pakistan's Desire for Strategic Depth in Afghanistan

Shalini Chawla

As 2014, the deadline for the US' and North Atlantic Treaty Organisation (NATO) troops' withdrawal approaches, the anxiety regarding the future of Afghanistan would grow and, most importantly, the future role of Pakistan in Afghanistan would become extremely critical. The apprehensions regarding the role of Pakistan are obviously intensified given Pakistan's volatile domestic situation, growing extremism within Pakistan and its strained relationship with the United States. The shape of Afghanistan post US withdrawal would be determined by multiple factors, especially the role of other regional powers – India, Russia and China – which have significant stakes in the stability of Afghanistan. Pakistan's role in Afghanistan would certainly impact it the maximum.

Undoubtedly, Pakistan has been overly obsessed with the desire to gain strategic depth in Afghanistan. The all powerful military and the intelligence agency, the Inter-Services Intelligence (ISI), which authored and executed the policy of strategic depth since the late 1980s through the 1990s when it strongly backed the Taliban, till today, strongly believes in having strong control over Afghanistan. There has been slight change in the terminology regarding the military's policy in Afghanistan, but the bottom line remains pretty much unaltered. At no stage was the policy of "strategic depth" logical or viable for Pakistan, and its adoption of the doctrine of strategic depth and, thus, control over Afghanistan is considered a strategic blunder which has actually facilitated Pakistan's drift into extremism and not allowed it the option of altering its strategic calculus. In Pakistan's perception, the strategic depth policy has allowed it to maintain a conventional balance against India, but, on the other hand, this policy has made the tribal areas of Pakistan the hub of terrorism, and militancy and extremism are perhaps at their peak at present, resulting in loss of Pakistan's sovereignity. For the first time in the history of Pakistan, not only did the military General Headquarters (GHQ) suffer a terrorist attack in 2009 but by now, the establishments of all the three forces, the Army, Navy and Air

Force have been attacked. The latest one in the series has been the attack on Kamra Air Base during which the Pakistan Air Force (PAF) claimed to have suffered the loss of at least one JF-17.

The doctrine of strategic depth has been considered outdated and outcast by several scholars who believe that with the overt nuclearisation of Pakistan, the doctrine has lost whatever meaning it had. But for a better understanding of the issues related to Pakistan's 'strategic depth' and its endorsement in Pakistan's policy-making, it will be useful to look into the concept of strategic depth.

Defining Strategic Depth

The concept of strategic depth has been interpreted differently by different policy-makers and scholars, but broadly two approaches can be classified.

First, and a more traditional approach to the concept of strategic depth is as it is understood in the pure military literature. Strategic depth, according to this interpretation, is the distance between the battle sectors and the combatant's capital cities, industrial areas, defence production units and other units of strategic importance. The military planners need to calculate the vulnerability of these assets in the case of a military offensive. The creation of strategic depth would allow a country's forces to move back deeper into their own territory, absorb the offensive thrust of the enemy short of his military objectives and also, apply power on the vulnerabilities of the attacking military. [1]

Strategic depth, when interpreted in purely military terms, can have three-fold offshoots: first is where the combatant seeks strategic depth in his own territory; second, when a state seeks strategic depth in the neighbouring country, extending its control in the foreign territory and the state is, thus, able to trade territory for a better partner; and third, when the state decides to create buffer states at its borders.

But strategic depth is not merely geographical and could have multiple dimensions: political, social or for that matter, even ideological (as in the case of Pakistan). The concept of strategic depth has been used in the past by Russia, Germany, Poland, and even Mao's 'people war' was a part of strategic depth. Mao's people's war relied on strategic depth within its own territory, China.

Russia did use its vast swath of space in its war against Napoleon and during World War II, when Hitler invaded it. During the Cold War era, the Central Asian Republics provided Russia strategic depth. When Hitler invaded Russia, in addition to *lebensraum*, he was looking for strategic depth. During World War II, Poland, a valiant force, although ill-equipped, lost due to lack of strategic depth. On the other hand, France was defeated but the nation survived as it had strategic depth which provided it with time and space to reorganise and resist the Germans.[2]

In the case of China, Mao's people's war was an all out war fought by land forces supported by a motivated population. The strategy was characterised by drawing in the enemy deep into own territory and ultimately destroying him by attrition of resources by guerrilla forces and aerial offensive. According to Air Cmde Jasjit Singh:

> Mao's "People's War" doctrine was premised on this philosophy, exploiting the strategic depth that China's geographical spread provided, to allow the attacker's offensive to peter out, with its logistic lines extensively stretched and vulnerable; followed by concerted offensive by the defender against an over-extended enemy and defeating it with a combination of guerrilla and conventional war.[3]

The second approach to strategic depth is ideological and religious where the state tries to extend its control and influence by spreading ideology or religious interpretation. In this context, China's efforts of spreading its Communist socialist ideology (through revolutions and war) for extending its control can be well understood. China went in for ideological control in the first 20 years of the formation of the People's Republic of China (PRC) before Mao got embroiled in his own "Cultural Revolution". China's revolutionary war and also its policies in Tibet can be exemplified as an extension of ideological control.

Pakistan's Desire for Strategic Depth

In the case of Pakistan, one must remember that the classical model of strategic depth in relation to India simply cannot work because all its key cities and industry are within 70-odd km from the Indian border. Hence, any withdrawal westward would leave the soul of Pakistan in India's hands. What we need, therefore, is to understand the contours of Pakistan's concept and motivation for strategic depth. Essentially, it has adopted a mix of both the military and ideological approaches in order to gain strategic depth in Afghanistan. If one has to trace the events and the evolution of Pakistan's polices and actions in order to gain strategic depth, both approaches can be seen as parallel for Pakistan. Pakistan has been overly concerned about having a hostile government in Afghanistan and over the decades has interfered in the Afghans' domestic politics. It has perpetually sought a 'friendly government' in Kabul. But, ironically, the relations between Afghanistan and Pakistan are scarred by turbulence and mistrust.

Pakistan's vision of strategic depth surfaced in the late 1980s with Gen Aslam Beg's announcement of "strategic depth" and the Pakistani elites began talking about strategic depth and also explored opportunities to replace the Afghan government led by Najibullah. For decades, Pakistan has bewailed the lack of strategic depth and, hence, the need to create it in neighbouring Afghanistan. Pakistan has always suffered a deep sense of insecurity, partially owing to its geographical limitations and to a great extent due to the fact that it was always apprehensive about India's policies which it perceived as 'hegemonic'. From the beginning, the Pakistani military and elites were concerned about the security of their major cities, like Lahore, and also communication lines, in case of a confrontation with a much larger, conventionally stronger India. Pakistan carried out the first aggression against India in 1947 and then again in 1965, leading to its defeat and further augmenting its threat perceptions. One can presume that the desire for strategic depth would have started to be nurtured after Pakistan's defeat in the 1971 War, in which it lost a significant portion of its military assets also. It was after 1971 that Zulfiqar Ali Bhutto propagated the concept of Pakistan being not just a South Asian state but also a West Asian state. The army under Gen Zia-ul-Haq (since 1976) projected itself as the defender of not only the territorial boundaries of the state but also its 'ideological boundaries'. Strategic depth in this respect was interpreted to include the Muslim nations in order to gain support on varied fronts (including funding for Pakistan's nuclear programme which commenced in 1971).

The Islamisation of the Pakistani state which was being propounded first by Bhutto and much more aggressively by Gen Zia-ul-Haq cannot be seen in isolation. The process is correlated to what was happening at the global level and has to be viewed in the context of the fact that the 1970s and 1980s witnessed the resurgence of Islam as a potent global force. It was the Iranian revolution that shattered the secular bias and expectations of modernisation and development theories. The revolution drew attention towards the significant changes that were taking place in many Muslim countries across the globe in the 1970s. Ironically, the revival of Islamic ideology was most prominent in the societies which were modern or in the process of modernisation, possessing a well-trained, Western oriented, secular elite, for example: Egypt, Lebanon, Tunisia, Turkey and Algeria.

In fact, post 1971, religious ideology manifested itself in a forceful manner, first by Bhutto and followed by the aggressive fundamentalist posture of Gen Zia. In the 1970s itself, Wahabi Islam was being propagated in Pakistan. Pakistan was influenced by this global trend and an Islamic University was built in Pakistan by 1979. Another important development comprised the funds flowing to the Islamic preachers, *maulvis*, in Pakistan from Saudi Arabia and the rising status of *maulvis* in the society. The trend for the adoption of stringent Islamic ideology was on, and Zia boosted it further.

Secondly, Pakistan, with its ambition to be the leader of Islamic states, was certainly keen to spread its influence into other Islamic countries. It succeeded in its efforts and Saudi Arabia provided direct support during the war. Also, Pakistan's nuclear programme launched in the early 1970s and its appeal in the Lahore Islamic Summit for grants fetched it substantial financial support from the Muslim world. So, there was an Islamic factor and Pakistan tried to get the support of the leadership of the Islamic world in its favour.

On the classical military aspect of strategic depth, one would believe that since Pakistan presents a comparatively narrow width, it probably needed the expansion westwards and also, eastwards (in Kashmir). Also, Gen Sunderji's doctrine of "deep strike" in the 1980s would have provided a justification to the Pakistani thinking on the criticality of gaining strategic depth.

On one side, in the 1980s one could see the merger of both approaches for strategic depth and, on the other, the Soviet influence, later followed by their occupation of Afghanistan, created a conducive ground for Pakistan to intervene in Afghanistan. Pakistan's engagement in the Afghan War had varied implications which actually impacted the balance of power in the country. In the 1980s, the ISI emerged as one of the most important decisive factors in Pakistan's power politics. Although the organisation had expanded during Ayub's time, the ISI gained much more strength under Gen Zia, as it was entrusted with the responsibility of recruiting and training the Mujahideen and also running the covert war against the Soviets in the 1980s. Reportedly, the ISI trained about 83,000 Afghan Mujahideen between 1983 and 1997 for the Afghan War. The ISI was responsible for the US equipment supplied (through the Central Intelligence Agency–CIA) to Pakistan for the Afghan War. The ISI received an enormous amount of equipment for the Afghan War but according to reliable Pakistani sources, around 60 percent of the equipment was retained by the ISI and was later used in the covert war against India.

The ISI became a state within a state, answerable to no one, neither the Prime Minister, nor the President. The ISI, which has been an extension of the army, fully supported the Rabbani government in the early 1990s in Afghanistan. The Afghan War provided a legitimate infrastructure to Pakistan for preparing *jihadis* and using them for covert war. As Pakistan was anyway following the covert war strategy with India, the Afghan War reinforced the existing strategy which intensified in the coming decades. The democratic regime in Pakistan was further weakened with this extended military takeover and the ISI gaining strength.

Pakistan's border regions, the Federally Administered Tribal Areas (FATA) and Northwest Frontier Province (NWFP) (now Khyber Pakhtunwa–KPK) became the staging posts for *jihad* because of their proximity to the eastern and southeastern Afghan provinces of Paktika, Paktia, Nangarhar, Kunar, Zabul and Kandahar. The lawless tribal areas served as transit posts for weapons, narcotics and Islamist zealots pouring in from all over the world to join the anti-Russian *jihad* inside Afghanistan. These areas became the training ground for the Mujahideen and ideal location of factories (e.g. Dera Adam Khel) to manufacture arms and narcotics, to feed the insurgency. Dozens of training camps flourished in FATA, NWFP and also Baluchistan. Apart from this, hundreds of *madrassas* mushroomed in these areas, preparing the future warriors dedicated to *jihad*. The seminaries or *madrassas* catered to the Afghan refugees and also recruited volunteers for the Afghan War.

Pakistan was also now able to realise its long-cherished dream of securing *strategic depth* in Afghanistan. With its involvement in the Afghan War, the ISI was able to gather enough expertise in waging guerrilla war and also obtain sufficient equipment to accelerate and intensify the war in Kashmir and other parts of the Indian territory. While the ISI gained experience and expertise in waging insurgency, the insurgent Afghan groups also gained experience, expertise, money and weapons to wage insurgency. Some of these insurgents have remained loyal to the ISI and the Army, even though the Pakistan Army is now compelled to carry out counter-insurgency operations against some of the old groups.

In the 1980s, Osama bin Laden, the world's most wanted terrorist, found sanctuary on the fringes of Miranshah in North Waziristan, the tribal agency that borders the eastern Afghan province of Paktia. So Afghanistan and the frontier borders of Pakistan became the perfect training ground for terrorists for Pakistan where thousands of *jihadis* could be trained to carry on the military's covert war against India not only in Kashmir but also other parts (Punjab). In order to continue this process, Pakistan needed a favourable governance in Kabul and, thus, the need for having the Taliban regime whose radical ideology was preferred in Islamabad. Having a Pashtun dominated government in Kabul was like an insurance policy for Pakistan against the Indian factor. The policy-makers in Pakistan somehow assumed that India had plans to occupy Pakistan with full military force. It will not be incorrect to say that the threat from India was overhyped to be able to justify or legitimise control over Afghanistan. Pakistani policies in the late 1980s and 1990s amounted to rendering Afghanistan a satellite state and had a clear strategy of, firstly, denying India any political or economic influence in Kabul, and, secondly, facilitating a favourable government in Kabul which would not allow the Pashtun nationalism simmering on the frontier borders of Pakistan to secede.[4] Pakistan, under the leadership of Benazir Bhutto, created the Taliban (to replace the Mujahideen government it had installed in 1992) and provided full political, logistical and military support to them, who then finally captured Kabul in 1996, establishing their complete control over Afghanistan.

At no stage was strategic depth really viable for Pakistan. Looking at the classical (military) interpretation of strategic depth, Pakistan's case in Afghanistan is irrelevant. Strategic depth in the classical sense can be used if there is substantive territory which the country is willing to give up or which the country might occupy. Pakistan needs strategic depth because, in case of an Indian invasion, major Pakistani cities would be lost and Pakistan would cease to exist. So what strategic depth are the Pakistanis talking about? In fact, Pakistan's entire struggle and its desire for taking control of Kashmir during the aggression in 1947 was due to the fear that in case Jammu and Kashmir (J&K) acceded to India, the Indian Army would be sitting on the border. As Akbar Khan said:

> One glance at the map was enough to show that Pakistan's military security would be seriously jeopardised if Indian troops came to be stationed along Kashmir's western borders. Once India got the chance, she could establish such stations everywhere within a few miles of the 180 miles long vital road and rail route between Lahore and Rawalpindi. In the event of war, these stations would be a dangerous threat to our most important civil and military lines of communications......the possession of Kashmir would enable India, if she wished, to take the war directly to Hazara and Muree—more than 200 miles behind the front.[5]

The 1947 Pakistani aggression can be seen as an attempt to create "strategic depth" eastwards. In 1947, the Pakistani leadership clearly understood the implications of their cities and lines of communication being close to the border. Therefore, when Pakistan talks of strategic depth, it is not based on the classical historical model.

By using the term strategic depth, Pakistan seeks rationalisation of its control and influence in Afghanistan for a number of reasons which can be listed as follows:

- One of the most important factors in determining Pakistan's policies in Afghanistan is the lingering Afghanistan-Pakistan border issue based on the Durand Line, which separates the tribal areas of the NWFP of Pakistan from Afghanistan. No Afghan regime, including the Rabbani government, has ever accepted the legitimacy of the border drawn by the British in 1893 – the so-called Durand Line.[6] The Durand Line Agreement was to last for 100 years and expired in 1993. It was very clear that the Afghan regime would not recognise the agreement and would seek to incorporate the Pashtun areas east of the Durand Line, into Afghanistan. As the Soviets were leaving in 1989 and the timeline for the expiry of the agreement (1993) was also closer,

Pakistan publicly pursued the doctrine of strategic depth, creating Afghanistan as a satellite state for Pakistan. Benazir Bhutto oficially authorised the creation and launching of the Taliban in 1991.

- Pakistan has faced the issue of Pashtun nationalism which demanded a separate Pashtunistan from the 1940s. There have been concomitant calls for an independent Pashtun homeland in FATA, KPK and parts of Baluchistan. These areas have been alienated and grossly underdeveloped for decades and the state has always had unique administrative and legislative arrangements which successive governments have used to administer the region. The Pakistani leadership which anyway was extremely dissatisfied with the small size of the country, that Jinnah had called a "moth-eaten" Pakistan, certainly wanted to prevent the creation of Pashtunistan and thus, further disintegration of Pakistan. Control and influence over Afghanistan by a Pashtun dominated (essentially Taliban) government would, therefore, reduce the demand for Pashtunistan and yet have the Pashtuns under Pakistan's control.

  What is also interesting to note is that FATA's anachronistic status was sustained by the military in Pakistan and, thus, the region provided space and liberty to the military to maintain its influence among the Pashtun tribes in neighbouring Afghanistan.[7] Also, "FATA acted as a buffer against predatory Afghan influence while allowing the military to interfere freely in Afghanistan. This became critical in the 1980s when the CIA-ISI arms pipeline to the Afghan Mujahideen went through FATA."[8]
- During the 1965 War, Pakistan managed to move its aircraft to the Iranian airfields of Zahedan across the Baluchistan border. Pakistan was not certain that the same facility would be available in the future. Therefore, for protecting its aircraft against Indian strikes, Pakistan looked at the airfields in Afghanistan, but their use by the Pakistan Air Force (PAF) would be conditional to the government in Kabul agreeing to it. Pakistan's military objective was to use the Afghan territory and air bases as a sanctuary for Pakistan. The Afghan territory would also provide the military with a much larger space for combat training without the risk of being monitored by the radars on the Indian side.
- Pakistan has followed the strategy of covert war through terrorism against India for more than 25 years now. The strategy is not new and Pakistan's first aggression in 1947 was initiated in the name of tribal revolt and, thus, the same was repeated in Operation Gibralter in 1965. Pakistan's covert war against India has been much more active since the late 1980s which can be correlated to the expertise gained as a frontline state during the Afghan War and also acquisition of nuclear technology in

1987 which was to act as a shield for terrorist activities in India and prevent Indian retaliation in response to terrorism.

Afghanistan provided Pakistan a safe haven to train the Islamist militants such as Harakat-ul-Mujahideen (HuM), Jaish-e-Muhammad (JeM) and Lashkar-e-Tayyeba (LeT), which were to conduct terrorist activities in Jammu and Kashmir and, eventually in other parts of India, including Punjab. A pro-Pakistan government in Kabul would certainly be much more supportive of Pakistan using Afghanistan to nurture these groups.

- Undermining Indian influence in Afghanistan has always been a priority for Pakistan. A former French diplomat, Fre'de'ric Grare, has said, "According to Pakistan, whatever India does in Afghanistan is a ploy against Pakistan, be it economic investment, infrastructure, or any related matter....As a result, Pakistan has ensured that Indian interest would be blocked whenever and wherever possible".[9]

  India obviously has interest in Afghanistan as it is India's route to Central Asia and India has always shared good relations with Afghanistan. But the Pakistani leadership refuses to believe that India has any other interest in Afghanistan other than destabilising Pakistan. Islamabad has always viewed India's actions in Afghanistan as a policy of encirclement and, thus, in its view, a radical Islamist regime–the Taliban – would help to cut down India's role in the region.
- Pakistan's control over Afghanistan gives it access to the Central Asian Republics. Pakistan is undoubtedly keen to expand its options for energy transportation due to the increasing demand for energy within Pakistan. It wants to occupy the commercial and strategic space in the Central Asian Republics before India can expand its influence.
- Lastly, and very importantly, by using the normally not well understood terminology "strategic depth", which sounds impressive, the Pakistani leadership could influence the public opinion to support its polices.

Success of Strategic Depth ?

How successful Pakistan's policy of creating strategic depth in Afghanistan has been is, obviously, a matter of discussion, although the general consensus is that Pakistan's Afghanistan policy has been, by and large, unsuccessful. Pakistan supported the Taliban regime in the 1990s for strategic objectives but did not get the desired results. The Pakistani leadership miscalculated that the Taliban regime in Afghanistan would lead to recognition of the Durand Line and also, Pashtun nationalism would be much more under control. But, obviously none of the Pakistani assumptions came true: the Durand Line issue remained, and Pashtun nationalism was, in fact, further nurtured by the Taliban.

Pakistan's Relations with Afghanistan

Pakistan had some success in keeping the government in Kabul weak and under some control. It has managed to create bilateral trade relations with Afghanistan and, at present, is Kabul's leading trading partner. The long awaited Afghan-Pakistan Transit Trade Agreement (APTTA) which was signed in October 2010, was implemented in June 2011. As a landlocked nation, Afghanistan is compelled to use the Pakistani route for its imports and exports – reportedly, goods worth $ 2 billion are imported by Afghanistan through Pakistan, and Pakistan exports about $ 4 billion worth of goods to the Middle East through Afghanistan. [10] Reports suggest that Pakistan often delays the Afghan containers which has added to the existing tensions between the two countries.

Pakistan's continued support to the Afghan Taliban and other extremist factions allowed the insurgency to resurface in 2003, during the Musharraf regime. Continued Pakistani support has not allowed the insurgency to dissipate. But despite continued intervention by Pakistan, it has been unable to control a large part of Afghanistan. It has been unable to exercise its soft power influence in the neighbourhood. The general opinion in Afghanistan resists Pakistan's involvement in the country and the Pakistani elites are well aware of this. *Dawn*, a leading Pakistani daily reported: "...how can Afghanistan be our 'strategic depth' when most Afghans hate our guts, not only the northerners, but even those who call themselves Pakhtuns*?"* [11]

Pakistan's strategies in Afghanistan have proved ineffective and not has only Pakistan failed to sustain its strategic depth but has become very unpopular in Afghanistan. There has been an increasing number of border skirmishes between Pakistan and the Afghanistan security forces. The latest incident began on May 13, 2007, when the Afghan ground soldiers reportedly attacked Pakistani posts, resulting in the killing of eight Pakistani soldiers, and again in 2011, when Pakistani missiles began shelling Afghanistan territory. In July 2011, there were massive protests by Afghans resisting the continuous shelling by Pakistan in Afghanistan's eastern provinces. In June 2012, again, a fresh round of skirmishes was reported and the Afghan leadership blamed Pakistan of opening rocket fire on Afghan posts and Islamabad, in turn, accused Kabul of allowing Afghan soldiers to enter Pakistan.[12] The Afghan leadership has actually threatened to approach the UN against the Pakistani shellings on Afghan villages, particularly those in the Kunar province.[13] Both Pakistan and Afghanistan blame each other for flaming insurgencies in their respective territories. The US has been been trying hard to reduce tensions between Afghanistan and Pakistan over cross-border skirmishes but not with much success.[14]

The Pakistani leadership has tried hard to establish control over Afghanistan but the reverse has happened. Karzai continues to be dissatisfied with the military's and ISI's interference in the functioning of Afghanistan. The military's support to the Haqqani network which has continued instability in Afghanistan has been an irritant to Karzai.

Pakistan's Relations with the United States

Pakistan's policies in Afghanistan have not been received well by the US and presently, the two nations probably stand at the worst phase of their relationship. Despite a decade-long involvement in the war on terror and provision of approximately $22 billion of the American aid and sophisticated defence equipment to Pakistan, the American ability to persuade Pakistan to alter its strategic calculus is restricted. The alliance has been edgy in the last two years and the US has been repeatedly expressing its frustration on the lack of success in the war on terror due to "lack of will" from the Pakistani military side and also its unwillingness to expand military operations in the tribal areas. Pakistan's support to Hafiz Saeed and also to the Haqqani network has added to the mistrust and distress in Washington. The US-Pakistan tensions reached a peak after the killing of Osama bin Laden in May 2011. Later, in November 2011, a US air strike on two posts on the Afghan border resulted in the killing of two dozen Pakistani soldiers, leading to closure of the supply routes by Pakistan.

The US defined its relationship with Pakistan in the past as being based on trust, but in December 2009, President Obama talked about the strategy for Pakistan:

> In the past, we too defined our relationship with Pakistan narrowly. Those days are over. Moving forward, we are committed to a partnership with Pakistan that is built on a foundation of mutual interest, mutual respect, and mutual trust. We will strengthen Pakistan's capacity to target those groups that threaten our countries, and have made it clear that we cannot tolerate a safe haven for terrorists whose location is known and whose intentions are clear...........These are the three core elements of our strategy: a military effort to create the conditions for a transition; a civilian surge that reinforces positive action; and an effective partnership with Pakistan.[15]

A year later, by 2010, the US had narrowed down its strategic ambitions in Pakistan and the President said:

> Pakistan is central to our efforts to defeat Al Qaida and prevent its return to the region. We seek to secure these interests through continued, robust counter-terrorism and counter-insurgency cooperation and a long-term partnership anchored by our improved understanding of Pakistan' strategic priorities, increased civilian and military assistance, and expanded public diplomacy.[16]

The US-Pak alliance post 9/11 started on a modest note and Pakistan became an immediate beneficiary of the international aid. Pakistan, obviously, had little option, and gave the nod to its cooperation in the war on terror, without actually realising that it would effectively imply that the military in Pakistan alters its strategic calculus and stops supporting terrorism as a tool of foreign policy. The alliance grew and Pakistan as a "major non-NATO ally" received colossal US aid, close to $22 billion, and the much desired defence equipment which would neutralise the Indian conventional military superiority. The initial US supplies to Pakistan consisted of items like UH-II utility helicopters, VHF/UHF aircraft radios, air traffic control radars, night vision equipment, and equipment and support systems, including intelligence gathering devices. Eventually, Pakistan managed to receive the F-16 A/B, F-16 C/D and the P-3Cs.

In 2007, after five years of alliance, various questions were raised regarding the use of the American aid and, reportedly, the Bush Administration and military officials said they believed that much of the American money was not making its way to frontline Pakistani units.[17] A report released in June 2008 by the US Government Accountability Office (GAO) discovered widespread accounting irregularities with the Pentagon spending in Pakistan.[18] Despite much debate on the misuse of the funds, the American aid continued at a rapid pace. Pakistan's resistance to act against the targeted terror groups clearly projected its partial and selective approach in counter-insurgency operations. Dissatisfaction in Washington led to a shift in the US posture and, consequently, it did initiate military moves to reduce its reliance on Pakistan to rein in the Islamists militants on the tribal belt. The US drone strikes were accelerated in 2008 despite tremendous resentment from the military and also the civilians, and these strikes remain a great source of tension between the two nations.

Pakistan has been equally disenchanted and this has been evident in the last two years in an increasing number of crises, including closing of a vital border crossing to NATO supply convoys in 2010 and also the military's and ISI's opposition to the continued drone strikes and presence of CIA agents within Pakistan. Anti-Americanism within Pakistan had started to increase in 2008, following the civilian and military casualties, and it continues to do so.[19] The Pakistanis blame the US for the spillover of violence in their country and the majority views the American aid as sheer compensation for the hardship and killing the nation has gone through due to America's war on terror. Although the Americans have never been bothered about the civil society's sentiments and have been comfortable dealing with the military, their trust in the military has been shaken, and the secret operation of Osama's killing was an ultimate manifestation of the mistrust.

The US has announced the suspension of further aid to Islamabad, but neither the military nor the civil regime appears to be bothered about the suspended aid. The increase in tensions between the US and Pakistan would lead to stronger Pakistan-China ties as Pakistan would naturally increase its reliance on China. The suspension of the US assistance would have security and economic implications for Pakistan. It would dangle the US equipment and training coming into Pakistan and also the developmental programmes based on the US funding would be put on ice. Also, the US moving away from Pakistan would impact Pakistan's ability to negotiate in international financial institutions like the International Monetary Fund (IMF) and the World Bank.

Pakistan Has Failed To Exclude New Delhi's Role

Pakistan has been extremely conscious of relegating India's role and growing influence in Afghanistan. For decades, it has carried the perception that India's sole objective in Afghanistan is to destabilise Pakistan.

India has played an active role in rebuilding Afghanistan and India-Afghanistan ties have improved significantly. India signed a strategic partnership agreement with Afghanistan in October 2011 and has pledged to invest upto $2 billion in the development of Afghanistan. India has been actively involved in Afghanistan and gets good support from the Karzai government and also the Afghan nationals. India's assistance in Afghanistan covers sectors such as power generation, education, infrastructure development, transport, health and diplomacy. India has till now restricted its involvement in development and commerce, avoided appearing intrusive and has not shown any interest in having an Indian military presence in Afghanistan. This was apparent from the statement made by S. M. Krishna, India's Foreign Minister, in a conference held in New Delhi in June 2012: "We need to offer a narrative opportunity to counter the anxiety of withdrawal, uncertainty, instability and foreign interference……..Let the grey suits of company executives take the place of olive green or desert brown fatigues of soldiers; and CEOs the place of generals."[20]

Since 2001, India has been playing an extremely significant role in Afghanistan's reconstruction. India's investments in various sectors make it the sixth largest donor in Afghanistan. Approximately 100 Indian companies have invested in different sectors in Afghanistan and the total amount of investment reaches nearly $25 million.[21] A major percentage of this investment goes to the construction and services sector as compared to the industries.

Afghanistan became a member of the South Asian Association for Regional Cooperation (SAARC) in 2007 with India's support and this has obviously made Afghanistan once again the crossroad between South Asia and Central Asian, linking them by trade, transportation and energy transformation.[22] Trade between India and Afghanistan which stood at approximately $80 million in 2001 has gone up to about $ 280 million in 2010. With the improvement in the economic and political ties between the two nations and also build-up of India's goodwill amongst the Afghans, the Karzai government has recently awarded the mining rights of the Hajigak iron ore, Afghanistan's biggest iron ore deposit, to a consortium of seven Indian companies for an investment of $ 6.6 billion. [23]

The US has been very keen on India taking up a more active role in Afghanistan.[24] Washington is worried about the political and security vacuum post 2014. Although, Pakistan has tried its best to keep India out of Afghanistan, India's economic, trade and cultural ties with Afghanistan have been stregthened in the past ten years.

Pakistan's Policy of Support to Terrorism has Backfired

Pakistan is currently facing a broad landscape of militancy. A vast variety of terrorist groups operate from Pakistan and share a varied relationship with the state. Some of these, the military is willing to target, some it was compelled to target, and a few it wants to protect. For the first time, the militancy has managed to penetrate the interiors of Punjab and Sindh, and the Army GHQ became one of the terror targets in the recent past. The impact of the Afghan War has allowed the Al Qaeda, Haqqani network and the Taliban inside Pakistan where they have been trying to expand their influence. The Pakistan military and ISI have nurtured some of the terrorist organisations which they categorically grade as their "strategic assets" and are clearly not willing to act against them. These so-called "friendly"[25] groups, as Ayesha Siddiqua Agha terms them, include the Good Taliban, Lashkar-e-Tayyeba (LeT), Jamaat-ud-Dawa (JuD), and Jaish-e-Muhammad. The Haqqani network which has strongholds in the bordering Afghan districts of Paktia and Khost and is involved in anti-US and anti-NATO operations, has enjoyed state patronage for a long time.[26] The military has desisted from acting against these groups and has been "selective and partial" in its counter-terrorism approach.

The frontier borders – NWFP and KPK – have become the breeding ground for terrorism and the region presents a conglomeration of various insurgent and terrorist groups to the Pakistani military and NATO forces. Al Qaeda, Haqqani and the Taliban have established their sanctuaries in these areas. The NWFP and KPK which have been a troublesome region even in the best of times, are now embroiled in a full-blooded insurgency. Insurgency in Baluchistan, which became active in 2004, has aggravated much more after the killing of Akbar Bugti in 2007. The Baluch have long suffered a deep sense of alienation from the state and have frequently resisted it, which the national leadership tried to curb with brute military force in the past, starting in the 1940s. Added to this deadly mix of extremism, is the Tehrik-e-Taliban-e- Pakistan (TTP) whose avowed aim is to revolt against the presence of US and NATO forces within Pakistan and to establish the Sharia as the rule of law within Pakistan. The TTP has taken up the battle against the Pakistani state and has been very selectively targeting the army. The TTP probably tops the list of deadly terrorist attacks, including the assassination of Benazir Bhutto in 2007 and the attack on the Marriott Hotel in Islamabad in 2008. Although some Pakistani scholars hold the view that the TTP is losing its 'brand value', the fact remains that the attacks by the TTP pose a significant challenge which the Pakistan Army is trying to counter militarily but not much success has been achieved.

Shift in the Policy of Strategic Depth?

Lately, Pakistan has projected a shift in its Afghan policy since very clearly its doctrine of gaining strategic depth in Afghanistan is being held responsible for the continued instability and raging insurgency in Afghanistan. Not only Afghanistan, but Pakistan too is currently facing a wide mosaic of militancy, where the state has a different nature of relationship with different terrorist groups. Pakistan's resistance to patronise the Afghan Taliban and its distinction between the Good Taliban and the Bad Taliban is more out of strategic calculation than ideological sympathy.

Gen Kayani has stated that Pakistan did not want strategic depth in Afghanistan as it is generally perceived in pure military-strategic terms, and the army's position is that Pakistan wants a "peaceful, friendly and stable" Afghanistan. He added that strategic depth is not about "controlling Afghanistan" but ensuring that Pakistan does not have long-term security problems on its western borders. [27]

Today's geo-political environment is very different from that of the 1990s and, thus, some shift in Pakistan's stated policy in Afghanistan is not surprising. In the 1980s and 1990s, when Pakistan intervened in Afghanistan, few actors had vested interests in Afghanistan, but today, probably more than 30 nations have vested strategic interests in the stability of Afghanistan. Thus, the projection of Pakistan's strategic depth and its role in Afghanistan needs some modification. Pakistan has suffered a massive blowback of radicalisation owing to its past policies and, thus, not only for the international community but also for the domestic community within Pakistan, the leadership cannot afford to hold on to the old form of strategic depth.

According to a recent report by the Jinnah Institute on the Perceptions of Pakistan's Foreign Policy Elite:

> Pakistani foreign policy elite are generally critical of their country's traditional, security-centric approach to Afghanistan. The security establishment, which has dominated the country's policy throughout, is seen as being overly concerned about an antagonistic Afghanistan. This fear has led to interference in sovereign Afghan affairs for years.....Pakistan's security-centric approach has caused the state to lose goodwill among Afghans ....Pakistan's interference in Afghanistan's affairs over the past two decades has left many Afghans alienated and resentful of what they view as Islamabad's hegemonic tendencies.[28]

According to the report, which has inputs from around 50 leading Pakistani foreign policy elites, Pakistan has two defined overriding objectives in Afghanistan:

First, the settlement of Afghanistan should not lead to a negative spillover which contributes to further instability in Pakistan.

Second, the government in Kabul should not be antagonistic to Pakistan and should not allow its territory to be used against Pakistani interests. [29]

The report recommends an inclusive government in Kabul which is formed as a result of a politically negotiated configuration with adequate representation that is recognised by all ethnic and political stakeholders in Afghanistan. This signifies that Pakistan is not looking for the return of the Taliban regime in Afghanistan. For the first time, the foreign policy elites have come up with some recommendations which are not distinctly different but are less aggressive, and give space to Afghan sovereignty. Whether the army adheres to these is not known.

Certain conclusions can be drawn based on the study of Pakistan's desire of obtaining strategic depth in Afghanistan :

- Pakistan's obsession with gaining strategic depth in Afghanistan is unlikely to change as the objectives which existed behind the rationale still exist. For example, the Durand Line factor still lingers, the Pashtun nationalism in Pakistan is not less, and FATA and KPK, the troublesome regions even in the most peaceful times in Pakistan, are engaged in full-blooded insurgency, Pakistan has not altered its strategy of covert war and support to the anti-India terrorist organisations continues, but India's image in Afghanistan has gone up and its role has further expanded into development.
- With these realities still existing, Pakistan is unlikely to change totally unless the military establishment actually alters its strategic calculus and seriously analyses the outcome of its own policies.
- Pakistan has talked about change in its Afghan polcies but there are contradictions in its position and it is still not clear which route it wants to adopt.

- Strategic depth will remain an integral part of the Pakistani military strategy and now, strategic depth means a pro-Pakistan government in Afghanistan which will allow it to exercise influence over Afghanistan. According to various reports, the Pakistani military is still trying to popularise its notion of strategic depth. A local daily in Pakistan has reported about Zaid Hamid who is apparently been patronised by the military to propagate strategic depth among the rich and influential families in the major cities of Pakistan.[30] Pakistan has also been extremely keen on playing an active role in the peace talks among the Taliban, Karzai and the US. Although Pakistan finds it difficult to stick to the old interpretation of strategic depth which it propagated in the 1990s, its objectives are not very different.

Notes

1. Air Cmde Jasjit Singh, "Strategic Search-Strategic Depth and the Question of the IAF's Strategic Posture", *AIR POWER Journal*, Vol 2, No. 2, Summer 2007, pp 11-26.
2. Brig M. S. Chaudhary "Pakistan's Strategic Depth", USI, at http://www.usiofindia.org/Article/?pub=Journal&pubno=577&ano=283
3. Air Cmde Jasjit Singh, "Pakistan and its Search for Strategic Depth: Prospects for Af-Pak Region in Post War Period," paper presented at a CAPS-Manipal University National Seminar at Manipal University, "Pakistan's Future: Implications for the Region", November 14-15, 2011.
4. Shehzad H. Qazi, "Pakistan's Afghanistan Plan: Strategic Depth 2.0," November 3, 2011.
5. Maj Gen Akbar Khan, *Raiders in Kashmir* (Delhi: Army Publishers), p. 9.
6. The British accepted the traditional boundary roughly established by Ranjit Singh along what came to be known as the Durand Line based on the agreement between Emir Abdul Rehman, the ruler of Afghanistan, and Sir Henry Mortimer Durand, British Foreign Minister, in 1893, leaving the majority of the Pashtun population and tribes in India.
7. See Ahmed Rashid, *Descent Into Chaos: How the War Against Islamic Extremism is Being Lost in Pakistan, Afghanistan and Central Asia* (London: Penguin, 2008), p. 266.
8. Ibid., pp. 266-267.
9. Fre'de'ric Grare, "Pakistan", in Ashley Tellis and Aroop Mukharji, eds.,*Is a Regional Strategy Viable in Afghanistan* (Washington, D.C: Carnegie Endowment for International Peace, 2010), p. 21.
10. "Pakistan Ignoring Transit Agreement (APTA) With Afghanistan", Ariana News, November 23, 2011,at http://ariananews.af/regional/pakistan-ignoring-transit-agreement-apta-with-afghanistan/
11. Kamran Shafi, *Dawn*, January 19, 2010.
12. Anita Joshua, "Afghanistan Pakistan Cross Swords on Border Row", *The Hindu*, July 3, 2012.
13. Ibid.
14. See "US Trying to Ease Afghan-Pakistan Border Tension: Pentagon", *The Nation*, July 25, 2012.
15. Transcript of President Obama's West Point Address on Afghanistan, White House, December 1, 2009. Available at http://www.whitehouse.gov/the-press-office/remarks-president-address-nation-way-forward-afghanistan-and-pakistan
16. "Overview of the Afghanistan and Pakistan Annual Review", White House, December 16, 2010. Available at http://www.whitehouse.gov/the-press-office/2010/12/16/overview-afghanistan-and-pakistan-annual-review

17. David Rohde, Carlotta Gall, Eric Schmitt and David E. Sanger, "US Officials See Waste in Billions Sent to Pakistan", *The New York Times*, December 24, 2007.
18. See "Combating Terrorism; Increased Oversight and Accountability Needed over Pakistan Reimbursement Claims for Coalition Support Funds", GAO Report, June 2008. at http://www.gao.gov/new.items/d08806.pdf
19. "Pakistan Now or Never? Anti-Americanism in Pakistan", *Reuters*, May 11, 2008.
20. "India Hosts Summit to Push Investment in Afghanistan", *The Express Tribune*, June 28, 2012.
21. "Economic Links Between India and Afghanistan", at dsafghan.in/pdf/India-Afghanistan.pdf
22. Ibid.
23. Ibid.
24. Julian E. Barnes, "US Seeks Larger Role for India in Afghanistan", *The Wall Street Journal*, June 5, 2012.
25. Ayesha Siddiqua Agha, "Pakistan's Counterterrorism Strategy: Separating Friends from Enemies", *The Washington Quarterly*, Winter 2011, pp.149-162.
26. Ibid.
27. "Kayani Speaks" *Dawn,* at http://archives.dawn.com/archives/29601.
28. "Pakistan, the United States and the End Game in Afghanistan: Perceptions of Pakistan's Foreign Policy Elite", A Jinnah Institute Research Report, 2011, pp. 20-21.
29. Ibid., p. 22.
30. "Zaid Hamid and Strategic Depth" *Daily Times*, February 13, 2010.

5

Nuclear Waste: India's Gordian Knot?

Sitakanta Mishra

The Nuclear Power Corporation of India Ltd. (NPCIL) has planned to launch 16 more reactors – eight 700 MW Pressurised Heavy Water Reactors (PHWRs) and eight Light Water Reactors (LWRs) – at an outlay of Rs 230,00 crore during the 12th Five-Year Plan period (1012-17).[1] This is in addition to NPCIL's four 700 MW PHWRs under construction at an outlay of Rs 22,000 crore. In the pursuit of ensuring energy security and harnessing the nuclear source as a viable option in the national energy mix, around three dozen more nuclear plants have been proposed. But, the addition of single megawatt electricity from the nuclear source during the years ahead will add to the existing radioactive waste. Apprehensions have been raised about the safe disposal of radioactive waste generated in India.[2] Allegedly, there is no official disclosure about the volume of radioactive waste generated so far. The report of the Comptroller and Auditor General (CAG) on the Activities of the Atomic Energy Regulatory Board (AERB) (2012) observes that "although a large number of consents for transport of radioactive material for safe disposal had been given so far, there was no proper mechanism in place to verify whether the sources had actually been disposed of in accordance with the safeguards prescribed ...."[3] This raises one obvious question: will the nuclear waste generated in India be India's Gordian knot?

The Process and Basics

In India, radioactive materials are used in many sectors like medicine, industry, agriculture, energy, etc. During all these activities, some amount of 'waste' – "material left over for which no further use is foreseen" – is produced which needs to be safely disposed of. "The underlying objective that governs the management of all such waste is protection of man and environment today and in the future."[4] This study examines only the waste generated in the Indian nuclear energy sector during the various stages of the nuclear fuel cycle which includes mining and milling of uranium ore, fuel fabrication, reactor operation, and spent fuel reprocessing. In India, waste out of reactor operation includes waste generated from PHWRs, Boiling Water Reactors (BWRs) and other activities, waste that may arise out of an accident condition and waste generated out of decommissioning of plants all of which needs safe disposal.

Safe disposal denotes "emplacement of waste in a repository without the intention of retrieval or approved direct discharge of waste into the environment with subsequent dispersion". The technical process, starting from the origin of the waste till the final process of safe disposal, involves many coordinated steps. Most important is the 'conditioning' or 'treatment' that transforms the waste into a form suitable for transport and/or storage and/or disposal. The chain of administrative and operational activity involved in the handling, treatment, conditioning, transportation, storage and disposal of the waste is called 'waste management'. Broadly, radioactive waste is generated in three forms – liquid, solid and gaseous – which are further characterised on the basis of their degree of radioactivity and hazard involved: (a) High Level (HL), (b) Intermediate Level (IL), and (c) Low Level (LL). Each category requires a separate process of handling. In India, "the safe and effective management of radioactive waste has been given utmost importance from the very inception of the nuclear industry".[5]

Global Scenario

Each year, nuclear power plants worldwide produce about 200,000 cubic metres (m3) of low and intermediate level waste and 10,000 m3 of high level waste.[6] But no country has been able to find an amicable solution for the highly radioactive waste which remains dangerous for hundreds of years. However, the nuclear industry claims it can 'dispose' of nuclear waste by burying it deep underground.

The United States, having the largest number of reactors, has not been able to start the deep geological depository yet. There is strong public opposition to the Yucca Mountain Repository initiative. Around 65,000 metric tonnes of spent reactor fuel is scattered around at 70 locations. The waste confidence that the US Nuclear Regulatory Commission (NRC) issued in 2010 expressed the commission's confidence that spent fuel can be safely stored for at least 60 years after a reactor's operating licence expires. However, this was struck down by another verdict by the US Court of Appeals for the District of Columbia on June 8, 2012, which said that Spent Nuclear Fuel (SNF) stored on-site poses a dangerous, long-term health and environmental risk.

The Blue Ribbon Commission has recommended immediate efforts to commence development of at least one geologic disposal facility and at least one consolidated storage facility, as well as efforts to prepare for the eventual large-scale transportation of spent nuclear fuel and high-level waste from current storage sites to those facilities. It outlined a strategy that contains three crucial elements: first, the commission recommends a consent-based approach to siting future nuclear waste storage and disposal facilities, noting that trying to force such facilities on unwilling states, tribes and communities has not worked; second, the commission recommends that the responsibility for the nation's nuclear waste management programme be transferred to a new organisation that is independent of the Department of Energy (DoE); third, changing the manner in which fees being paid into the Nuclear Waste Fund – about $750 million a year – is treated in the federal budget to ensure it is being set aside and available for use as Congress initially intended.[7] Despite all these efforts, nuclear waste disposal remains one of the most contentious issues in the US.

In Canada, reportedly, there are two million high level radioactive fuel bundles sitting at temporary storage sites, as the Nuclear Waste Management Organisation (NWMO) struggles with the mandate of finding a community to host a central storage facility for the waste.[8] Aboriginal organisations have come out against a proposal to bury nuclear waste in Northern Ontario. Earlier, in 1998, a federal environmental assessment rejected the geological storage option. People involved at the time with the Seaborn Panel were convinced that the science was good but the central storage option did not have public support, as people feared accidents and contamination. However, in 2002, the NWMO was mandated by the federal government to find a site.

The situation in Australia is not favourable either. Currently, nuclear waste from the medical and mining industries is stored in more than 100 "temporary" sites in universities, hospitals, offices and laboratories. The Australian government has passed legislation aiming to create the country's first nuclear waste dump, despite fierce opposition from environmental and Aboriginal groups. The passage of the National Radioactive Waste Management Bill 2010 through the Senate paves the way for a highly controversial plan to store nuclear waste in Muckaty Station, a remote Aboriginal community in the arid central region of the Northern Territory.[9]

China has a plan to dispose the High Level Waste (HLW) in the national centralised geological repository.[10] According to the guidelines approved by the Chinese government, an underground research laboratory should be constructed before 2020, while the construction of a national HLW repository will begin around 2040.[11] The site selection is in progress and granite is being considered as the candidate host rock for the repository.

The process started in 1985 and the Beishan area, Gansu province, has been selected for building the repository.[12] Though China has made progress in this field, there is still a long way to go. Also, China is reportedly building a nuclear waste processor to solve its nuclear waste problem. The Changsha Boiler Plant (CBP) Co. Ltd. started building the plasma furnance in central Hunan province.[13] The furnance is co-developed by the CBP and Shenzhen-based China Nuclear Power Technology Research Institute which will transmute nuclear waste into less harmful waste.

The existing nuclear facilities in Russia are already facing problems in the storage and safe disposal of their wastes. These problems arise because of limited on-site capacity for storage and the paucity of waste processing facilities. According to reports, around 34 large and 257 small disposal sites are available. However, Russia's attempts to ameliorate the impacts of discharge to important water sources have had variable success. Also some of the procedures used have been found technically unsound. The Russian Navy has traditionally dealt with virtually all of its radioactive waste by disposal at sea. Enormous quantities of decommissioned Russian nuclear reactors and radioactive waste were dumped into the Kara Sea in the Arctic Ocean north of Siberia over the course of decades, according to documents given to Norwegian officials by Russian authorities and published in the Norwegian media.[14] In July 2011, then Russian President Dmitry Medvedev signed a federal law on radioactive waste management.[15] The new Bill establishes a legal framework for radioactive waste management in Russia and formally creates a unified state system for this task. The law includes provisions on the treatment of certain types of waste and regulates radioactive waste management activities, including a ban on the construction of new facilities for disposal of liquid waste in geological formations. Further legislation dealing with high level waste is still to come.

By 2030, Britain will have generated approximately 1.4 million m3 of Low Level Waste (LLW), 260,000 m3 of Intermediate Level Waste (ILW) and 3,000 m3 of High Level Waste (HLW).[16] The UK is planning a £13.8 billion underground facility to host the radioactive wastes. In this pursuit, the UK has adopted an innovative approach – instead of politicians or experts choosing a location, the local authorities were invited to volunteer to host the deep underground repository, but so far, just a few local councils in west Cumbria – Copeland and Allerdale – have shown any interest in hosting it. Thirteen local councils which inquired about it, decided not to go any further, according to a report by the Committee on Radioactive Waste Management (CoRWM). That raises questions over the policy of "voluntarism" which was designed to prevent a backlash, with host communities feeling unfairly picked on.[17]

France had an inventory of radioactive wastes totalling some 1.32 million cubic metres in 2010, according to the latest data released by the National Radioactive Waste Management Agency, ANDRA. This is a 12.9 percent increase from the 1.15 million cubic metres in 2007.[18] Reportedly, the amount is likely to double by 2030. The current 45 million cubic feet of nuclear waste in France is likely to reach 95 million cubic feet in the next 18 years.[19] The HLW, accounting for just 0.2 percent of the total waste volume in 2010 (2,700 m3), represents 96 percent of its radioactivity. The amount of HLW that France has increased by 400 m3 between 2007 and 2010. HLW, which mainly comes from the reprocessing of used fuel from nuclear power plants, is destined for disposal in the Centre Industriel de Stockage Géologique (Cigeo) repository in Bure in northeast France being designed by ANDRA, which is testing the soundness of the rock and the technologies to contain the waste in the €1-billion underground laboratory under construction. ANDRA scientists are convinced that the rock formations can safely house highly radioactive waste, and plan an industrial-scale facility that would open deep below a 30-sq km site nearby, in 2025.[20]

Several parallel efforts are also on across Europe to prepare a permanent home for the long-lived radioactive waste accumulating at temporary storage sites. Finland and Sweden plan to open deep geological repositories in about 2020–25, whereas Germany hopes to open its own long-term repository in 2035. Several smaller European countries have banded together to form a European Repository Development Organisation to work on the concept of a shared facility. An important question that is likely to reverberate in India in the decades ahead, is: will India be able to manage the radioactive waste that will be increasingly generated as it marches ahead on the nuclear energy road?

Volume of Waste in India

Much concern has been in the air regarding the volume of radioactive waste India would generate and whether it can amicably dispose of it when the major nuclear power countries have not been able to do so. In the Parliament, questions have been repeatedly raised about "whether Government has … assessed the quantity of nuclear waste likely to be generated by the nuclear power plants in the country"?[21] And, the standard explanation furnished during all these debates is that "the quantity of this waste in our country is much smaller due to our adoption of the closed fuel cycle".[22] The interim storage facility is adequate and can store waste generated for 30-40 years by which time, it will lose some radioactivity. Therefore, it is asserted that "nuclear waste is not an immediate problem for India", and at the current level of nuclear power generation, India will not have any problem related to waste management. However, India may face such problems by 2020-30.[23]

Undoubtedly, considering the previous and current rate of nuclear energy production, the volume of waste already generated in India could be very small. The nuclear waste disposal issue in India at present, therefore, cannot be compared with the situation in the United States. Deliberately or otherwise, there is no exact information available in the public domain on the current inventory of radioactive waste in India and the amount that will be added in the decades ahead. Therefore, the issue has become a subject of intense speculation. Answering a question by N.R. Govindarajar on the handling of nuclear waste in the Rajya Sabha, Prithviraj Chavan, the Minister of State in the Prime Minister's Office (PMO) and Ministry of Personnel, Public Grievances and Pensions, revealed on February 26, 2009 that:

> In India about 500-600 litres of high level waste is generated per tonne of spent fuel processed. Also about 1,000 litres of intermediate level waste is generated per tonne of spent fuel. The quantities generated depend on the type of fuel, cooling period before reprocessing and the process adopted in the reprocessing plants. Low level nuclear waste is generated during normal operation and maintenance of nuclear plants. About 20,000-30,000 m3 of low level of nuclear waste is generated from a typical twin 220 Mwe PHWR nuclear plants per year.[24]

To estimate the approximate amount of waste produced, one needs to rely either on secondary sources based on individual predilections or calculate the amount of fuel irradiated, taking into account the average figures revealed during the Parliament debate. Since the exact amount of fuel irradiated is again unknown, one needs to calculate backward from the amount of nuclear energy produced over the years. Mostly, the media and individual scholars have advanced their own estimations, at times, exaggerating, and other times, overestimating, leading to a public outcry. For example, according to the study by M.V. Ramana a decade ago (2001), waste produced out of uranium mining and milling was 4.1 million tonnes; waste generated out of fuel fabrication was 2,000 m3; low- and intermediate-level waste generated out of reactor operations was 22,000 m3 and 280 m3 respectively; from spent fuel storage (not to be reprocessed) 400 tonnes; from reprocessing, 5,000 m3 high-level waste, 35,000 m3 intermediate-level waste, and 2,10,000 m3 low-level waste was generated.[25]

Table 1: Total Nuclear Waste Generation in India

Steps in Nuclear Fuel Cycle	Waste Estimate (2 Significant Digits)
Uranium mining and milling	4.1 million tonnes
Fuel fabrication	2,000 m3
Reactor operations (low-level waste)	22,000 m3
Reactor operations (intermediate-level waste)	280 m3
Spent fuel storage (not to be reprocessed)	400 tonnes
Reprocessing (high-level waste)	5,000 m3
Reprocessing (intermediate-level waste)	35,000 m3
Reprocessing (low-level waste)	210,000 m3

Source: M. V. Ramana, "Estimating Nuclear Waste Production in India", *Current Science*, Vol. 81, No. 11, December 10, 2001, p. 1461.

Table 2: Cumulative Low Level and Intermediate Level Waste Production

Nane	Date of commencement	Intermediate level waste (m3)	Low level waste (m3)
RAPS 1	December 16, 1973	35.1	2,700
RAPS 2	April 1, 1981	24.7	1,900
MAPS 1	January 27, 1984	20.8	1,600
MAPS 2	March 21, 1986	18.2	1,400
NAPS 1	January 1, 1991	13.0	1,000
MAPS 2	July 1, 1992	10.4	800
KAPS 1	May 6, 1993	9.1	700
KAPS 2	September 1, 1995	6.5	500
TAPS 1	October 28, 1969	49.6	3,875
TAPS 2	October 28, 1969	49.6	3,875
CIRUS	July 10, 1960	32.0	2,400
Dhruva	August 10, 1985	12.0	900
Total		**281.0**	**21,650**

Source: M. V. Ramana, "Estimating Nuclear Waste Production in India", *Current Science*, Vol. 81, No. 11, December 10, 2001.

According to N.S. Sunder Rajan, the former head of the Waste Management Division, Bhabha Atomic Research Centre (BARC), with the aim to produce 10,000 MWe by the year 2000, India would generate 107,000 m3 of primary solid waste, 77,100 m3 of low-level waste concentrates, 19,900 m3 of intermediate level waste, and 8,000 m3 of high level waste.[26] The production rate estimated by him for the year 2000 is in sharp contrast to the figures during 1985.

India's Estimated Waste Arisings

Primary solid wastes and low-level waste concentrates constitute the bulk of the estimated waste arisings in India up to the year 2000, at a projected electric power production of 10 000 megawatts. These consist of contaminated process equipment, protective clothing, used particulate filters, concentrated precipitates, and sludges from the low-level liquid waste treatment plants. The volume of the intermediate- and high-level waste generated is small, yet it constitutes the bulk of the radioactivity.

	1985	2000
Installed capacity (megawatts-electric)	1350	10 000
Primary solid wastes* (cubic metres)	1850	107 000
Low-level waste concentrates (cubic metres)	3000	77 100
Intermediate-level wastes (cubic metres)	800	19 900
High-level wastes (cubic metres)	450	8 000

* Up to 10^4 röntgen per hour.

Source: N.S. Sunder Rajan *IAEA Bulletin* (Spring), 1986, p. 40.

If the above trend is followed to estimate waste generation out of India's envisaged nuclear energy programme, by 2020, India would pile up double the volume of waste currently reserved in different facilities. If the government's assurance on existing facilities' sufficient waste storage capacity is to be believed, India can manage additional nuclear wastes for the next three decades comfortably. But, as India has expedited domestic uranium exploration activities in recent days, the waste out of mining and milling would increase manifold over the previous decades. The commercial uranium recovery plant at Jaduguda treats around 1,000 tonnes of ore per day from the Jaduguda mine, containing around 0.05 percent U3O8.[27] Taking into account the low quality of uranium ore in India, the amount of tailings out of extensive mining would pose the "reclamation" challenge of tailing ponds.[28] The negative perception of the public about mining as a polluting industry would complicate it further.

As India follows a closed fuel cycle and the second stage of its three stage programme will start soon where plutonium produced during the first stage as waste will be used as fuel, the amount of high level waste will reduce drastically. India has around 40 years of experience in the spent fuel reprocessing based on the PUREX process which has given the confidence that this technology can be successfully employed for the recovery of both uranium and plutonium with yield exceeding 99.5 percent.[29] Moreover, the high-level waste in India, essentially generated at reprocessing plants, is "much smaller due to the closed fuel cycle" it follows. These wastes are "vitrified into a glassy form, contained in multiple barrier containers and stored for an interim period of three to four decades in engineered vaults with necessary surveillance facilities".[30] The Indian government is aware and has carefully assessed the quantity of nuclear waste generated, and, accordingly, systematic management guidelines and philosophy have been adopted for integrated recycling, management, and geological repository in the long-run.

However, there are fundamental contentions over the issue of whether SNF comprises a resource or poses a dangerous, long-term health and environmental risk. Many cite the American verdict delivered on June 8, 2012, that struck down rules framed by the Nuclear Regulatory Commission to extend the storage period for SNF at the plants from 30 to 60 years. On the other hand, the Madras High Court's endorsement of the Department of Atomic Energy (DAE) assertion that SNF is not a waste, but a resource which could be reprocessed for separating plutonium and uranium and can be utilised in a closed cycle to generate more nuclear power, has been criticised. The allegation is that India has not been able to build a national repository yet and the capacity at Kudankulam to store spent fuel is for no more than the fuel discharged "during seven years of full power operation of the reactor".[31] Whatever the efficacy of the reprocessing option, the Supreme Court of India has observed that irrespective of the money already spent, it would not hesitate to stop nuclear projects if they are found wanting in the safety aspects.[32]

Guidelines and Philosophy

As per the Atomic Energy (Safe Disposal of Radioactive Wastes) Rules, 1987, the responsibility for safe disposal of radioactive waste is placed on the licencees and the Atomic Energy Regulatory Board (AERB) has the mandate of ensuring that the licencees perform their responsibilities. To keep the effective doses of radiation to the individual and the environment As Low As Reasonably Achievable (ALRA), the AERB prescribes necessary codes and safety guidelines (2004) on safe handling, treatment, storage, transport and disposal of radioactive waste in conformity with the formulations by the International Commission on Radiation Protection (ICRP). The guidelines prescribe that a Waste Management Plant (WMP), along with a nuclear surface disposal facility shall be available prior to the commencement of nuclear power plant operation as a mandatory "operational requirement".[33] The plant management interacts with the designer of the WMP during the design and construction phases to ensure plant capability to meet waste management objectives. So far, all seven Indian WMPs are co-located with waste generating facilities which helps in avoiding undue radiation exposure during transportation.[34]

The first philosophy followed in India is "waste minimisation" (clause 2.3.1 of Guidelines No. AERB/NPP/SG/O-11) at all stages of design, operation and maintenance through "volume reduction" and an innovative treatment process. India's overall policy is based on the universally adopted philosophy of (i) delay and decay of short-lived radionuclides; (ii) concentration and containment of radioactivity as much as practicable; and (iii) dilution and dispersion of low-level activity to the environment well below the nationally accepted levels.[35] As listed by the Nuclear Recycle Group of BARC, India's national policy for radioactive waste management broadly includes the following:

- Discharge through gaseous, liquid and terrestrial routes is as low as reasonably achievable.
- Low and intermediate level solid/solidified wastes are emplaced in specially engineered near surface shallow land repository.
- High-level and alpha contaminated liquid wastes from spent fuel processing and other radio metallurgical operations are immobilised in a suitable matrix and stored in an interim storage facility with appropriate cooling and surveillance for the period necessary. Thereafter, these waste products will be emplaced in a suitably engineered deep geological repository.
- Alpha contaminated waste not qualifying for nuclear surface disposal is provided suitable interim storage pending its disposal in a deep geological repository.
- Spent radiation sources are either returned to the original supplier or handed over to a radioactive waste management agency identified by the regulatory body.
- Co-location of near surface disposal facility with the nuclear installations.
- As spent fuel is a resource material in India and needs to be processed for recovery and recycle of fissile material, each reprocessing plant has a collocated vitrification plant.
- The regulatory body determines the period for which active control for the shallow land repository should be maintained by the waste management agency. The institutional control may span a period of 300 years comprising 100 years of active control and 200 years of passive control so as to allow decay of most of the radionuclides.

The waste generated out of uranium mining and milling requires separate management. As Indian uranium ores are mined by the method of wet mining, proper ventilation is ensured to protect against undue radiation concentration. According to N.S. Sunder Rajan, the then head, Waste Management Division of BARC, "the 'barren liquor' produced from the uranium recovery process is treated with lime and barites for precipitation of radium and other uranium daughter products. Along with the mill tailings, it is disposed into a tailing pond, which is a natural depression to ensure settling".[36]

Process and Technique

In answer to an unstarred question by Vinay Kumar and Nishikant Dubey in the Lok Sabha, the Minister of State for Personnel, Public Grievances and Pensions and Prime Minister's Office, V. Narayanasamy, on March 9, 2011, and August 17, 2011, respectively, informed that the government has "an effective plan in place for the disposal of nuclear waste" and the "latest technology" is used for safe management of nuclear waste.[37] The entire process is claimed to be "a transparent" system and "efforts are continuously on to update and have a balanced Nuclear Waste Management System (NWMS)".[38] For example, extensive efforts are made in the field of research and development for new technologies to manage wastes generated in the future from the new reactor systems like advanced Heavy Water Reactors (HWRs) and Fast Breeder Reactors (FBRs).

The high level radioactive wastes in India are stored temporarily within the plant boundary, and with regard to Low- and Intermediate-Level Waste (LILW), India's experience has been claimed to be fairly good.[39] This is mainly because of the comprehensive stages of the waste management process, that include characterisation, treatment, conditioning, storage, disposal, surveillance/monitoring, etc., adopted. Characterisation is the first process to determine the physical, chemical and radiological properties for record keeping, segregation of materials for reuse, exemption and disposal or storage. Storage of wastes in designated facilities is mainly undertaken to ensure isolation and environmental protection. Some wastes require a short storage period for decay of radionuclides, and many other types are stored for an interim period for the subsequent treatment. In the process, waste is collected, segregated and decontaminated through chemical adjustments. Some waste requires conditioning to transform radioactive waste into a solid form suitable for handling. It involves immobilisation of the waste and putting it in containers, and additional packaging. The final step in the process is the emplacement of radioactive waste in a repository with a reasonable assurance of safety. As per current practice, most types of wastes are disposed of by concentration and containment but some effluents are discharged into the environment within authorised limits, specific to sites, and vary from coastal to inland sites, with subsequent dispersion.[40]

India practises a variety of "self-reliant" management and treatment procedures for all type of radioactive wastes generated during the operation of its nuclear facilities. For treatment of gaseous waste, it is ensured that all nuclear installations have an elaborate off-gas cleaning system. Indian scientists claim to have developed "very efficient gas cleaning techniques employing different types of wet scrubbers like venturi, dust, packed bed, cyclone separators, high-efficiency low-pressure drop demisters, chillers and High-Efficiency Particulate Air (HEPA) filters to practically retain most of the particulate radionuclides".[41] All Indian nuclear facilities have emergency air clean-up systems, indigenously developed filter banks, ruthenium absorber, particulate respirator like the HEPA filters, charcoal impregnated sampling filter, and stack-sampling cartridges. The HEPA filters are provided in the exhaust systems which are standard filters of capacity m3 /h with collection efficiency of more than 99.97 percent for submicron particles.[42] To contain effectively the environmental release of radioactive-iodine – the main radiological concern – proper ventilation and containment systems of combined particulate and iodine filters are deployed. To absorb and retain the radio-iodine, coconut shell-based activated charcoal impregnated with potassium iodide and potassium hydroxide is used.[43]

A large volume of low and intermediate level liquid waste is generated from reactor operations, off-gas scrubbers of nuclear facilities, fuel reprocessing facilities, active floor drains, decontamination centre, laboratories, drains from change room and showers as well as during the management of high and intermediate level waste. For the treatment of this type of waste, chemical precipitation/coprecipitation process, ion exchange, evaporation, reverse osmosis, etc., are employed.[44] Some of the liquid waste management plants in India are:

- Effluent treatment plant in Trombay.
- Solar evaporation pond in Rajasthan.
- Ion exchange plant in Tarapur.
- Waste immobilisation plants in Trombay and Kalkakkam.
- Rasin fixation plants in Narora, Kakrapar and Tarapur.
- Reverse osmosis plant in Trombay.
- Vitrification facility in Trombay.

The high level liquid wastes generated during reprocessing of spent fuels are managed by a three-step strategy: (1) immobilisation of waste oxides in stable and inert solid matrices; (2) interim retrievable storage of the conditioned waste under continuous cooling; (3) disposal in deep geological repository.[45] First, these wastes are concentrated by evaporation, stored in stainless steel tanks and kept under constant cooling and surveillance. India is claimed to be "one of the seven countries in the world to have mastered the technology of high level waste management".[46]

The management of solid waste has been in practice in India since the early Sixties and six solid waste management sites are presently under operation.[47] Depending upon the nature of the waste generated, different methods of treatment and disposal are adhered. All solid waste management plants are equipped with segregation, repacking, compaction, incineration and embedment processes.[48] All spent radiation sources from radiography units, hospitals, industry, agriculture, medicine, research centres, etc. are collected at Trombay or Kalpakkam and packed in standard steel drums. As some wastes, like contaminated equipment or components, are not amenable to any treatment, they are packaged in appropriate containers. To reduce the volume of the waste, the compaction and incineration method is followed. Presently, incinerators are in operation at Trombay, Kalpakkam, and Narora.

The approach followed in the disposal of solid waste is multi-barrier: first, beta gamma emitting wastes are disposed of in an earth/stone lined trench, RC trench and the tile hole (waste packages up to radiation field of 200-500 mGy/hr). Alpha contaminated waste is disposed of along with beta gamma waste. The trench is an unlined shallow excavation in soil for disposal of low level waste, covered by one metre of soil and backfill materials like vermiculite and bentonite to uptake the radionuclides and prevention of spread of radioactivity.[49]

The wastes with higher alpha activity are temporarily stored to be finally deposited in a permanent geological site in the future. But before they are shifted to the permanent repository, they need to be cooled to a level where transportation and disposal become viable. One such storage and surveillance facility co-located with a vitrification plant is operational at Tarapur with a capacity for storing nearly 1,700 overpacks with an inventory of nearly 80,000,000 TBq of radioactivity.[50] Extra precautions are being taken for temporary storage sites at Narora and Rajasthan, considering seismic and less soil coverage respectively. The trenches are constructed totally or partially above the ground with sufficient arrangements for remote handling and preventing ingress of rainwater. For viewing the hot cells, either the direct viewing systems such as radiation shielding windows or radiation resistant CCTV systems are used. A radio controlled remote inspection device with remote traction and steering capability has been developed for in-service surveillance of storage tanks for high and intermediate level waste tanks.

India has also begun experimenting on a new technological option, the accelerator-driven sub-critical reactor systems (ADS), which will incinerate nuclear waste.[51] Such a programme has been evolved for stage-wise development of systems and technologies in India. This is based on proton linear accelerator development in the first stage and cyclotron as a complementary one.[52] The ADS system "merges accelerator and fission reactor technologies into a single system that has the potential to efficiently generate electricity for nuclear fission and/or transmute the long lived waste material".[53]

Waste Out of Decommissioning

India is known to have considerable experience in the field of decommissioning of nuclear facilities and major systems and has successfully replaced several times the coolant channels after deconditioning.

Nuclear waste out of decommissioning of nuclear facilities needs special care; therefore, the AERB has made it mandatory for all nuclear installations to incorporate provisions for *in situ* decontamination and decommissioning provisions from the design stage until the end of the operational phase. Keeping the future need for decommissioning of nuclear plants in India in view, a six-axis gantry servo robot has been developed, especially for decommissioning of glove boxes or similar equipment.[54]

The thorium plant at Trombay, commissioned in 1955, was planned to be decommissioned in the year 2000 due to ageing, structural weakness, extensive corrosion, and build up of radiation dose on the process equipment. The decommissioning was planned so as to minimise both the radiation exposure to working personnel and the generation of radioactive waste. The steps taken were decontamination of tanks and equipment, removal of the tanks and equipment from the plant and subsequent removal of civil structures, segregation of waste, and disposal of the radioactive waste in the dykes. The radioactive solid waste, about 2,150 m3, consisting mainly of 70 percent concrete and 30 percent metallic waste, was disposed of in the dykes of size 25m x 25m x 3.5m and 33m x 37m x 3.5m.[55] During the decommissioning, about 300 m3 of contaminated soil excavated from three main drains was disposed of in the dykes. A total of about 3,465 man-days were required for decommissioning, with a radiation exposure of 122 person-mSv.[56]

En Masse Coolant Channel Replacement

A major portion of the Indian nuclear power programme consists of PHWRs which require En-Masse Replacement of Coolant Channels (ECCR) of each unit with zirconium niobium tubes. The main components of this coolant channel that need disposal are End Fittings (EF), Pressure Tubes (PT), and garter springs. The disposal of waste material out of this process requires meticulous planning and concerted efforts due to high radiation fields, and large quantities and odd dimensions of the components. This requires creation of additional facilities for their handling, transport, cutting, sizing, disposal and conditioning for which India has developed new technologies and existing technologies, have also been improved upon.

Radioactive waste management during many ECCR campaigns has been carried out safely in India. Removal of coolant channels was carried out for the Madras Atomic Power Station (MAPS)-II during May-July 2002 and for MAPS-I during January-March 2005. ECCR of unit-2 of the Rajasthan Atomic Power Station (RAPS-II) was carried out during April-September 1996.[57] During all these operations, valuable experience has been gained. As a result, according to the Nuclear Recycle Group of BARC, "technology for the management of decommissioning of reactors and other facilities is getting established in the Indian nuclear power programme."

Integrated Nuclear Recycle Plant and Geological Repository

With a long-term perspective, India has a plan to set up three indigenous and state-of-the-art integrated nuclear recycle plants, with facilities for both reprocessing of spent fuel and waste management. The design of the first plant at Tarapur has been started and is expected to be functional by 2017. The remaining plants will be commissioned with a gap of two to three years.[58]

With the aim to develop capacity for permanent disposal of radioactive waste that may arise in three-four decades ahead, research activities for the development of a geological repository have been undertaken, though no substantial headway has been achieved. While answering the unstarred question, "Whether the Government has any proposal to set up underground laboratories to study the effects and desirability of storing nuclear waste in deep underground sites," V. Narayanasamy informed the Lok Sabha:

> Presently, work related to host rock characterisation with a view to develop comprehensive data bases is in progress. The DAE has a proposal to construct an Underground Research Laboratory during the XII Five-Year Plan. The proposed laboratory will be of generic nature. Such laboratories are used for development of methodology and technology related to emplacement of solidified waste in the repository. Experiments in such laboratories will form a basis for the development and construction of an underground geological repository for storing high level nuclear waste in the future.[59]

Reportedly, India has begun scouting for deep underground sites to build a repository about 1 km below the land surface and is also setting up a laboratory to develop the required technology.[60] The waste is planned to be disposed "at a depth of 800-1,000 metres to isolate radioactivity from the environment".[61] According to the then Atomic Energy Commission (AEC) Chairman Srikumar Banerjee, the nuclear establishment is "looking for a rock formation that is geologically stable, totally impervious and without any fissures". In that case, the site should not have experienced any event in recorded history and should have a cooling mechanism using air draft. The Department of Atomic Energy (DAE) scientists have begun looking for options that vary from underground storage in rocky central India to plains where the storage may be housed inside layers of clay. Dr Banerjee is quoted as saying, "We will use an existing underground mine to study conductivity, heat management and percolation and rock stability. The site has to be totally impervious, geologically stable and without any fissure."[62] In their search for such a future repository, scientists have reportedly screened some 600,000 sq km of India's landmass, mainly zones having granites, and have found a few zones, of between 5 sq km to 25 sq km, for more detailed studies.[63]

According to K.K. Prasad, the former head of the Back End Technology Development Division of BARC, the geo-scientific studies for an Underground Research Laboratory (URL) have already been completed.[64] The work related to the repository programme in India includes (1) heating experiments by multi-heaters and single heaters in an abandoned underground mine at the Kolar Gold Fields (KGF); (2) site screening, selection and characterisation of the host rock are ongoing programmes; (3) ongoing programmes include design and construction of a URL in a captive site. The main goals of the URL programme are:

- To develop engineering technology for repository construction, operation and closure;
- To develop the disposal technology and validation of the disposal concept with modelling;
- To develop site characterisation techniques and methodology; and
- To demonstrate the geological disposal to the public, and confidence building.

Geologically, India is endowed with a number of suitable rocks to serve as host rocks for a geological repository. A few promising areas lying in northwest and central India, which have good quality granites have been systematically investigated. According to BARC, for assessment of the rock mass response to the thermal load from disposed waste overpack, an experiment of 8-years duration was carried out at a depth of 1,000 metres in an abandoned section of the Kolar gold mine.[65] Some more *in situ* experiments pertaining to testing of full-scale engineered barriers i.e. simulated waste overpack, bentonite clay buffers and clays sand admixture, are planned to study the behaviour of thermal, chemical, mechanical and hydraulic processes around the overpack. Also, for development of methodology and technology for characterisation of field scale fractures as pathways for radionuclide and gas migration, experiments are planned in abandoned underground mines in the future.[66]

However, no site for such a repository has been finalised. According to news reports, there were several unsuccessful attempts by the authorities during the last few years in Madhya Pradesh's granite belt, in Karnataka's Kolar gold mines, and in Sanawada village in Pokhran district in Rajasthan.[67] To that extent, so far, no country in the world has succeeded in preparing a deep geological repository for nuclear waste. The United States has found no politically acceptable site yet. Work on the proposed site at Yucca mountain has been controversial. However, if DAE succeeds in such an endeavour, "India will help boost people's confidence in nuclear energy" says C. Ganguly, former head of the nuclear fuel cycle and materials section at the International Atomic Energy Agency (IAEA) in Vienna.[68]

Uranium Mining and Waste Disposal

At present, India does not have sufficient domestic uranium supply that is capable of supporting its nuclear energy expansion programme. India's target to produce 10,000 MWe by 2020 would be entirely unachievable without a three-fold increase in uranium supply. In this pursuit, India is building up civil-nuclear cooperation networks with around 20 countries. Meanwhile, it is exploring new uranium reserves within the country. Indigenous output can only triple if the mines located in different states are approved and achieve full production, although presently they are only in the initial stages of exploration. However, there are many difficulties in exploring the new found reserves. Technologically, there are constraints in locating large tonnage high grade uranium deposits in the country; this may lead to dependence on more exploitation of low-grade, low-to-medium tonnage deposits. Socially, the negative perception about mining as a polluting industry, exaggerated safety concerns regarding tailing ponds, and spread of misinformation by activists are major hurdles that require effective and urgent solutions.[69]

Fig 1: State-wise Uranium Reserves in India

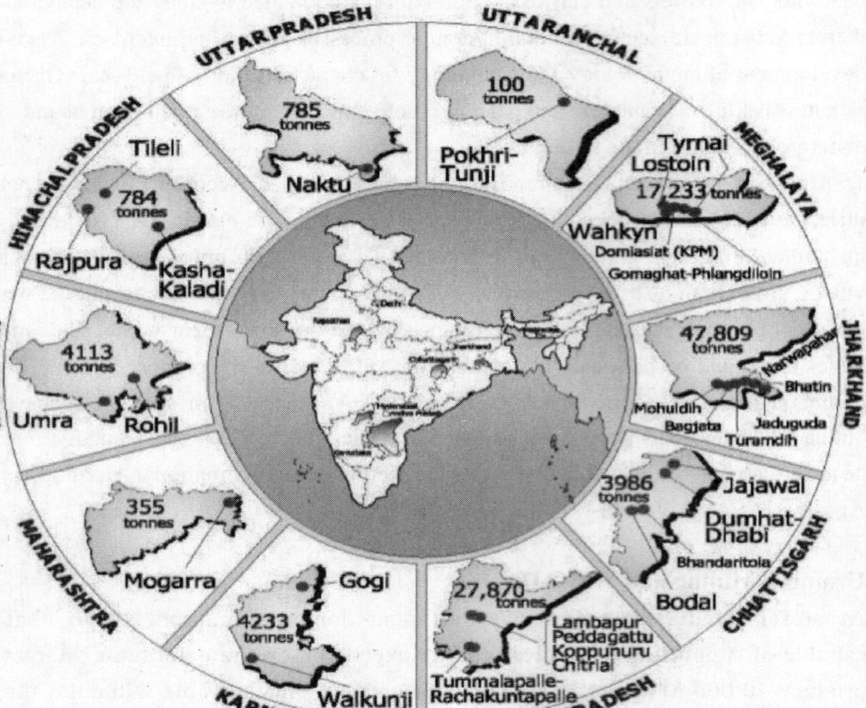

Source: http://www-pub.iaea.org/mtcd/meetings/PDFplus/2009/cn175/URAM2009/Session%20 1/9_63_Gupta_India.pdf

As per the IAEA *Red Book*, the total uranium reserves in India as on March 2007 comprise 1,07,268 te. In 2011, the DAE, after several years of survey, found that the Tumalapalli mine near Hyderabad (Andhra Pradesh) could be world's largest uranium reserve. It could provide up to 49,000 tons and there are indications that the total quantity could be as large as three times that amount (150,000 tons).[70] The Uranium Corporation of India Limited (UCIL) has commissioned in late 2011 an underground mine and processing plant at Tummalapalle. But, anti-mining protests were triggered by the reported large-scale deaths of fish in the Ranikor river, allegedly from toxic waste caused by drilling and dumping into the river. The local government officials ruled out radiation poisoning as the cause—rather some officials claimed that miscreants had dumped poisonous materials into the river to create a scare and scuttle the mining project.[71]

Such incidents are no longer sporadic in India these days. Since 1996, the Domiasat uranium mining project has been stalled by large public protests, triggered by concerns over radiation. The National Alliance of Anti-Nuclear Movements (NAAM) organised a rally in Delhi in October 2009, supporting the Khasi Students Union's anti-uranium mining crusade. At Jantar Mantar, speakers from Meghalaya, Karnataka, Andhra Pradesh and Jharkhand highlighted the ill-effects of uranium mining and the dangers of setting up nuclear power plants.[72] In Karnataka, the Gogi and surrounding village residents demanded relocation before the start of the uranium mine as they are worried about the consequences for the future generations.[73]

There have also been reported incidents of mining and waste management related incidents that have spread panic and resentment among the local population: for example, an accident that occurred on December 24, 2006, near Jaduguda when one of the pipes carrying radioactive wastes from the uranium mill to a tailing pond burst, and thousands of litres of radioactive waste spilled into a nearby creek for nine hours before the flow was shut off.[74] While the DAE officials have called it a "small leak" and of no risk to anyone, the local population and the anti-nuclear lobby viewed it as a threat to the health of thousands of villagers who are "living in the deadly shadow of uranium".[75] There are many other reported issues like uranium mill tailings spillover during flash floods, concentration of uranium in local water sources, congenital deformities, sterility, and cancer among people living within 2.5 km of the mines that have generated critical debate on uranium mining safety and waste management in India.

The nuclear establishment asserts that the operations at all the uranium mines, including Jaduguda, are safe.[76] Contrary to the allegations that no independent survey is conducted by UCIL or DAE, there have, in fact, been two independent surveys commissioned: the first one was by the faculty from the Radiotherapy and Radiology Department of the Patna Medical College and the second was undertaken by a medical team composed of the civil surgeon, physician and nuclear medicine specialists from the Tata Main Hospital, Jamshedpur, and a senior medical officer from the Mercy Hospital. Both surveys found that all the reported diseases were caused due to thalassaemia, chronic malaria, malnutrition and consumption of alcohol..[77] The Environment Survey Laboratory collects the environmental samples for analysis and it found that concentration of uranium in the Gara Nala, Subernarekha river, Gara river, etc. has always been less than the limit set by the AERB and World Health Organisation (WHO). The Health Physics unit regularly monitors the concentration levels and discharges, if any, and ensures that the activity is not polluting the environment in any way.[78]

Advanced and systematic techniques are followed in the waste management at uranium mining areas: (1) waste rocks of mines are used for back-filling of stopes; (2)

coarser fraction tailings (deslimed) are used for back-filling; (3) slimes are stored in the impoundment facility (tailing pond); and (4) plant effluents are treated before discharge to the public domain. The tailing ponds are well engineered with natural barriers on three sides; channel ways and well-laid drainage system for discharge of effluents; and reclamation of tailings pond after use with soil cover and plantation is strictly carried out.[79] Newer concepts like the Thickened Tailings Disposal (TTD) system are under implementation to minimise the tailings pond area as the production and processing of large quantity of ore results in generation of large volumes of tailings.

India's Gordian Knot?

Problems associated with radioactive waste management in the long term are major ones that humanity has not been able to come to terms with so far. Although there are undoubted technical solutions to finding various disposal routes for radioactive wastes, like shallow burial, deep mines, disposal under the sea-bed, and even shooting them to the sun, amicable disposal options are comparatively limited. Even in the USA, the shallow burial sites have been closed following the discovery of poor containment of wastes and sloppy management. In January 2012, the Blue Ribbon Commission concluded that there is no alternative to burying the waste underground. Sweden, France, the UK, etc. are opting for deep burial as well. However, there is no international consensus regarding the best technological solution for waste disposal. The options available are also enmeshed in the dichotomy between scientific understanding and human values.

India, in this context, is not facing an acute problem of nuclear waste at this stage as the volume piled up is comparatively small, but it may become a Gordian knot in the decades ahead due to many unique issues. First, with the increasing institutionalisation of anti-nuclear movements in India, the trend in opposition is likely to shift from "Not In My Back Yard" (NIMBY) to "Not In Anyone's Back Yard" (NIABY). Though India has a variety of land and rock forms to build a geological repository, the issue of burying hazardous waste for future generations and guaranteeing an institution which can survive and be responsible for 1,000 years to safeguard the repository would pose serious hurdles in arriving at a national consensus. Second, the management of waste generated out of the reactor operations in India, is perceptibly well planned and unlikely to pose a problem for the next few decades, but waste out of uranium mining projects and new exploration activities may experience strong social discontent. As the quality of uranium reserves in India is poor and a larger amount of ore has to be processed to obtain a small quantity of uranium, the amount of tailings produced in the process would be much more. This would pose a bigger challenge for the industry. Third, most of the uranium reserves in India are located in areas inhabited by the tribal population who may not agree to vacate the areas. As rehabilitation issues related to developmental projects in India in the past have become contentious, uranium exploration induced displacement of the local population in the future would lead to further escalation of public resentment. Fourth, rampant corruption in every sector in India brings home the fear that nuclear waste management too may not be spared. Will India be able to set up an institution for the upkeep of deep buried radioactive waste, which has to survive for centuries, without dilution of its integrity? According to the CAG report, "The existing mechanism for safe disposal of radioactive material reveals weakness in verification of compliance and the lack of enforcement by AERB".[80] However, AERB assures that once the advanced web-based interactive system for the management of the radioactive source becomes operational, it would be easier to track the cradle to grave cycle of a radioactive source.

Lastly, uranium is a strategic mineral and is the property of the union government; but as state governments are poised to play a greater role in the future, conflict between the states and the union government over the management of 'social acceptance' of nuclear projects may arise. This would further delay the nuclear energy programme. India has already missed its five-year nuclear power generation target by 74 percent mainly owing to the protests at Kudankulam and other nuclear plant sites. The NPCIL could add only 880 MW nuclear power over the past five years to the 3,900 MW capacity at the start of the 11th Five-Year Plan in 2007.[81] Therefore, instead of slicing hurriedly the nuclear waste management spiral, India must untie the knot deftly and painstakingly before it becomes a Gordian one. This can be managed by evolving a well-structured 'nuclear information management system' and a value-based 'corporate social responsibility culture' in the country.

Notes

1. "Nuclear Power Corporation of India to Launch 16 New Nuclear Reactors", *The Economic Times*, June 01, 2012.
2. Rashme Sehgal, "India Needs Proper N-Waste Disposal Tech", *The Asian Age*, May 13, 2008.
3. Union Government, Department of Atomic Energy, "Report of the Comptroller and Auditor General of India on Activities of Atomic Energy Regulatory Board for the Year Ended March 2012", Report No. 9 of 2012-13, p. 51.
4. K. Raj, K.K. Prasad, N.K. Bansal, "Radioactive Waste Management Practices in India", *Nuclear Engineering and Design*, March 11, 2004, p. 914.
5. Ibid.
6. "Radioactive Waste", International Nuclear Societies Council, http://www.ne.jp/asahi/mh/u/INSCAP/Radwaste.html
7. "Blue Ribbon Commission on America's Nuclear Future Issues Final Report to Secretary of Energy", http://www.prnewswire.com/news-releases/blue-ribbon-commission-on-americas-

nuclear-future-issues-final-report-to-secretary-of-energy-138140713.html, January 26, 2012.

8. Brian Kemp, "Storing Nuclear Waste a $24-billion Problem", http://www.cbc.ca/news/canada/story/2009/08/18/f-nuclear-waste-storage.html, August 18, 2009
9. Oliver Milman, "Australia Passes Controversial Nuclear Waste Bill", http://www.guardian.co.uk/environment/2012/mar/13/australia-nuclear-waste-aboriginal, March 13, 2012.
10. "Radioactive Waste Management (RWM) in China", www.fnca.mext.go.jp/english/rwm/news_img/rwm_cr03-02_r004.pdf
11. Ju Wang, "High-level Radioactive Waste Disposal in China: Update 2010", *Journal of Rock Mechanics and Geotechnical Engineering*, Vol. 2, No. 1, 2010, p. 10.
12. "Chinese Nuclear Waste Management Program", www.nwtrb.gov/meetings/1996/jan/wang.pdf
13. "China Builds Home-made Nuclear Waste Processor", *China Daily*, March 07, 2012.
14. Charles Digges, "Russia Announces Enormous Finds of Radioactive Waste and Nuclear Reactors in Arctic Seas, http://www.bellona.org/articles/articles_2012/Russia_reveals_dumps, August 28, 2012.
15. "Russian Radioactive Waste Law Signed", *World Nuclear News*, July 15, 2011.
16. "Where to Dispose of Britain's Nuclear Waste," http://www.ccg.leeds.ac.uk/teaching/nuclearwaste/nuclearwaste.html
17. Rob Broomby, "UK Nuclear Waste Strategy in Jeopardy", *BBC News*, July 17, 2009.
18. "France Details Nuclear Waste Inventory", *World Nuclear News*, August 06, 2012.
19. "Nuclear Waste in France Set to Double", http://www.upi.com/Science_News/2012/07/13/Nuclear-waste-in-France-set-to-double/UPI-21671342208921/, July 13, 2012.
20. Declan Butler, "France Digs Deep for Nuclear Waste", http://www.nature.com/news/2010/100810/full/466804a.html, August 13, 2010.
21. During the last four years (2009-12), four unstarred questions were raised in the Lok Sabha and Rajya Sabha on February 26, 2009; July 28, 2010; August 17, 2011; and March 14, 2012, specifically regarding the quantity of nuclear waste generated in India.
22. Lok Sabha Debate, Unstarred Question No. 2747, "Nuclear Waste", asked by Nishikant Dubey, answered by V. Narayanasamy on August 17, 2011.
23. "Nuclear Waste not an Immediate Problem for India: Ramesh", *The Times of India*, January 03, 2011.
24. Rajya Sabha Debate, Unstarred Question No. 1012, "Handling of Nuclear Waste", by N.R. Govindarajar, answered by Prithviraj Chavan, on February 26, 2009.
25. M.V. Ramana, "Estimating Nuclear Waste Production in India", *Current Science*, Vol. 81, No. 11, December 10, 2001, p. 1461.
26. N.S. Sunder Rajan, *IAEA Bulletin*, Spring 1986, http://www.iaea.org/Publications/Magazines/Bulletin/Bull281/28104693740.pdf, p. 40.
27. G.V. Rao and S. Prakash, "An Approach to Reduce Load on the Acid Leaching Circuit of the Commercial Uranium Recovery Plant at Jaduguda, India", *Magnetic and Electrical Separation*, Vol. 9, 1998, www.downloads.hindawi.com/archive/1998/032360.pdf, p. 27.
28. UCIL, "Uranium Mining and Milling Industry in India", http://www-pub.iaea.org/mtcd/meetings/PDFplus/2009/cn175/URAM2009/Session%201/9_63_Gupta_India.pdf
29. http://www.barc.ernet.in/publications/eb/golden/nfc/toc/Chapter%206/6.pdf, p. 51.
30. n. 22..
31. Monoj Mitta, "Spent Nuclear Fuel: A Danger or Resource?, *The Times of India*, October 03, 2012.
32. Dhananjay Mahapatra, "Kudankulam Nuclear Plant can be Shut if Found Unsafe: Supreme Court", *The Times of India*, September 28, 2012.
33. AERB, *AERB Safety Guide – Management of Radioactive Waste Arising from Operation of*

Pressurised Heavy Water Reactor Based Nuclear Power Plants, "Operational Requirements", Clause 2.3.1, Guidelines No. AERB/NPP/SG/O-11, March 2004, p. 3.

34. Raj, et al., n. 4.
35. Ibid., p. 915.
36. Rajan, n. 26, p. 38, n. 26.
37. Lok Sabha Debate, "Nuclear Waste", Unstarred Question No 2747, asked by Nishikant Dubey, answered by V. Narayanasamy on August 17, 2011; Lok Sabha Debates, "Disposal of Nuclear Waste", Question No 2088, Question asked by Vinay Kumar, answered by V. Narayanasamy on March 9, 2011.
38. Rajya Sabha Debate, "Nuclear Waste Management System", question raised by Ramachandra Khuntia, answered by the Minister of State for Parliamentary Affairs, Personnel, Public Grievances & Pensions and PMO V. Narayanasamy on March 10, 2011.
39. Rajan, n. 26, p. 37.
40. Ibid., p. 917.
41. Ibid.
42. S. Kumar, S.S. Ali, M. Chander, N.K. Bansal, K. Balu, "Integrated Radioactive Waste Management from NPP, Research Reactor and Back End of Nuclear Fuel Cycle – An Indian Experience", Waste Management Division, BARC, IAEA-SM-357/38, p. 8.
43. Ibid.
44. Ibid.
45. Raj, et al, n. 4, p. 920.
46. Rajya Sabha Debates, Unstarred Question No. 1012, "Handling of Nuclear Waste", by Shri N.R. Govindarajar, answered by Shri Prithviraj Chavan, February 26, 2009.
47. M.P. Gupta, et al, "Indian Experience in Near Surface Disposal of Low Level Radioactive Solid Waste", Proceedings of the Symposium on Experience in the Planning and Operation of Low Level Waste Disposal Facilities, IAEA, Vienna (1996),
48. Kumar, et al, n. 42. p. 4.
49. Ibid., p. 5.
50. Raj et al, n. 4, p. 928.
51. G.S. Mudur, "Site Hunt for Nuclear Graveyard", *The Telegraph* (Kolkata), February 15, 2012.
52. S.S. Kapoor, "Accelerator-driven Sub-critical Reactor System (ADS) for Nuclear Energy Generation", *Panama Journal of Physics*, Vol. 59, No. 6, December 2002, p. 948.
53. A. Stanculescu, "Accelerator Driven System (ADS) and Transmutation of Nuclear Waste: Options and Trends", IAEA, http://users.ictp.it/~pub_off/lectures/lns005/Number_2/Stanculescu.pdf
54. "Waste Management: Remote Handling & Transportation", Nuclear Fuel Cycle, *BARC HIGHLIGHTS* http://www.barc.gov.in/publications/eb/golden/nfc/toc/Chapter%2014/14.pdf, p. 95.
55. S. Kumar, P.M. Satya Sai, S. Manohar, R.R. Rakesh, "Studies for Onsite Disposal of Waste from Decommissioning/Revamping of Nuclear Facilities and NPPS in India", in IAEA, *Disposal Aspects of Low and Intermediate Level Decommissioning Waste Results of aCcoordinated Research Project 2002–2006*, December 2007, http://www-pub.iaea.org/MTCD/publications/PDF/TE_1572_companion_CD_web.pdf, p. 54.
56. Ibid; P.B. Savant, et al, "Health Physics Experience on the Decommissioning of Thorium Plant of I.R.E. Ltd at Trombay", BARC/2004/I/011 (2004).
57. For more details on India's capabilities on onsite disposal of waste from decommissioning, see Kumar et al, n. 55.
58. Lok Sabha Debate, "Integrated Nuclear Recycle Fuel", Unstarred Question No 389 by PT Thomas, answered by Prithviraj Chavan on November 10, 2010.

59. Lok Sabha Debate, "Nuclear Waste", Unstarred Question No. 3419, answered on April 25, 2012.
60. "India to Get First Underground Repository for N-Waste", *The Times of India*, May 06, 2012.
61. Lok Sabha Debate, Unstarred Question No.3419, "Nuclear Waste", answered on April 25, 2012. http://www.dae.gov.in/parlqa/2012/budget2012/lsus3419.pdf, p. 2.
62. Kalyan Ray, "India Keen on Having Nuclear Waste Repository", *Deccan Herald*, February 12, 2012.
63. G.S. Mudur, "Site Hunt for Nuclear Graveyard", *The Telegraph* (Kolkata), February 15, 2012.
64. K.K. Prasad, "Underground Research Laboratory (URL) Programme In India", http://www.iaea.org/OurWork/ST/NE/NEFW/WTS-Networks/URF/documents/Status/2004/MS/India.pdf
65. "Waste Management: Disposal of Radioactive Waste", Nuclear Fuel Cycle, *BARC HIGHLIGHTS*, http://www.barc.ernet.in/publications/eb/golden/nfc/toc/Chapter%2017/17.2.pdf
66. Ibid.
67. Rashme Sehgal, "India Needs Proper N-Waste Disposal Tech", *The Asian Age*, May 13, 2008.
68. Ray, 2012, n. 62.
69. "Uranium Mining & Milling Industry in India", http://www-pub.iaea.org/mtcd/meetings/PDFplus/2009/cn175/URAM2009/Session%201/9_63_Gupta_India.pdf
70. "Largest Uranium Reserves Found in India", *The Telegraph*, July 19, 2011.
71. "Uranium Projects Show India's Nuclear Ambition Undiminished", http://www.cleanbiz.asia/story/uranium-projects-show-india%E2%80%99s-nuclear-ambition-undiminished May 02, 2012.
72. *The Telegraph*, October 02, 2009.
73. *Deccan Herald*, September 10, 2011.
74. U.A. Shimray, M.V. Ramana, "Uranium Mining in Meghalaya: Simmering Problem", *Economic & Political Weekly*, December 29, 2007, pp. 13-17.
75. Harsh Kapoor, "TS: Living in the Deadly Shadow of Uranium", *The Toronto Star*, October 10, 2010.
76. "Jaduguda Operations Safe", *The Hindu*, April 09, 2000.
77. Ibid.
78. Ibid.
79. "Uranium Mining & Milling Industry in India", http://www-pub.iaea.org/mtcd/meetings/PDFplus/2009/cn175/URAM2009/Session%201/9_63_Gupta_India.pdf
80. n. 3.
81. India had set the target of adding 3,380 MW of additional nuclear power by 2012. Charu Sudan Kasturi, "India's Ticking Nuclear Crisis: Part I", *Hindustan Times*, September 30, 2012.

6

Indigenisation of Aerospace Industry Through Jonah's Thinking Process

P.V. Athawale

The world we have created is a process of our thinking. It cannot be changed without changing our thinking

— Albert Einstein

Introduction

Indian Industry

Until independence, India had remained significantly isolated from the industrial revolution around the world[1]. Independent India gradually began on a progressive path of industrialisation with a firm resolve. A poor nation with a large population and little design and manufacturing infrastructure chose the socialist route to industrial growth through the public sector. Even after the economic reforms of the 1990s, the hi-tech aerospace design and manufacturing have been left relatively untouched by the private sector. This can be attributed to the inherently high costs and the lack of a market. The public sector has contributed only sporadically with products for use primarily by military aviation. The defence production units viz. Defence Public Sector Undertakings (DPSUs) and Ordnance Factories (OFs), having made their contribution, seem to have tapered to saturation. Their qualification and ability to undertake Design and Development (D&D) tasks, however innovative and efficient, do not inspire great confidence. If there is anything that will bring about a rejuvenation, it is competition.

In keeping with a socialist ideology , the country kept itself isolated from external suppliers until the 1980s. Clearly two generations behind those in the world market, cars made by Hindustan Motors and Premier Automobiles managed to transport Indians who wore hmt watches. But, on the subject related to defence of our skies, we required machines that could match the adversaries' assets. Having the latest technology in cars may not have been a necessity but when it came to aircraft, it was imperative to keep pace with the world. There was a limit to which the genius of our pilots would have offset deficiencies in our aircraft. We were, therefore, compelled to acquire aircraft and systems from foreign sources. This proved to be sufficient justification for scrapping the indigenous Maruts (HF-24) to make way for the British Jaguars even as the decision hurt the sentiments of many air warriors. With the surrender of indigenous military aerospace design and manufacture to foreign purchases, the Indian industry was left with no option but to be satisfied with manufacturing under licence.

The opening of Indian markets after the 1990s changed the economy but the industry remained under a distinct hangover from the past, so much that the typically Indian fear of manufacturing has endured through this long phase of economic growth. The economy has been propelled primarily by the service sector, which suited the Original Equipment Manufacturers (OEMs) from abroad. By outsourcing routine work to India, they got access to our markets while safeguarding key design and manufacturing acumen. Most industrial sectors, after having gone through these long phases of services and partial manufacturing/assembly under licence, are now attempting to break free to enter into independent design and manufacturing.

However, the aerospace industry's predicament has continued even in the post 1990s scenario. Unlike others, the aerospace industry cannot develop its own market segment, especially in view of the distinctly higher cost and technology involved in the face of an extremely restricted and uncertain market. Therefore, state sponsorship has been essential for growth in this sector where the entry of new players is almost impossible without government support. The public sector has justifiably been favoured for the last few decades. But, the DPSUs have gradually gone into a state of virtual happiness with licensed manufacturing. They are going down further to seek the routine maintenance of Air Force inventories in the field, shifting their focus from D&D. Ordnance factories, tucked well behind the Ministry of Defence (MoD) show little respect for accepted production tasks. At the same time, the Defence Research and Development Organisation (DRDO) has not succeeded in bringing out competitive technologies with acceptable standards of reliability and product support from manufacturing partners. The most disappointing part has been the lack of adherence to time schedules. The Air Force, amidst this national industrial incapability, has found justification in looking out for arms purchase from foreign vendors.

Around the world, only a few global companies supply aircraft and equipment to most civil airlines and airport authorities. The civil aerospace sector is also like any other commercial field e.g. motor cars manufacture. The lack of indigenous control here does not have a far-reaching strategic impact as in the case of defence aerospace. Different airlines as buyers find it suitable to purchase from the best globally available. In comparison, **institutionalised measures by the MoD to promote indigenisation** and provide for offsets in defence procurements have particularly encouraged the industry including the private sector. Therefore, the entire indigenisation focus of the Indian aerospace industry hinges on defence supplies, resulting in raised expectations from the defence establishment.

Where does Air Power Reside?

The Air Force, without doubt in anyone's mind, is the measure of air power. It is the front end. It is the agency which is ultimately responsible for effective deployment of air power on call by the national leadership. Technically, a reference to the Air Force should not include the air arms of the Army and the Navy. But, for the sake of simplicity, we may call the combined air arms the '*Air Force*'. As we ponder upon 'where the foundation of air power lies', we are called upon to look well beyond the Air Force. Even though behind the scenes, indigenous defence Research and Development (R&D) and industry begin to play a distinctive role as expectations from air power rise.

Fig 1

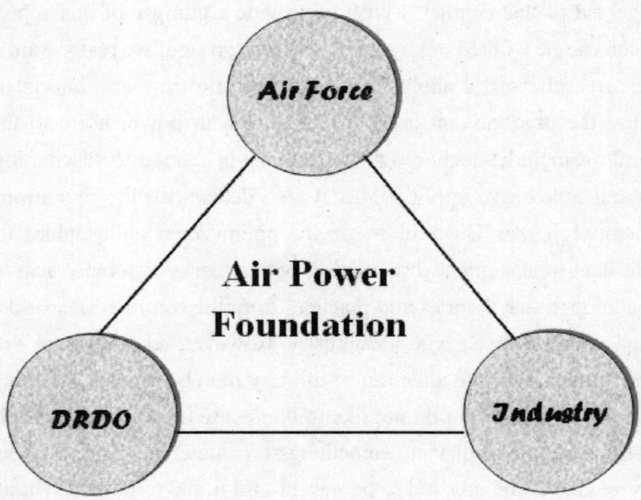

The defence aerospace power can be perceived to rest on a triangular foundation made of the three vertices viz. DRDO, Industry and Air Force (**Fig 1**). The reach and influence of this aerospace power is determined through a non-linear relationship with the three determinants. This is held in a precarious balance as each contributing element works towards maximising its own effectiveness to feel constrained by the lack of contribution of someone else - 'the problem is always somewhere else! The biggest positive is the fact that everyone wholeheartedly agrees with the objective of indigenisation. And yet, everyone finds so many hurdles in decision-making and execution. These conflicts paralyse us in status quo and we remain unable to take action to change things for the better under the fear that the situation may turn for the worse.

The conventional view serves to protect us from the painful job of thinking.

— John Kenneth Galbraith

Transformation of Conflict into Synergy

While all involved may be well meaning and working relentlessly towards organisational goals, conflict arises because the efforts do not synergise. There is no inherent conflict among people. And, therefore, the triangle of conflict can easily be transformed into the triangle of synergy. In my opinion, the Theory of Constraint's (TOC's) thinking process can help us get rid of this conflict. I wish to provide a glimpse of this approach here, the details of which can be worked out by a separate task group if we really want a change.

Defence researchers and analysts are left with no time and energy for industrial issues, because the predominant combat element of air power hogs all their attention. Military literature includes technology issues usually related to fascination with future possibilities and innovative applications. It also deals with the operational aspects of logistics and supply chain. But seldom are the optimisation philosophies for acquisition and life cycle fleet management discussed in books that are globally acknowledged and sold. It is a relief then that theories and practices from the commercial world apply equally to the military, which in itself is a big industry. However, research from the commercial arena does not attract adequate attention of military men because of references to *market, money, profit, customer*, etc. We do not like to be diverted from air power related strategic or tactical battle space vocabulary to something so commercial. The text, therefore, needs to be suitably modified and adapted to be meaningful to the military. I will attempt to link the TOC expressions with our air power context in a limited sense to break the conflict related to indigenisation.

Introduction to Theory of Constraints

Before a detailed discussion in the context of indigenisation, it will be useful to present an overview of the Theory of Constraints (TOC). Elliyahu M. Goldratt developed the 'Theory of Constraints' as a management and improvement philosophy. He introduced it through his many books including *The Goal* (1984)[2], *The Goal II - It's Not Luck* (1994)[3], *Critical Chain* (1997)[4] and *Theory of Constraints* (1999)[5].

Goldratt saw organisations as systems with resources and processes to perform. TOC asserts that "any manageable system is limited in achieving more of its goals by a very small number of constraints, and there is always at least one constraint". This constraint may be related to machines, equipment, people or policy. A five-step process for improvement is suggested by this theory as listed below:

- Identification of constraints.
- Decision on how to exploit the constraint (to get the most capacity out).
- Subordination of everything else to support the decisions.
- Elevation of the constraint (break through other major changes).
- When the constraint is broken and it moves, getting back to step 1 and not letting inertia become a constraint.

The logical conflict between the society and industrial processes has been explained by Kelvyn Youngman[6]. He says that our everyday beliefs and mental fixations of social networks block us from understanding the industrial processes. This is what he calls the '*error of logical type*'. Social networks call for optimising individual outputs to maximise group achievement. On the other hand, industrial systems are more sequential, where the system output is limited by the weakest element called the constraint. Parts other than the constraint have excess capacity. Therefore, optimising all parts for maximising individual output would lead us to no enhancement. In fact, the usual state of the system is such that it is unable to even produce to the maximum capacity of the constraint. That is why we have to maximise the constraint instead of maximising every system element.

Thus, the theme of '*maximising almost all while subordinating a few*' from the social world has to give way to *'maximising only the constraints while subordinating everything else to that*'.

The Theory of Constraints covers many things, including some of the following:

- **Five focussing steps** for solution (listed in above para).
- **Drum Buffer Rope:** The *drum* is the rate at which the constraint resource is able to process. The correct loading of the constraint is ensured by the '*drum beat*'. The Murphy is looked after by a buffer set up in front of the drum in such a way

that work is always waiting to be taken up by the constraint. The constraint is never required to wait for work otherwise the output would go below the capacity of the constraint itself. The important aspect is that the buffer capacity is measured and set up in units of time required by the constraint. The *rope* is the schedule that ties all parts of the system together to enable subordination of the capacities of all nonconstraint parts to the constraint.

- **Critical Chain:**. Project managers estimate the time required as the arithmetic sum of estimates of different parts. The different parts tend to estimate requirements with their own safety margins pushed in. The result is that the benefit of specific parts finishing early hardly ever goes to the subsequent stages, but the delays are shared. Therefore, Critical Chain Project management was developed by Goldratt to solve the problems of projects' time as well as cost overruns. The longest dependent path is identified as the '*Critical Chain*' as against the '*Critical Path'*. A project buffer is kept to account for the overall delay. Feeding buffers (of time) and resource buffers (of people and skills) are kept for the critical chain. Finally, the tasks are measured in terms of their remaining duration rather than percentage completion.
- **Thinking Process:** Goldratt put forward the *'Thinking Process' to* find solutions to systemic problems. The process breaks *the constraint of our thinking paradigm*. The identification of the root cause of the systemic problem, its solution and implementation are achieved by addressing three fundamental questions: *'What to change', 'What to change to' and '**How** to cause the change'?*

The Goal

The clarity of the 'goal' of an organisation is the starting point for every related action and most certainly actions related to transformation and improvement. Therefore, before we identify constraints, the following prerequisites are essential.

- System definition and its *goal* (purpose or objective).
- Determination of a metric or a measure to evaluate the efficacy of the system meeting its purpose.

For all business organisations, Goldratt suggested the purpose or goal in simple language as, "*Making more money now as well as in the future*". To amplify further, he suggested, "*To provide a secure and satisfying environment for employees now and in the future*" and "*To provide satisfaction to the market now as well as in the future*" as the other two primary objectives for sustenance of the business. Each one of the three can be seen as complementary to the other two.

Here the contrast between business and the military is obvious. The military is not interested in making money today or tomorrow! But, the armed forces most certainly are concerned about reducing operating expense to maximise the use of the available budget. The military has a goal which must be kept sight of at all times. As an example, one may say that the goal of the Air Force is to match (or better) the capabilities of adversaries (individual or combined). Alternatively, one may say the goal of the Air Force is to be a regional air power or an air power with global influence. The next important issue is *whether the achievement of the goal is measurable*. Military men are known to be proud of their discipline and ethics. Above all, we are fond of a different set of rules to determine the behaviour of our men as well as machines. We don't like the civilian business world to cast its shadow on our systems and would, therefore, quickly close our minds to '*sales and profit*' talk as simply *'not applicable'* to us. At this stage, therefore, I wish to reiterate the relevance. It won't be justifiable to close up by saying no yardstick of measurement of efficacy applies to us. Oversimplification by measuring percentage serviceability or flying effort as per current norms could be misleading. The number of squadrons maintained, average fleet serviceability and flying effort are all incomprehensive measurements. These must be made to relate to force structure, fleet availability (not unit percentage serviceability), training and war potential.

Goldratt considered business companies to be making money when they created value add to bought out material faster than the expenditure. He identified three ways of categorisation with Throughput, Operating Expense and Rate of Return. In essence, the measure of value generation is vital for making decisions regarding process refinements, whether the organisation makes money or generates output in different units. For military requirements, the throughput measured as war potential generated (per unit of constraint per unit time) must govern all decisions. **Can we then measure war potential like the bottom line of a business balance sheet?** Like the throughput, we can certainly devise appropriate metrics, but that perhaps will have to be the outcome of a separate study.

Jonah's Thinking Process

A fictitious character by the name of Jonah was created by Goldratt in his story-like books to illustrate TOC. The thinking process has accordingly been popularised as Jonah's Thinking Process. In line with the scientific approach, this process verbalises the cause and effect relationships so that the assumptions can be verified. These assumptions are challenged and either invalidated to relieve the conflict or accepted to gain renewed understanding of relationships. The following fundamental beliefs are at the core:

- Nature has **inherent simplicity** and not complexity.
- Nature has **inherent harmony** and **no conflicts**.
- All problems converge to a **single root cause** or **core conflict**.
- There are **no bad people**; we only have **bad assumptions**.

The thinking process uses six methods to enable focussed improvement. These are discussed briefly here to enable appreciation of the concept. The retention of some of the original terms may make the text a little intricate. But, the examples of our domains will make things easily comprehensible later on.

Current Reality Tree (CRT)-1

The thinking process starts with precise articulation of the problems named as *Undesirable Effects* (UDEs). As per the guideline, articulation of UDEs does not require an explanation; no cause, no blame is to be assigned and no solution is required to be offered. With UDEs, we build a Current Reality Tree connecting the cause and effect relationships of all problems. An example is shown in **Fig 2**.

Fig 2

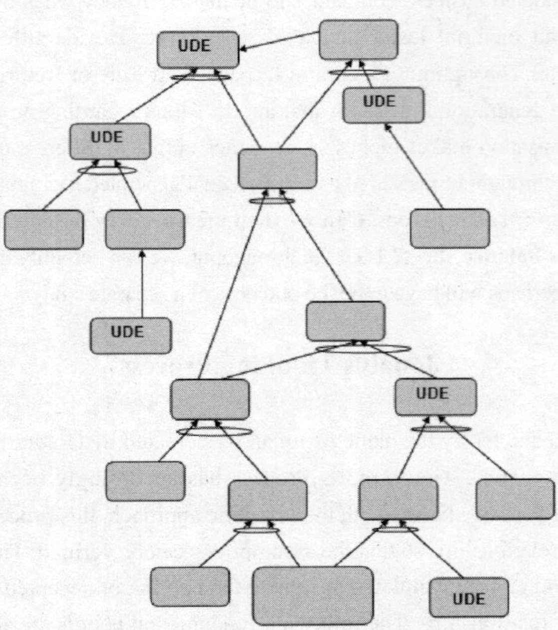

Evaporating Cloud or Conflict Diagram-2

The systemic cloud is drawn as shown below in **Fig 3** for breaking the conflict surrounding a given problem. Here the prerequisite is an objective, which is a positive systemic objective agreed upon by all parties. **B** and **C** are needs; both are positive and supportive of the objective. The prerequisite actions and wants at **D** and **D'** individually support the needs at **B** and **C** respectively, leading to the objective. But, these conflict with each other and cannot exist together. At the same time, **D** jeopardises the need at **C,** while **D'** jeopardises the need at **B**; this is what makes the conflict really tight. These are real life situations as we will see later.

Fig 3

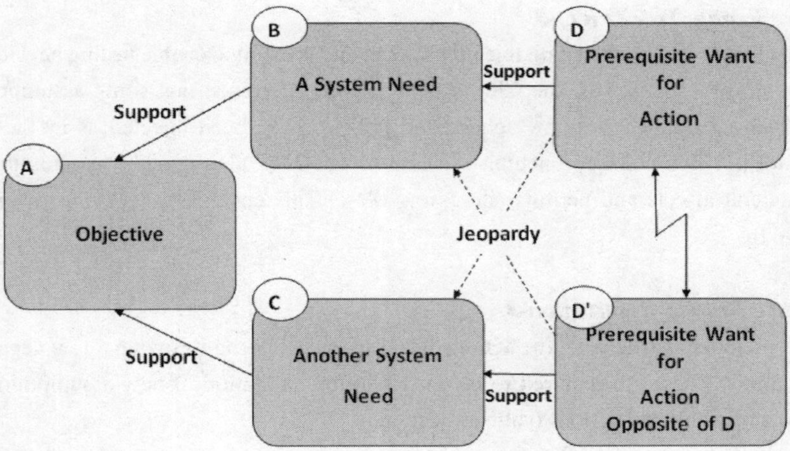

Now, all linkages from one block to the other are verbalised listing *assumptions* for each as shown below:

- In order to have **A**, we must have the requirement **B** because *<reason l>*
  In order to have **A**, we must have the requirement **B** because *<reason m>*
- In order to have **B**, we must have the action **D** because *<reason l>*
  In order to have **B**, we must have the action **D** because *<reason n>*
- In order to have **A**, we must have the requirement **C** because *<reason l>*
  In order to have **A**, we must have the requirement **C** because *<reason p>*
- In order to have **C**, we must have the action **D'** because *<reason l>*
  In order to have **C**, we must have the action **D'** because *<reason q>*

- If action **D** is carried out, then we cannot get **C** because <*reason 1*>
  If action **D** is carried out, then we cannot get **C** because <*reason r*>
  AND
- If action **D'** is carried out, then we cannot get **B** because <*reason 1*>
  If action **D'** is carried out, then we cannot get **B** because <*reason s*>

As we verbalise our assumptions and carry out a rigorous check, we begin to invalidate many assumptions leading to the conflict. Injections (or actions) can be then generated for insertion in the Current Reality Tree (**CRT**) to remove conflicts to turn Undesirable Effects (UDEs) into Desirable Effects (DEs). Evaporating clouds bring out and confirm **'what to change'**.

Future Reality Tree (FRT)-3

The FRT is constructed with injections taken into account to enable testing new ideas. This is drawn exactly like the CRT except for the difference that some assumptions have been invalidated and new actions and policies have been injected. Now the tree looks all positive and approaching a solution. The FRT also reveals any possibility of collateral affects and permits addressing these. This enables us to know '**what to change to**'.

Negative Branch Reservation-4

As members participate, the actions listed in the FRTs can throw up a few negative reservations. These are required to be dealt with by validation of new assumptions or insertion of additional actions (called injections).

The Prerequisite Tree (PRT)-5

The third step deals with implementation of the solution i.e. *'how to change'*. Towards this, the PRT helps in identifying obstacles in the way of implementation. The FRT with injections and trimmed negative branches is the input to the PRT. People who are intuitive in their respective fields can visualise obstacles in implementation and also Intermediate Objectives (IOs) to achieve. With their participation, the PRT is made to indicate sequential actions to achieve objectives.

Transition Tree (TrT)-6

Finally, the Transition Tree describes how to execute. Here, the interfaces, actions, intermediate states and outcome results are depicted. The action plan TrT (**'how to**

change') connects all the elements like the existing reality, an unfulfilled need, a specific action to be taken, an unexpected effect of the preceding three actions and the rationale of the need.

Insight into Evaporating Clouds

Crises and deadlocks, when they occur, have at least this advantage that they force us to think.

— Pandit Jawaharlal Nehru

Kelvyn Youngman has called the conflict shown in **Fig 4** '*The Lieutenant's Cloud.*' Here the lieutenant wishes to perform a task but is stopped by a rule which prohibits him. **D** has something that we have, but we don't want. And **D'** has an action that we wish to take, but cannot. It is quite amazing then that there is something negative in **D**, but we carry on suffering from it because it also satisfies a positive need (or so we feel) towards the achievement of the *goal*. At the same time, it is intriguing that knowing well about the good outcome of a positive change or action in **D'**, we continue to be paralysed, and fail to change. The result is a status quo because of our fear that if we take action at **D'** (and change), it will jeopardise the need at **B** and the *goal*. It is here that verbalisation of our assumptions (which have made us believe a certain outcome) can help us in challenging some beliefs. Verbalisation can also help us to understand and strengthen a few assumptions which were only vaguely perceived hitherto.

Fig 4

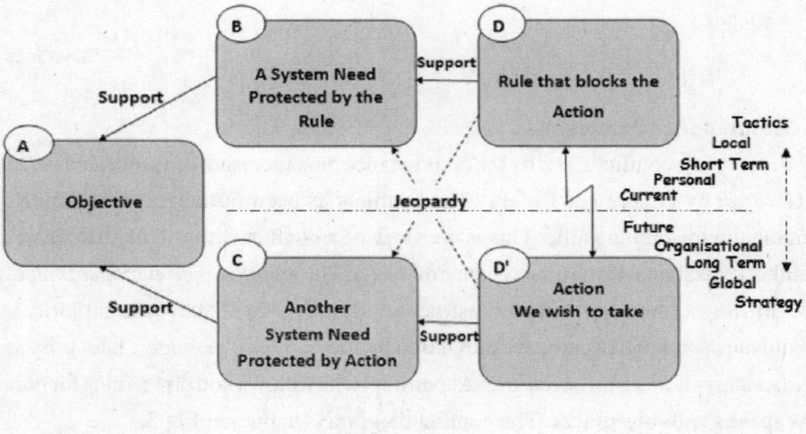

Conventionally, the box D is used to write the UDE; an undesirable rule that blocks the action, we wish to take listed in **D'**. These two wants or actions are, therefore, mutually exclusive. Kelvyn Youngman suggests dividing the diagram with a horizontal line drawn from box **A** across. This virtually divides the space occupied by **B** and **D** from that of **C** and **D'**. The upper and lower part of the dashed line can now be seen as separating two different worlds of logic, as shown in the diagram. The conflict is created fundamentally because the local begins to influence the global view instead of aligning with the '*MAIN*'; short-term policies restrict long-term vision because of the fear of failure, the current affects the future adversely.

It's Not a Compromise

This system of belief has one special approach. A *solution does not lie in compromises* as the outcome of compromises is further undesirable effects. The answer is not in giving up short-term gains totally to build avenues for long-term achievements. The resolution of conflict is *not intended* as one side giving up (**lose-win**); forcing the other side (**win-lose**) or even a compromise **(lose-lose). The intended solution is win-win.**

The quest is for a simple and elegant solution rather than a sophisticated one. According to Goldratt, "Human based environments are governed by simple common sense logic". There is no conflict about the system goal and the needs when we set out to analyse. Only the assumptions either fulfilling or obstructing these needs may have inconsistencies, causing conflicts.

> *Simple can be harder than complex: you have to work hard to get your thinking clear to make it simple. But, it is worth it in the end because once you get there, you can move mountains.*
>
> — Steve Jobs

The Maintenance Manager

The story of a conflict faced by the maintenance manager has been presented in *Deming and Goldratt* by Lepore and Cohen[7]. The conflict has been further explained by Kelvyn Youngman in his online guide. This is the story of a conflict between the responsibilities and authority assigned to the maintenance manager. The *maintenance manager is measured by the* '**uptime**' of his production infrastructure. But, he does not have the authority to buy the requisite spares. The spares are purchased by the *purchase manager*, who is *measured by the least expenditure on purchases*. Accordingly, he follows laid down rules for purchase of **cheapest available spares**. The conflict diagram is shown in **Fig 5**.

Fig 5

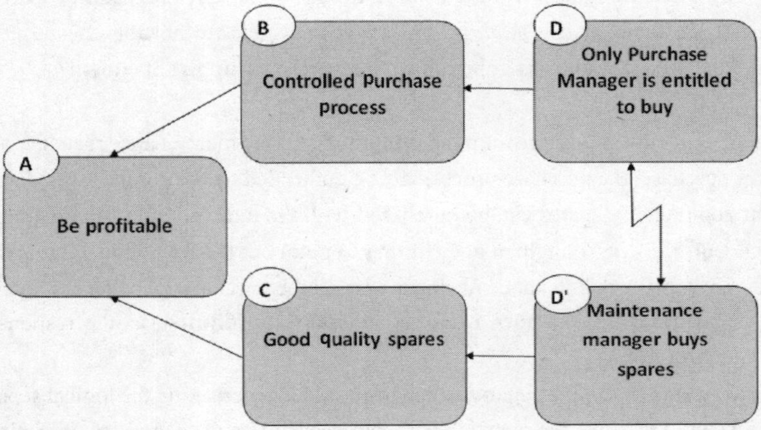

We can verbalise dependencies and assumptions as given below:

- **AB:** In order to keep the company profitable (**A**), we need control on the purchase process (**B**), because increased purchase costs would reduce profits.
- **BD:** In order to have control on the purchase process (**B**), we have to authorise only the purchase manager to buy (**D**), because only he can strike the best deal, following the laid down norms.
- **BD':** If the maintenance manager buys spares (**D'**), accountability would be lost and we cannot (**jeopardy**) exercise control over the purchase process (**B**).
- **BD':** If the maintenance manager buys spares (**D'**), he would wish to buy costly spares for his perceived reasons of reliability of spares and the control would be lost (**jeopardy**) on the purchase process (**B**).
- **AC:** In order to keep the company profitable (**A**), we need to have good quality spares (**C**) because good spares will give us high uptime and, consequently, higher production and profits.
- **CD':** In order to have good quality spares (**C**), the maintenance manager must buy spares (**D'**) because only he can assess the quality.
- **CD:** If the purchase manager buys spares (**D**), we cannot (**jeopardy**) be assured of quality (**C**), because he would go for the least price.

The assumptions can now be examined:

(i) Is it true that **only the purchase manager can strike the best deal?**

(ii) *If the maintenance manager* **advises** *the purchase manager for spares* (instead of himself buying), will the control on the purchase process still be lost?

(iii) If the maintenance *manager buys spares* which are not the cheapest, will it really end up in costs going up so much as **to bring profits down**?

The first two questions throw up the solution that if the maintenance manager advises on spares purchase, the purchase process can be controlled by the purchase manager. And also that good quality spares can be purchased with the intervention of the maintenance manager. But, Kelvyn Youngman goes further to point out the following anomaly:

- Even if the maintenance manager advises the purchase manager for spares, the **accountability of both remains substantially diluted**, as the responsibility gets divided.

The answer to the above negativity can be provided by breaking the logical separation between **D** and **D'**. Now, the question (iii) also needs to be answered about profit really reducing if the maintenance manager recommends spares which are not the cheapest. The answer, therefore, lies in **throughput accounting** for the system rather than local optimisation for individual performance measures. In this case especially, it turns up as given below:

- Good quality spares may increase the cost of spares.
- But good quality spares will enhance uptime and reduce breakdowns.
- Good quality spares will need fewer replacements.
- Enhanced uptime will increase throughput of the system.
- With increased Throughput (T), enhancement of profits can be ensured even if the Operating Expenditure (OE) goes up marginally (Profit = T - OE).

The change enables the maintenance manager to extend advice for spares purchase. But, he is now responsible for the throughput, which is systemic rather than uptime of machines. And in the purchase process, instead of only purchase cost being of concern, the operating expense which is a systemic parameter, now becomes the measure. So, the *maintenance manager,* while *advising for spares,* can be made responsible for *both*, **maintaining high throughput as well as controlling operating expenditure**. The purchase manager goes conveniently out of the conflict. Here, a further change in approach is possible if the functions of the maintenance manager turn more comprehensive to overall logistics. He would better buy spares following the laid down norms. The system block diagram would then reduce to the one shown at **Fig 6** with no conflicts.

Fig 6

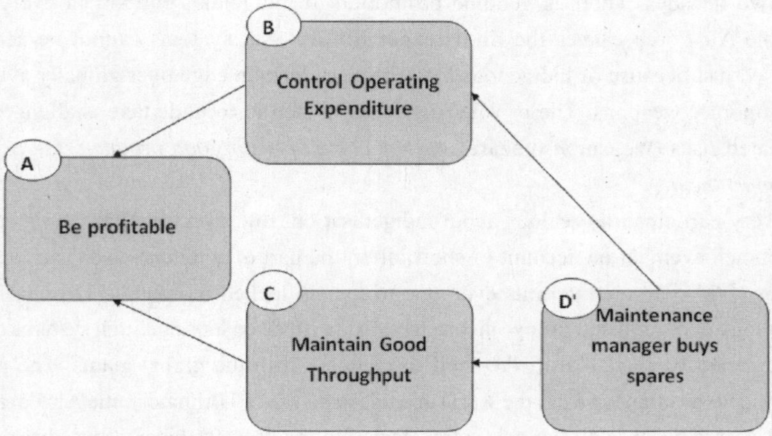

Is Indigenisation Our Goal?

At this point, it would be worth examining whether '*indigenisation of the aerospace industry*' is our goal. If yes, we need to reaffirm that this is **our collective goal -** of the three participants: DRDO, industry (public as well as private) and Air Force. We may have to articulate it with assumptions for justification. We will also need to articulate the measure of accomplishment of our goal. Hypothetically, let me put down below a few words for each of the three elements as an academic exercise.

DRDO: The organisation exists for the development of indigenous defence technology. The aerospace arena is no different. Indigenisation is the goal for the aerospace industry as well. However, for accomplishment of the goal, to a great extent, it *depends on the users' inherent acceptance of indigenous designs.*

Aerospace Industry: The **DPSUs** would also see indigenisation as their intrinsic goal. For its accomplishment, however, they would feel dependent on MoD support for Transfer of Technology (ToT), DRDO support for indigenous designs and *users' support for acceptance* without being fussy. The **private sector** would see great opportunity for the aerospace sector in manufacturing, Maintenance, Repair and Overhaul (MRO) as well as services, beginning with an entry through defence offsets and then diversification. They would see the success depending largely on *promotion by the government, accommodation by DRDO and DPSUs*, and *in principle acceptance by the users*.

Air Force: Indigenisation has been the Air Force's especially focussed effort for over two decades. There is genuine promotion of indigenous support in everything. But, the Air Force carries the **final responsibility**—so, systems cannot be acquired and used just because of indigenous D&D if these lack an edge over globally available contemporary weapons. The private sector has to step in to undertake challenges with associated risks (we can also share). *If they come up with good products, we are here to support them.*

Every participant is zealous about indigenisation. But, everyone has strong reasons for non-achievement on account of shortfall on the part of someone else. The '*problem is elsewhere*' syndrome permits everyone to remain locked in conflict. Original R&D, technology evolution and follow-up production are time consuming. Such systems cannot be indigenously available off-the-shelf to compete with the global giants. The private sector needs assurances from the R&D agencies and users. Ultimately, the Air Force is in a tight corner because all the risk is transferred to the user. In this conflict, the measure of success (indigenisation effort) is determined by each part to suit its own local logic. Each one makes an effort to optimise one's own sphere within the local logic, hoping that global benefits would naturally accrue. On the contrary, without the constituents being conscious of it, the global conflict continues to exist. Therefore, for all three constituents it would be pertinent to identify and align with the global goal. Then, together as they diffuse the conflict in the logic, they can also find measures of achievement, which also align with the systemic measures.

Whose Need is it?

Peter Senge reminds us[8] about our mental models and experiences from the past which shape up our behaviour. In a situation of conflict, we are locked between the local view and the system or global view. The lock gets tighter as we develop our measurement yardsticks conforming to our local or departmental needs. The department doing well by these yardsticks is delightfully satisfied under the assumption that the system optimum is a mere arithmetic sum of the local optima. We stay firm in our local view, in a state of conflict with the global needs—locked in our current state without gathering courage to change the future—fixations of the kind that if we don't continue with the present approach, the situation may worsen, actually paralyse us. The vital thing pointed out by Kelvyn Youngman is that we apply the logic of our department to the whole system, and fail to adopt the system's logic for the parts. Actually, most often, we are not even aware of it, believing "**my department's local view is God's own view**". "God's view" brings me to the fundamental question of 'whose need is it anyway'? I recall an experience when a renowned *swamiji* came to address us at the College of Defence Management (CDM). In just a few minutes, he introduced us to the fundamental conflicts in life as he explained the *'dog pattern'* and *'cat pattern'* of human behaviour. A dog and a cat separately live happily, very well taken care of by their respective masters. But their views of life are entirely different. The dog acknowledges that it is blessed with great life under the care of its master because the *master is God.* On the other hand, the cat believes that it has a great life and, is taken well care of because *it is God.* I venture to suggest that *'I am God'* is well entrenched in the local view projected by everyone of us. We continue to suffer from this myopia with a **sincere belief that my view is the system's need**. As per the Theory of Constraints, the system's logic has to be applied to all parts. And all parts have to be subordinate to the **system's needs which are governed by the constraint**.

Maturity Levels of Air Power

In my opinion, there are three distinct levels of aerospace power equations. These are governed by the state of maturity levels and predominance of the three participating elements as shown below.

Fig 7

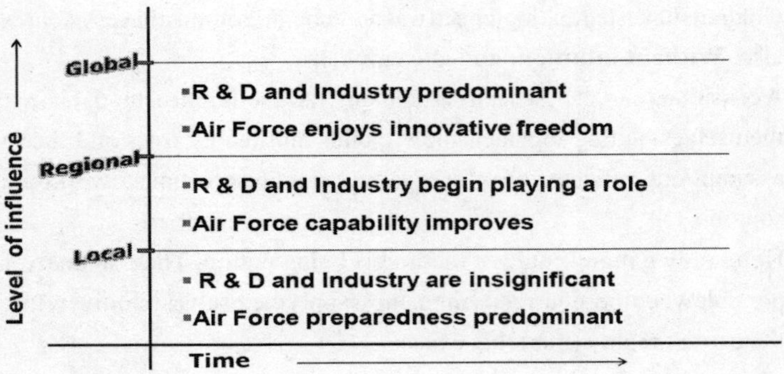

- ***Air Power with Local Influence***
  - Air Force assets, management, training and operational preparedness are predominant elements which determine the level of influence.
  - Indigenous R&D and industry are insignificant.
- ***Regional Influence***
  - The Air Force remains proficient and agile and derives strength for maintenance and upgrades backed by strong R&D and industry.

  - Indigenous R&D and industry begin to play an increasingly significant role.
- ***Global Influence***
  - Indigenous R&D and industry assume predominance and enable the Air Force first use of the globally best technology.
  - The Air Force gains further proficiency and agility strategising the use of hi-tech forces while validating tactics under indigenous control.

The Indigenisation Clouds

Logic and Intuition

An intuitive mind is a sacred gift and a rational mind is a faithful servant. We have created a society that honours the servant and has forgotten the gift.

—Albert Einstein

Before drawing indigenisation clouds of conflict and even remotely attempting to indicate a possible strategy for evaporating these, I should clarify the following few things explicitly.

- This is not merely elementary arithmetic that a consultant can use to break logic and provide straight answers.
- Goldratt suggested that logic itself was not enough. You must have system experience also. **Without intuition, no logic can help**.
- A consultant can, at best, lead participants into a solution method. The participants themselves, sitting together, draw clouds and reality trees and then verbalise assumptions, validate, check for negative branch reservations to work out a win-win solution.
- Here, only a representative method is being put up. The real analysis is only possible when those currently in business apply themselves intuitively to relate with the current reality (tree) that exists.

The Undesirable Effects

The formulation of the problem is often more essential than its solution, which may be merely a matter of mathematical or experimental skill.

—Albert Einstein

The following is an attempt to list out the Undesirable Effects (UDEs) in the process of acquisition and indigenisation. These are only academic to represent a process wherein a few participants from different areas would sit together to voice their concerns without assigning causes, pointing blame or giving instant solutions. The UDEs are also not listed in any sequence.

- We can't get state-of-the-art weapon systems from Indian manufacturers.
- The General Services Qualitative Requirements (GSQRs) are often unrealistic.
- The requirements go on changing.
- Adversaries are raising their potential steadily.
- Our assets are getting obsolete.
- Users are unable to gather courage to try out indigenous designs.
- We have tremendous hurdles in operationalising indigenous products.
- We are under pressure to modernise.
- Life cycle cost of foreign acquisitions is high.
- After foreign purchases, we remain dependent for maintenance.
- We get stuck for spares even in cases of licensed manufacture.
- Foreign procurements take a long time.
- We have to buy from foreign sources.
- We are unable to build indigenous capability.
- Cost of spares and support is high for foreign weapon systems.
- Delays in indigenous projects upset our plans.
- We are unable to get indigenous products to meet our specifications.
- We are unable to get the desired support from DPSUs.
- DRDO has not been quite productive in the aerospace sector.
- We have no model to promote the indigenous private sector.
- DPSUs are neither treated as partners nor independent suppliers.
- DPSUs have little flexibility in costing products.
- DPSUs have to absorb uncertainties of vaguely contracted buy/make projects.
- We are unable to maintain high serviceability for most fleets.
- Weapon systems are becoming costlier by the day.
- ToT for manufacture or overhaul is not adequate to stand up on our own.
- Every major contract goes only to DPSUs.
- We are unable to get adequate control over foreign suppliers after production of DRDO designs.
- We have not been able to derive tangible benefits from the offsets policy.
- We are unable to get the right response and efficiency from DPSUs.
- The aerospace market is limited to the military.
- We are unable to feel secure in a long-term relationship with the private sector.

- We are unable to find a robust method of costing of private sector products.
- We cannot promote a few reputed companies only.
- Budgets remain tight.

From the above list of UDEs, a Current Reality Tree would be drawn providing a flow from causes to effects. Where required, additional blocks with statements not otherwise contained in the list of UDEs would be added. These steps have been avoided here because they involve details and also because analyses without the involvement of specialists may not truly represent reality. It suffices to say that the Current Reality Tree would throw up a few UDEs which would determine most others. These are the constraints we would need to focus on. As an academic exercise, I will pick up the following two examples as **core constraints:**

- Foreign procurements have inherent dependency.
- We have no model to promote private sector indigenisation.

The Cloud for "Foreign Procurements have Inherent Dependencies".

The cloud for this UDE can be drawn as shown in **Fig 8**.

Fig 8

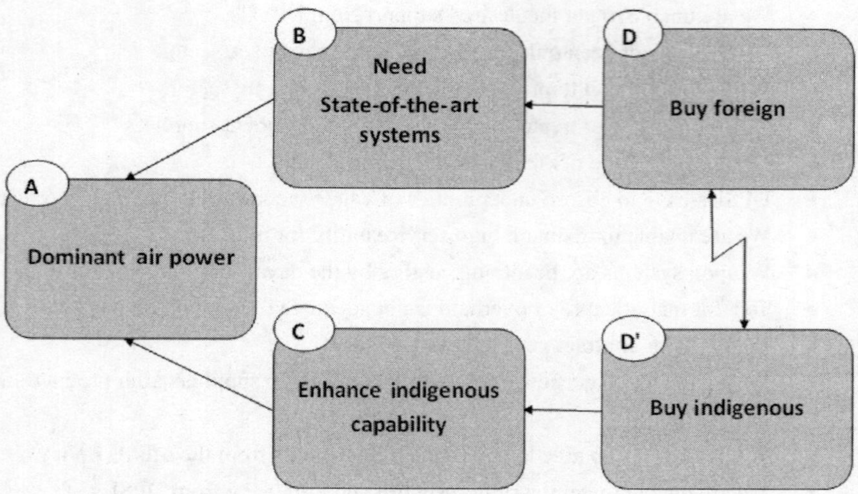

The assumptions may be listed out as shown below:

- In order to be a dominant air power, we need state-of-the-art systems, because an edge over adversaries' weaponry is necessary.
- In order to meet the need for state-of-the-art systems, we have to procure from foreign sources because only foreign manufacturers have such systems for sale.
- If we buy indigenous systems, we cannot (jeopardy) satisfy the need for state-of-the-art systems, because we have to usually compromise on desired specifications.
- If we buy indigenous systems, we cannot (jeopardy) satisfy the need for state-of-the-art systems, because indigenous developments involve undue and uncertain delays.
- In order to be a dominant air power, we need enhanced indigenous capability, because it would enhance logistic support and fleet availability.
- In order to be a dominant air power, we need enhanced indigenous capability, because it would provide us with flexibility to exploit systems.
- In order to be a dominant air power, we need enhanced indigenous capability, because we can assist friendly neighbours.
- In order to have enhanced indigenous capability, we must buy from indigenous sources so that indigenous R&D and industry can follow up.
- If we buy from foreign sources, we cannot (jeopardy) enhance indigenous capability, because we will always get limited visibility into designs and special manufacturing processes.
- If we buy from foreign sources, we cannot (jeopardy) enhance indigenous capability, because we will continue to be tied up with licensed manufacture at best.

As we begin to examine assumptions, conflicts will begin to dissolve with questions as shown below:

- Do we need all systems to be state-of-the-art?
- Do budget restrictions not make us look for a portion of inventory which is affordable and may be a generation older than top of the line?
- Can defence R&D and production adhere to timelines in case of projects where technology is within reach?

The Cloud for the UDE "We Have No Model To Promote Private Industry"

This conflict can be depicted as shown in **Fig 9**.

Fig 9

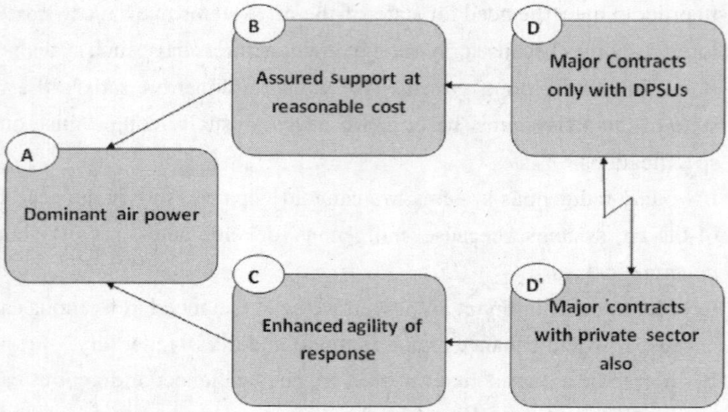

The assumptions could be as listed below:

- In order to be a dominant air power, we need assured support at reasonable cost, because logistics govern fleet availability and consequent power to exploit systems.
- In order to be a dominant air power, we need assured support at reasonable cost, because revenue expenditure has to be kept in check.
- In order to have assured support at reasonable cost, we must have major contracts with only DPSUs, because the MoD has control over these.
- In order to have assured support at reasonable cost, we must have major contracts with only DPSUs, because we can verify their costing methods.
- If major contracts are given to the private sector, we won't (jeopardy) be assured of support at reasonable cost, because once secure in business, companies will arbitrarily raise prices.
- If major contracts are given to the private sector, we won't (jeopardy) be assured of support at reasonable cost, because companies can arbitrarily withdraw support if not viable.
- In order to be a dominant air power, we need enhanced agility of response because better logistics support would enhance fleet availability.
- In order to have enhanced agility of response, we need contracts with the private sector, because the private sector has inherent flexibility.
- If major contracts are with the DPSUs, agility of response is lost (jeopardy) on account of bureaucratic delays and interferences.

- If major contracts are with the DPSUs, agility of response is lost (jeopardy), because public sector companies have inherent inefficiencies.

The assumptions could be questioned as shown below:

- **Can we have a shortlist of reputed private companies**, which can be considered for major contracts? All others can join in as sub-contractors.
- Can we not develop a model for engaging the private sector, so as to **get listed companies committed with assurances through contracts**?
- Can we not develop a suitable model of costing and partnership with trust? Can the costing models be revalidated periodically?
- Can we look for joint ventures to derive benefits from both public and private sector strengths?

Evaporating clouds would take us through to identification of the problem. The next few steps, as discussed earlier will, assist the change teams to eventually develop a solution. TOC did not, however, limit itself to only clinically finding out a solution for the identified problem. The implementation obstacles at each step were recognised and layers of resistance advised as listed below:

- Don't agree with the problem.
- Don't agree about the solution.
- Have reservations (negative effects).
- Implementation obstacles.
- Unverbalised fears.

The biggest resistance we face right in the beginning is in **acceptance of the problem** itself. It is most common to find a situation where an organisation wishes to hire a consultant to first identify the problem and accordingly suggest a solution. This approach is sure to fail because the most concerned remain unaligned with the whole process of identification of the problem, its solution and the implementation method. Therefore, at the national level, it is vital to first accept that *we have a problem*. Only then, can a task group find solutions, whichever method it uses.

Indigenisation and Interdependence

Before I conclude, I must clarify that enhanced indigenisation of the aerospace industry cannot expect cessation of all foreign industrial activity connected with aerospace in India.

Today, no worthwhile industrial house can be tagged with one nationality. Industries have truly gone global, taking advantage of the ability to establish different processes or divisions of business at different places around the world. The current global equations govern that no large industry anywhere in the world can remain profitable if it is completely indigenous for all parts. Accordingly, indigenisation of the aerospace industry in India should strive to create interdependence with foreign sources where Indian defence interests are legitimately protected, bringing substantially increased strategic independence.

Give me a lever long enough and a fulcrum on which to place it and I shall move the world.

— Archimedes

Archimedes told us of the importance of the high leverage point. Peter Senge tells us about an example of *'trim tab'* to explain the big effect with a small effort. That is mathematical. But, Peter Senge also tells us about these *high leverage areas* in every system being the *least obvious*. The theory of constraints tells us that *the core constraint* is the place to act. In my opinion **'our inability to develop a model to involve the private sector in a major way'** ***is the*** **core constraint** for the indigenisation of the aerospace industry. We have to pull ourselves out of the paralysis, push the fear out, and act. We can effect a change if we begin with sincere acceptance of the problem and break conflicts to implement win-win solutions.

References

1. Air Cmde Jasjit Singh, *Indian Aircraft Industry* (New Delhi: KW Publishers Pvt Ltd, 2011).
2. E. M. Goldratt and J. Cox, *The Goal* (The North River Press, 1984; Reprint by Productivity & Quality Publishing).
3. E. M. Goldratt, *Goal II -It's not Luck*' (The North River Press, 1994; Reprint by Productivity & Quality Publishing).
4. E. M. Goldratt, *Critical Chain* (The North River Press 1997; Reprint by Productivity & Quality Publishing, 2012).
5. E. M. Goldratt, *Theory of Constraints* (The North River Press, 1999).
6. Dr. Kelvyn Youngman, "Online Guide in Implementing TOC 2008-2009," //www.dbrmfg.co.nz
7. Domenico Lepore and Oded Cohen, *Deming and Goldratt* (Reprint by Productivity & Quality Publishing, 2010).
8. Peter Senge, *Fifth Discipline* (1990, London: Reprint by Random House, 2006).

7

Technology Advancements in the Unmanned Era

Manoj Kumar and Dhanasree Jayaram

The first step towards securing national interests, as the realists would suggest, is to have unrivalled military strength. The basic constituents of this military strength include the arsenal/armoury and human power. The very idea of possessing the most advanced arms gives any nation-state an edge over the rest; to add to it, if the nation-state also has the best military personnel to put those arms into use in the most effective manner, then the stature of the nation-state gets enhanced. If you eliminate one, the other is rendered redundant. Is this actually so? If you go by the accounts of several Hollywood actions films, you would come to the conclusion that human beings may not actually play as big a role in future warfare as they have in the past. Unmanned Vehicles (UVs) have become symbols of military strength primarily because they are considered cost-effective, using the most advanced technologies and reducing dependence on human power, thereby, not putting the lives of soldiers at risk. The UVs have been traditionally used for Intelligence, Surveillance and Reconnaissance (ISR) and sometimes as force-multipliers during conventional conflicts or wars. It was after World War II that the need for developing UVs started to be stressed upon heavily. To involve human beings in dirty, dangerous and repetitive tasks began to be looked upon as not only unnecessary but also derogatory.

However, substituting manned platforms with unmanned ones will take much more time than expected considering the fact that the technology is yet to mature to a level at which the UVs can function completely independent of human engagement, apart from the fact that the debate on the ethics of using such platforms in warfare has not been settled yet. The most common definition of a superpower is a country that is in a position to send its troops and weapons to any corner of the world at any point of time. The time is not too far when a superpower would be defined by its ability to send its Unmanned Platforms (UPs) to any part of the world without causing any harm to its troops.

The success stories of the 'drone attacks' in Afghanistan, Pakistan and Yemen in killing some key terrorists and destroying certain terrorist hubs have brought the attention of militaries across the globe to the importance of UVs in both conventional and non-conventional situations. What the operations led by the International Security Assistance Force (ISAF) in Afghanistan and Pakistan have shown is that the only way in which the terrorists elements can be eliminated in such a hostile environment is to carry out pre-decided strikes using UVs over long distance. Their stealthy nature plus the ability to bring down the scale of hostilities have also been recognised by the armed forces. The next leg in the technology advancement would be definitely termed 'the great leap forward' as this would ensure that UVs attain complete autonomy.

Before going into the various specifics of the UV technology, it requires to be clarified that the term UV is used in a very restrictive sense in this paper. Use of these platforms as long range missiles can actually be termed as a UV. In this paper, the use of the term UV is restricted to machines akin to manned machines. Therefore, many UVs such as kamikaze drones have been left out of the purview of the paper since they are not reusable. Ethical issues in connection with the use of UVs in warfare or otherwise such as 'man versus machine' and sovereignty have not been addressed. Yet another disclaimer that needs to be put forth at this stage is that the attempt is not to enlarge the scope of the paper by looking very deeply into the dual-use characteristics of this technology, particularly since the UVs are extensively used in the civilian, specifically the commercial, spheres, including oil exploration, disaster management, fire-fighting, and so on. An overwhelming portion of the paper would be contextualised in the military milieu. Since developments in Unmanned Aerial Vehicles (UAVs) have been relatively more in terms of both quality and quantity, a significant part of the paper has been dedicated to covering UAVs. The primary objective of the paper is to reflect on the evolution of these technologies over time, the future of UV technologies and the state of UV programmes in India.

Ground to Start With

Unmanned Ground Vehicles (UGVs) operate while in contact with the ground and are usually referred to as 'military robots'. They are used even on the frontlines, as seen in Iraq. These robots are generally equipped with sensors, means of propulsion and a power source. The most common UGVs used by the military are small and flat and can be mounted on miniature tank treads. They have in-built sensors – audio and video surveillance and chemical detection. For example, TALON – a man-portable and amphibious robot – was used for rescue operations at the World Trade Centre Ground Zero after the 9/11 terror attack and in Bosnia, Afghanistan and Iraq mainly for disposing of live grenades and explosives. Larger military robots come in the form of trucks or tanks. One such robot is the Armoured Combat Engineer Robot (ACER) that has multiple uses – clearing explosives, mines and other obstacles, pulling immobile or inoperable vehicles, serving as a weapons platform and even as a fire-fighting/decontamination platform. In addition, the Robotic Armoured Assault System (RAAS) and Armed Robotic Vehicle (ARV) are being developed by the US military.[1]

The Sea Without the 'Old Man'

Unmanned Surface Vehicles (USVs) began to be used as early as during World War II in which Canada had planned to deploy COMOX – a torpedo USV – to lay a smokescreen during the Normandy invasion. The US is also reported to have developed USVs for clearing mines and other obstacles. After the war, the US Navy began to use 'drone boats' to collect radioactive water samples in the aftermath of the atomic bomb blasts (tests) as well as for minesweeping. The use of USVs as target drones began to gain prominence in the US with the induction of the Mobile Ship Target (MST), the QST-33 and QST-35/35A SEPTAR Target, and the High Speed Manoeuvrable Seaborne Target (HSMST) in the US Navy. During the Vietnam War, minesweeping drones were used extensively and such systems were then developed by a number of countries, including Denmark (STANFLEX), Germany (Troika Groups), Netherlands, the UK (RIM drones), Sweden [Self-propelled Acoustic/magnetic Minesweeper (SAM) II ACV drones], and Japan (SAM ACV drones).[2] The most recent cases are the US operations in Iraq and Afghanistan, which saw the use of the Spartan USV "a modular, reconfigurable, multi-mission, high-speed, semi-autonomous USV capable of carrying payloads of 1.5 and 2.5 t for 7 m and 11 m craft, respectively, with approximately 8 hours of autonomy." Stealthy USV sensor platforms are now being considered by the surface fleet, especially for littoral combat missions. Besides, USVs could be used for force protection, surveillance, mini-warfare, anti-submarine warfare, riverine operations and Special Forces operations. They are being equipped with acoustic sources and towed array sonar systems for anti-submarine warfare.[3]

The transition from semi-autonomous to autonomous USVs in terms of fuelling has also been accomplished with the development of the Unmanned Ocean Vehicle (UOV) that does not need fuel, depends on solar power and, therefore, has high endurance. However, its low speed makes its operational scope restricted to data gathering applications in oceanography and surveillance, etc. The Israeli Navy uses the Stingray whose applications range from target identification to ISR. It can be run autonomously or be remote controlled by an operator. It is equipped with "autonomous navigation and positioning capability, cruise sensors, and a stabilization system which prevents capsizing."[4]

The Unmanned Underwater Vehicles (UUVs) are being used by the most advanced navies in the world. For example, the Royal Navy has positioned them in the Gulf region to prevent Iran from mining the Sea Lanes of Communication (SLOCs) and is now thinking of extending their use in the pirate-infested seas off the coast of Somalia.[5] Its purposes range from finding and sinking submarines to providing intelligence to maritime forces. This is also a time when a majority of countries in the West are going through one of the worst economic/financial phases, with the world economic meltdown taking a heavy toll on most of their economies. Therefore, countries like the UK are now thinking of designing and developing UUVs instead of dedicating exclusive ships to operations such as the anti-piracy ones that would undoubtedly be cost-intensive. Since UUVs are already being used commercially for purposes like oil exploration, their transformation for employment in the military milieu would not be difficult. India also tested its first UUV in 2010 that is meant for coastal security operations.[6] Countries like the US have now embarked upon the path of heavy investments as far as maritime UVs are concerned. In the UUV master plan released by the US Navy in 2004, nine missions have been outlined. They are: "ISR; mine countermeasures; anti-submarine warfare; inspection/identification; oceanography; communication/navigation network nodes; payload delivery; information operations; and time-critical strike." In fact, "the Pentagon's budget request for unmanned maritime systems (including unmanned surface) research, development, testing, procurement, operations and maintenance is approximately $641 million for the 2011 to 2015 period."[7]

The Sky Is the Limit

The US Department of Defence defines UAVs as "powered aerial vehicles that do not carry a human operator, use aerodynamic force to provide vehicle lift, can fly autonomously or be piloted remotely, can be expandable or recoverable and can carry a lethal or non-lethal payload."[8] Various letters are assigned to the UAVs/drones on the basis of their operating capability in the US, that is, R = Reconnaissance, Q = Predator, M = Multi mission. Surveillance is done mostly with the support of the RQ-1 Predator; close air support is taken care of by the MQ-1C Grey Eagle and Hunter Killer, and the RQ-9 Reaper is used in combat as well as reconnaissance.[9]

The Predator UAVs usually comprise "a colour nose camera used by the operator flying the drone to guide it in flight, a day variable aperture TV camera, a variable aperture infrared camera (for low light/night), and a Synthetic Aperture Radar (SAR) for looking through smoke, clouds and haze. The cameras produce full motion video and the SAR still frame radar images."[10]According to General Atomics, the Predator drones can fly at an altitude of up to 25,000 feet, with an endurance of 40 hours. Predators incorporate numerous payloads, including Electro-Optical/Infrared (EO/IR) video cameras, laser designators, and Hellfire missiles.[11]

UAVs currently operated by the US are capable of destroying targets with onboard weapons capability; these are mainly the Predator and the RQ-9 Reaper. These UAV systems can be armed with AGM-114 Hellfire missiles, which are helicopter-launched fire and forget weapons. They are basically air-to-ground anti-armour missiles. The UAVs may also contain a laser designator which is used to guide laser-guided bombs on targets. Drones, especially the MQ-9 Reaper, can carry up to four Hellfire II anti-armour missiles and two laser-guided bombs (GBU-12 or EGBU-12) and 500lb GBU-38 JDAM (Joint Direct Attack Munitions). In May 2008, a US Air Force (US AF) Reaper successfully test dropped four Raytheon GBU-49 Enhanced Paveway II 500 lb bombs, which have laser and Global Positioning System (GPS) guidance.[12]

Surveillance has been a key element in warfare for decades. Like the USVs, the Vietnam War saw extensive use of UAVs as well, mainly to monitor troop positions over the opponents' region. After the Vietnam War, the US military, especially the US Air Force, started to employ small, long-range, experimental drones called Fireflies for the purpose of reconnaissance in Southeast Asia.[13] In the 1960s and 1970s, the US flew more than 34,000 surveillance flights using the **AQM-34 Ryan Firebee**, a UAV launched from a host plane and controlled by operators within the same plane. The US also placed UAVs called Lightning Bugs that were released from airborne C-130s for missions over China and Vietnam. Engineers from the manufacturing entity operated the UAV with a joystick control.[14] During the Gulf War of the early 1990s, UAVs were used on a large scale for the first time. Two types of remotely piloted vehicles were used – one known as the Pointer and the other, the more sophisticated one, called the Pioneer.[15] In the late 1970s and 1980s, Israel developed the **Scout** and the **Pioneer**, which represented a shift towards the lighter, glider-type model of UAV in use today. The Predator drones began to be used widely in Bosnia since 1995 as well as in some of the other UN, US or North Atlantic Treaty Organisation (NATO) operations such as Operation Enduring Freedom in Afghanistan and Operation Iraqi Freedom, "flying over 500,000 flight hours on over 50,000 flights."[16]

Continuous flying missions, especially for surveillance, continue to be one of the topmost priorities of militaries and civil agencies across the globe. In this respect, endurance assumes great significance. Take for instance, the US Army's MQ-9 Reaper that is furnished with highly accurate laser-guided AGM-114 Hellfire missiles, infrared cameras, and electro-optical cameras on stabilised gimbals. It has made direct operation from the ground for customs and border protection possible 24 hours a day. Boeing's Phantom Eye is also designed to fly at 65,000 feet for up to four days straight. UAVs are increasingly being utilised in disaster management operations as well. For example, the Yamaha RMAX helicopter, a crop-dusting helicopter, is capable of flying to a disaster-stricken area, searching for survivors and even collecting data on the extent of damage. This could be specially useful in case of a nuclear disaster in which the disaster management team will not be exposed to the radioactive environment. Zephyr, a solar powered UAV produced by the British defence company QinetiQ, flew for two weeks straight without refuelling, thereby breaking a world record in the process. This is expected to be used for undertaking environmental research, remote communications and monitoring. Another example is that of the Tempest, a 10-foot-wide, 20-pound UAV that can move at 100 miles per hour and is outfitted with sensors that can measure air pressure, moisture, wind speed, temperature and other atmospheric conditions even during heavy rain, hail or even a tornado.[17]

In 2008, in yet another breakthrough in aviation technology, the Rockwell Collins Company successfully flight tested an unmanned FA-18 subscale model air vehicle that is equipped with an automatic system that not only gauges the cause and extent of damage caused but also readjusts the plane so that it can land safely. The US Defence Advanced Research Projects Agency (DARPA) awarded Boeing a $89 million contract for the development of the Solar Eagle that has a 400-feet wing span, quad-tail flying wing, can carry a payload of 450 kg and remain airborne at very high altitude of more than 60,000 feet for a period of five years. It is expected to be flight tested by 2014. It is like a low-altitude satellite that can provide intelligence, surveillance, reconnaissance and communications.[18]

The latest UAVs are outfitted with crucial sensors and missile system platforms that allow them to accomplish their tasks efficiently. Some of them include colour and black and white TV cameras, image intensifiers, radar, infra-red imaging for low light conditions and lasers for targeting. They can also be armed with laser guided missiles.[19] One of the biggest advantages of UAVs is that they have access to the remotest and most hostile settings. Hence, if the terrain is heavily forested or is located at high altitudes, UAVs can make the task easier and they also provide ample time for planning and effective execution of the operation. UAVs are known particularly to have played the role of a force multiplier in conflict scenarios. During times of conventional warfare, UAVs have been used as a diversion technique to subvert the opposing anti-aircraft armour. This technique was used by Israel in the 1982 War in Lebanon. UAVs can also act as effective vehicles for surveillance over the enemy's territory. This enables the armed forces to keep track of the enemy's positions as already mentioned in the case of the Vietnam War. Currently, UAVs are used in combating threats emanating from non-state actors and hostile forces which are not as strong as conventional forces.

In 2011, a new stealth drone called the Avenger was sent by the US to Afghanistan. It is an upgrade of the Predator and Reaper, which has an "internal weapons bay and four hard-points on each wing" that will give it "greater flexibility and will accommodate a large selection of next generation sensor and weapons payloads."[20] It can operate at speeds up to 400 KTAS (Knots True Air Speed), a maximum altitude of over 53,000 feet, and has 20 hours endurance. In addition, the fact that it can carry multiple sensors due to its greater payload capacity and its internal weapons bay house can store 3,000 lb of precision munitions[21] gives it an edge over the other existing drones.

UAVs have been employed successfully in conflict situations for their striking capabilities by three countries – the US, UK and Israel; the US has used this capability in Iraq, Af-Pak region and Yemen; the UK in Afghanistan; and Israel against Hezbollah and Hamas. The US has classified drone strikes into two: the signature drone strike and the personality drone strike. The former is generally used to target a group of suspected fighters or terrorists while they are in transit. Signature strikes are part and parcel of any counter-insurgency or counter-terrorist campaign carried out by the US, as evidenced by the cases of Afghanistan and Pakistan. The primary aim is to prevent the group from succeeding in fulfilling its intentions. On the other hand, personality drone strikes are used to target high value individuals who are deemed a threat to the functioning of the state. Some of the key terrorists such as the head of the Pakistan Taliban, Baitullah Mehsud and Al Qaeda's Anwar al-Awlaki in Yemen were killed in drone strikes that were specifically targeted at them.

It is a well-accepted fact that UVs can also have a significant role to play in peace-time. They can be used for saving lives during disaster management operations and can also aid in search and rescue missions. They can help tackle other illegal activities such as drugs and human trafficking across both land and sea borders. The drones have certain technology that can detect intrusions, and they carry thermal cameras which can spot human trafficking. Moreover, UAVs are being used by countries such as Brazil and Indonesia that are rich in natural resources like forests to prevent intrusions and illegal activities such as logging, hunting, smuggling, and so on. Interestingly, drones are also being considered by Canada for Arctic surveillance intended at claiming sovereignty in the region.

India: The Story So Far

A potent UV force is crucial for India's national security. UVs can be used to monitor border posts as the latest ones have the capability to work at any given point of time, even in low light conditions. India could also possibly use armed drones to carry out surgical strikes against terrorist elements taking refuge in hostile territories. Drones can provide the effectiveness of a conventional air strike without risking the life of the pilot who would otherwise be flying a conventional aircraft. India can also use the drones to monitor its vast coastlines. The threat of terrorism emanating from India's coasts has been highlighted by two events – smuggling of RDX to carry out the blasts in Mumbai in 1993 and the terrorist attack in Mumbai in 2008.

In the aftermath of the 1999 Kargil conflict and the 2002 Parliament attack, India began to invest heavily in acquiring UAVs from other countries as well as in developing its own indigenous programme. Israel has been one of the main beneficiaries of India's rigorous arms imports, especially those of UAVs. Israel's Searcher and Heron were inducted into the Indian armed forces for ISR. India recognised the multiple uses of UAVs principally since the country faces threats on all frontiers. Strengthening surveillance along the western, northern and eastern borders plus the long coastline remains one of the critical priorities of the Indian authorities. UAVs are being touted as a means of maintaining surveillance in Maoist-affected areas as well. UAVs can act as not only communication/ transmission devices but also as missiles for precision strikes. In fact, the Indian Army is currently using the Israeli Heron UAV to monitor the Line of Control (LoC) along the disputed region of Pakistan Occupied Kashmir (PoK) and Jammu and Kashmir. One such Searcher UAV was shot down by a Pakistani aircraft in 2002.[22] The Indian Navy has already deployed two squadrons of Israeli Herons – one at Kochi and the other at Porbandar, Gujarat, where the Navy is using the Herons to survey areas in the region, particularly those bordering Pakistan.[23] Herons navigate with the support of an internal GPS receiver plus it is equipped with a pre-programmed flight profile in which case the system would be fully autonomous from take-off to landing even when communication is lost from the ground station. Reports also categorically state that Indian UAVs have their Searcher IIs equipped with the standard day/night surveillance turret, while the Herons are similar to Israel's maritime patrol configuration, with an Elta Systems radar and a stabilised Tamam surveillance and targeting turret.[24]

On the one hand, the Indian authorities have time and again exposed their vulnerabilities during various terrorist attacks, and, on the other, the US has propitiously shown the way to tackle terrorism to the rest of the world by carrying out 'drone attacks' in Afghanistan and Pakistan. This has clearly given the Indian establishment a boost to go for UAVs, particularly since intelligence failures have, time after time, put the national security apparatus of the country under scrutiny. Yet another reason why the Indian authorities are keen on acquiring UAVs is Pakistan's desire to get hold of the US Predator drones as part of its military aid.[25]

One of the biggest hindrances to India's efforts to source UAVs from some of the leading producers of this technology such as the US and Israel is the technology regimes. The sale of the Medium Altitude Long Endurance (MALE) type of unmanned aircraft has been halted due to the Missile Technology Control Regime (MTCR) – an informal and voluntary association of countries that prevents transfer of unmanned delivery systems capable of delivering a payload of at least 500 kg to a distance of at least 300 km.[26] One of the questions that needs to be answered very clearly is whether all the UAVs can be regarded as part of the larger family of missiles, considering the fact that UAVs are multi-purpose and are not part of the problem that the MTCR was created to address in the first place. This has been countered by non-proliferation lobbies with the argument that any system that is capable of delivering Weapons of Mass Destruction (WMDs) should be treated under the MTCR guidelines. However, in the past, countries like the US have made special provisions to overcome these restrictions to transfer some of these technologies to their allies. In addition, all the UAVs are covered under the Wassenaar Arrangement that aims to impose export controls on conventional arms and dual-use goods and technologies.

In such a scenario, India has shifted its attention to its indigenous programme and developed and tested the Nishant and Lakshya successfully. The Nishant is basically a reconnaissance UAV and is capable of being launched from a hydro-pneumatic launcher without the need for a runway. It is supported by ground control station equipment mounted on 'Tatra' vehicles.[27] The Lakshya is a pilotless target aircraft meant to "tow flying targets, providing aerial target tracking and live-fire combat training."[28] Indian developers like the Aeronautical Development Establishment (ADE) collaborated with Israel to produce three UAVs – the Rustom, Pawan and Gagan[29] – out of which, the first is the MALE type while the other two are short-range. The Rustom can fly at an altitude of 9,000 metres or more for up to 24 hours and has a surveillance range of 250 km and is extendable beyond 1,000 km. However, the most important programme being run by India is that of the Autonomous Unmanned Research Aircraft (AURA) that intends to develop stealth Unmanned Combat Aerial Vehicles (UCAVs) capable of "firing missiles, bombs and Precision-Guided Munitions (PGMs)." Moreover, India is now looking forward to designing the solar-powered spy drone that is High Altitude, Long Endurance (HALE). It can act as a "pseudo-satellite"; it is also being looked upon as a way of reducing the carbon footprint of the Indian military; it is expected to fly for nearly a fortnight at a stretch; it scores high on cost-benefit analysis; plus it is touted to possess superior ISTAR (Intelligence, Surveillance, Target Acquisition and Reconnaissance) capability.[30]

Living in the Age of Complex Uncertainties

The UAVs in the current context can fly at high altitudes but this does not guarantee that they would not be detected by radars. They can become prey to enemy fire, especially in hostile territories, in a conventional conflict. Hence, it is equally important to achieve technology that can ensure that the UAVs can evade radars by reducing radar signature, thus, emphasising on the need for developing advanced stealth technology. As a case in point, a Central Intelligence Agency (CIA) stealth drone of the US, the RQ-170 Sentinel was downed by Iran through an alleged cyber attack on the GPS navigation of the craft. The Sentinel was on a pre-programmed mission of reconnaissance over the Afghanistan-Iran border. This was for the first time that an adversary had managed to get hold of such a craft. It also enabled Iran to lay its hands on vital information regarding radar-evading stealth drones.

One of the biggest threats to UV systems is virus attacks, especially since these are primarily controlled by computers that are vulnerable to such attacks. In 2011, the US Department of Defence was found wanting when the drone flight control centre at Creech Air Force Base, Nevada, of the US Air Force Space Command, was attacked by a computer virus that was introduced, interestingly by a portable USB hard drive.[31] Hacking is yet another threat that countries across the world have been facing of late in the cyber domain. Interceptions have been reported in the past and now, protection of communications signals from electronic jamming has also emerged as a challenge. In 2009, a few insurgents in Iraq managed to intercept live video feeds from US Predator drones. It was confirmed later by the US officials that the insurgents were in no position to meddle with the flight control system but they got access to information regarding the US military operations, thus, leaving loopholes that could help them evade these operations in the future. They did this with the assistance of very cheap software called SkyGrabber.[32] One of the ways in which such interceptions can be blocked is to add encryption but that has not proved to be easy as these networks are quite old. Therefore, the network connecting the UVs to the operators has to be upgraded.

Hence, UVs, especially UAVs, face two kinds of threats when they enter the enemy's territory. First, a UAV can be downed by firing. Second, the adversary can also tamper with the electronic communications system, debilitating it. A report of the C. S. Monitor reveals various other ways in which UVs can be targeted or attacked. For instance, the

GPS receiver can be fed with fake signals so that "it believes that it is located somewhere in space and time that it is not."[33] Some also contend that the success of UAVs against terrorists in Afghanistan, Pakistan and Yemen probably cannot be replicated in case of a sophisticated enemy in the form of full-fledged state-supported armed forces.

Full-scale deployment of UVs continues to be hampered by certain limitations in technology that have not been overcome yet. UUVs, for example, have faced several roadblocks in terms of technology. First, protection of electronics from various underwater conditions such as pressure, corrosion, waves, currents, etc remains problematic when the UUVs have to operate at sea for days or weeks. Therefore, the need for enhancing power and endurance becomes a priority. Second, launch-and-recovery remains a hurdle due to the low speed, lower endurance and short-range communication of the UUVs. For this, the solution is being touted as deployment of USVs that can stay close to the UUVs and relay information, thus, complementing the role of UUVs by overcoming the latter's limited communication capability as well as keeping the manned platforms away from the minefield. Third, UUVs can also carry weapons and act as mines or torpedo decoys themselves; and for this to materialise, advanced technologies such as synthetic aperture sonar and other sensors that provide greater resolution would be required. Greater propulsion, less power compulsion and superior autonomy are some of the other desired traits that the industry is attempting to infuse into these systems. Some of these issues are discussed in detail in the subsequent section.

A Peep into the Future: Autonomous Unmanned Vehicles

The future of UVs would see a few changes to give them an edge in the execution of the allotted task—an edge over human capabilities to perform an equivalent task. Analysing the areas where this 'edge' can come about, one immediately realises that long endurance, not having to design the machine around the human being at the controls, and higher 'G' loads acceptance for aerial vehicles are just a few of the things that make the unmanned vehicles special.

The future technological improvements would also have to provide fixes for some of the weaknesses that are so apparent in the present generation unmanned vehicles. First amongst these would have to be the need for constant controlling that the UVs require during their entire span of operations. Any break or 'take-over' in this control link would prove to be disastrous for any UV and may lead to its crash. To avoid this eventuality, future technologies would make the UVs increasingly autonomous in their operations. This aspect would be covered in greater detail later on. The second weakness in today's generation of UVs is the lack of manoeuvrability that makes them vulnerable to counter-attacks. Manoeuvrability can come with a better power/propulsion system and better skeletal designs. Therefore, research and development on these technologies has to be a priority. The third weakness in the system is lack of an enhanced armament role capability. To make the system truly an attack platform rather than predominantly an intelligence gathering and reconnaissance machine, this capability transfers the UVs across another generation. This role requires incorporation of the capability of a manned machine like radars/homing devices, lock-on, etc and, above all, autonomous decision-making ability on target mapping, leading to the launch of an onboard weapon. The fourth weakness that has restricted the use of UVs is their lack of the capability to avoid traffic. This is why the Federal Aviation Administration (FAA) has yet to give clearance to UAVs using the US air space. The last minute avoidance capability is always vested with the man at the controls. With unmanned flights, the delay in response can prove catastrophic, endangering lives. This would, thus, be the next concern of UV developers.

The race to make UVs autonomous has seen many incremental stages. It started with making the machine able to negotiate initial and terminal movements autonomously. In the context of a UAV, this implies being able to take off and land on its own. This is an extension of the autopilot control loop system and did not require a major leap in the UV software. The next stage would be to enhance the capability of the machine to be able to perform self-navigation. This would avoid the need to constantly control-manoeuvre the machine over long distances. The base navigation parameters in this controlled movement could come from satellite linkage, which the machine itself establishes at a certain point of time in its journey. Managing the propulsion and controls based on these inputs in the shortest time span in the case of UAVs is a challenging taks but is not insurmountable. The challenge is also in being able to put onboard computing and controlling devices that do not unduly add to the power loading as well as the weight penalty that would invariably accompany them. The autonomy would require the machine to return after the mission is over. The technological paradigm changes in the event the machine parameters are degraded due to technical defects or battle damage and then it has to decide by itself the best course of action for returning safely. This brings in the need for advanced computation and probably Artificial Intelligence (AI) based fuzzy logic programming.

The next stage of technological development would be the use of AI based computing in deciding the best position of a stand-alone or a swarm of UVs to undertake a mission. Working in a heterogeneous wireless communication architecture, the machines would get associated with the best available network, according to the task-based priority matrix, which may take into account user preferences, probability of achieving the task in the shortest time and most effectively, effortless handing-taking over, etc. This prioritisation may be carried out through a multi-variable auctioning mechanism. Another way to perform these computations may be through probabilistic modelling wherein the limitations of auction-based mechanisms are removed. In an auction-based mechanism, the best course of action is chosen which normally cannot take into account the acute need to utilise a resource later on; it only chooses the best resource at that juncture not realising that once it is used, it may not be available later. The probabilistic computing does away with this limitation to a large extent. It decides the probability of achieving a task with a particular resource, the developed scenario from that use, and, thus, the need to utilise the same resource if that path is so chosen.

The complex computations described above have to be done in the shortest possible time and the margin of error has to be almost nil. This brings us to the need for developing the technology through an interface of programmers and strategists together, by making them understand each other. This phase is currently on in the countries where huge forays are being made in developing UVs like the US, the UK/France/Germany (either individually or together), and Israel, to name a few. As usual, not much is known about the development profile of UV technology in China. The next change that advances in technology would showcase is that of autonomy in selection of the onboard weapon system, weapon-target matching and, finally, selection of target(s) in a pre-planned decision priority set but one that takes into account the real-time circumstances, which may require spur of the moment choices. This is a very sensitive issue because it brings us to the cusp of the dilemma: the machine deciding on what human targets to take on without the last minute interference by humans. Therefore, this kind of computation is still some time away but is required to ensure the battle effectiveness of UVs – especially as attack UVs; they would become more and more a part of futuristic battlefields, making this technology essential.

This leads us to the next generation onboard payload that UVs of tomorrow would need to carry to absorb the advances in computations and commensurate manoeuvring requirements. High onboard speed of communication and power devices that can prolong the UVs' endurance would be the need of the future. The advances in high speed computations and then linking these with physical applications like engine power management or control surfaces' movements is a field that is esoteric and highly technology intensive. Faster computations do not bode well for autonomous operations if the results are not communicated at the same rate; this capability brings the UVs close to a manned platform. The power management would not only be for the pre-planned mission but should be able to alter itself under duress of a defect or damage. The power to control all this is being provided through a variety of means.

Use of solar energy through cells placed on the body of the UV is one such source for slow moving UAVs and ground-based UVs. However, normal mineral fuel-based UVs are the norm for larger machines, increasingly available with onboard electrical generators being run as an engine accessory (like the Wolverine 3).[34] The electrical energy for the onboard payloads and even for electrically powered UVs is being sought to be provided through fuel cells, the latest power storage device that has revolutionised the concept of batteries. The Aeronautical Development Establishment (ADE) in Bangalore is developing one such system.

The UAVs normally have propellers and not jet engines for a variety of reasons, the primary one being the fuel efficiency provided, which aids long endurance. However, this reduces its speed and decreases manoeuvrability. To overcome this, in the future, UAVs would have jet engines with a provision of refuelling during the mission or even hybrid propulsion that may reduce the need for in-mission refuelling. This would incorporate the advances in power electronics[35] that are now driving hydraulics even in large airliners. Fast speed and faster computations, fast communication and decision-autonomy and, finally, the onboard weapons carriage make the future UVs a deadly concoction of fearsome war-machines.

Not only technological advances but the changes in utilisation of UVs would pose a challenge in the battlefields of tomorrow. The miniaturisation of UVs has provided them an opportunity to be used in groups with a locust-like attack. The movement in formation and computation of the best suited machine (or group) to undertake the mission has thrown up many possibilities, especially when these are being considered for underwater applications. Weaponisation and retrieval of the machine after the attack has added the lethality dimension to these machines, even allowing precision attacks in the urban environment, controlling the collateral damage. The miniaturisation of machines, payloads, and computing devices is nothing short of a technological marvel that has been seen till now only in science fiction motion pictures. Even with such small machines, the need of the hour has been to provide higher and higher endurance. This is now the next frontier to be achieved in miniaturisation. However, the advances in UAVs are also moving towards making the machines more like the manned jets of today. The following is an excerpt of a news article in *The Times of India*, New Delhi edition, of July 4, 2012.[36] The future development trajectory is clearly reflected in this piece.

Box 1: Flight of Next Generation of Unmanned Platform

LONDON: Pilotless fighter planes have come a step closer to reality as British Aerospace revealed that it would test such a new fighter jet next year. It is not a drone, but rather a robotic plane with a far wider range of equipment and capabilities, the company said.

The company is set to unveil a new super-fighter which can fly on its own for 24 hours with no cockpit and no human on board, *The Daily Mail* reported. If all goes as planned, the artificial intelligence could mean the end of fighter pilots in the UK and bring down the curtain on conventional aircraft like the F-35. And the robotic fighter plane, christened 'the Mantis', will be making its first flight in 2013 over Britain, as it is tested to see if it works.

Attack UVs: The Natural Progression

Attack UVs or in the field of aviation, UCAVs, have been mentioned earlier in the paper. As per Russian Air Force Commander-in-Chief Maj. Gen. Viktor Bondarev, "The technical progress and information technology development is occurring at such a pace that a man, pilot, operator already has to stretch himself to the limit of his physical and psychological abilities."[37] He goes on to say that the sixth generation aerial vehicles would be unmanned. Therefore, it is felt that the weapon payloads would increase in vehicles that are bigger and have the ability to carry more weight. South Korea has also been developing an attack drone but under the Korea-US missile guidelines, the military is restricted to a UAV payload size at the level of US drones from the 1990s.[38] This effectively means an engine power of around 150 HP (horsepower) and payloads under 500 kg. It is claimed that Korea has the capability of manufacturing (the US') Reaper-class UAVs that can carry 1,700 kg of payload. With such attack capabilities and higher horsepower engines (the Reaper is believed to have around 900 HP), the qualitative and quantitative aspects of weapon carriage would generate a large debate.

The focus of such a debate is not how much weapon payload these UVs can carry but the type of weapons they would carry. The carriage part is not merely restricted by the weight consideration but also by the onboard avionics that are required for integrating the weapon and acquiring the target. While the current limitations of speed and weight have resulted in the UVs being used more for reconnaissance and intelligence gathering purposes, the armed UAVs are mostly for air-to-ground usage. Weaponisation of underwater UVs is bound to happen but that is in the future. However, the next generation of UCAVs would have to be able to defend themselves from ground or air-based adversaries as well as attack air assets. This effectively also means being equipped with air-to-air missiles and compatible avionics. This is a quantum jump from the present generation of UCAVs. Once autonomy is built into defensive/evasive decisions and weapon attack systems, it would effectively mean that unmanned machines have now reached the level wherein they can replace their manned counterparts. Till that time, they would complement and augment the manned platforms.

Crossing the Seas, the Skies and the Frontiers

India has several lessons to learn from the world in the UV systems technology. As discussed above, the rapid technological changes are making UVs sleeker and more efficient and effective day by day. Some of these technological advances have made UVs the ultimate weapon of choice for future warfare. So much so, that there is even an active programme in the US that intends to develop nuclear powered drones.[39] Once operational, they would be able to fly and keep round the clock surveillance in remote areas for months. One of the fears associated with the project is that such technologies raise the risk of fissile material falling into the wrong hands if the drone crashes on the adversary's territory. One of the other important innovations occurring in these technologies is the miniaturisation of UVs. Countries are in the pursuit of developing smaller-sized UVs that can go undetected and can be used in specific missions. Camouflaging these systems to look like naturally occurring elements has also been pursued. In this paper, some of the developments have been quoted that are indicative of where the future of these technologies lies.

Being highly technology intensive, if the UV industry is to grow in India, the need for high end technology development, its absorption and innovations assume great salience. Such a process could be a potential game-changer for the growth trajectory of Indian industry and, indeed, for the economic growth of the nation. The case of the exceptional growth in India's automobile industry, with local industry coming up with products matching world standards and spurring huge exports in this sector could be cited as an example. A similar success story can be emulated in the UV industry with the requirement for Joint Ventures (JVs) being very strong due to the weak R&D base of our local UV industry. It would be prudent for the Indian industry to foray into the hitherto untouched, technologically intensive and operationally futuristic sectors of the UV industry. Lessons can be learnt from the US wherein small industries lead the way in innovative development and are then acquired by large firms like Lockheed Martin (in the case of the Predator development).

It can be stated that UVs comprise one of the most influential technologies that have changed the face of modern warfare in the 21st century completely, and as the technology develops, UVs will find an increasingly relevant place in the inventories of all major powers of the world, including India. However, until and unless some of the gaping holes in the technology that can prove to be disastrous for both the developer and the victim are filled, and some of the ethical issues are settled, unmanned platforms are not expected to be deemed as glamorous as manned ones. As long as they are not used as a war instrument, ethical issues would be partly solved. They cannot replace manned platforms if they do not attain complete autonomy. Should they form the bulk of the armoury or should they only act as force multipliers as is already the case in a few countries' military engagements? Militaries across the world would have to make a choice and if they work towards the first option, a fresh discourse on warfare would have to be written and imbibed.

Notes

1. Ed Grabianowski, "How Military Robots Work", HowStuffWorks.com, January 19, 2005. See http://science.howstuffworks.com/military-robot6.htm, accessed on September 3, 2012.
2. Volker Bertram, "Unmanned Surface Vehicles – A Survey". See, for more information http://www.skibstekniskselskab.dk/public/dokumenter/Skibsteknisk/Download%20materiale/2008/10%20marts%2008/USVsurvey_DTU.pdf, accessed on September 4, 2012.
3. Ibid.
4. Elbit Systems, "Stingray: Unmanned Surface Vehicle (USV)", *Defense Update,* November 21, 2006. See http://www.defense-update.com/products/s/stingray.htm, accessed on September 5, 2012.
5. Nick Hopkins, "Ministry of Defence Plans New Wave of Unmanned Marine Drones", *The Guardian,* August 2, 2012. See http://www.guardian.co.uk/world/2012/aug/02/ministry-defence-plans-unmanned-marine-drones, accessed on September 6, 2012.
6. "India Tests Unmanned Underwater Vehicle", *Mathrubhumi,* February 17, 2010. See http://www.mathrubhumi.com/english/news.php?id=30385, accessed on September 6, 2012.
7. Antoine Martin, "US Expands Use of Underwater Unmanned Vehicles", *National Defense,* April 2012. See http://www.nationaldefensemagazine.org/archive/2012/April/Pages/USExpandsUseOfUnderwaterUnmannedVehicles.aspx, accessed on September 2, 2012.
8. Jeremiah Gertler, "US Unmanned Aerial Systems", *CRS Report for the Congress* (Congressional Research Service: Washington, DC, 2012), p. 1. See http://www.fas.org/sgp/crs/natsec/R42136.pdf, accessed on September 2, 2012.
9. Joseph Morbi, "Modern Warfare: The Introduction of Predator Drones", *e-International Relations,* December 5, 2011. See http://www.e-ir.info/2011/12/05/modern-warfare-the-introduction-of-predator-drones/, accessed on September 1, 2012.
10. For more information, see http://www.notbored.org/UAV.html, accessed on September 6, 2012.
11. "Predator UAS", Aircraft Platforms, *General Atomics Aeronautical*, see for more information http://www.ga-asi.com/products/aircraft/predator.php, accessed on September 6, 2012.
12. "Predator RQ-1/ MQ-1/ MQ-9 Reaper, United States of America", airforce-technology.com, see for more information http://www.airforce-technology.com/Projects/predator-uav/, accessed on September 3, 2012.

13. Andrew Callam, "Drone Wars: Armed Unmanned Aerial Vehicles", *International Affairs Review* (USA: The Elliott School of International Affairs), Vol. 18, No. 3, Winter 2010. See http://www.iar-gwu.org/node/144, accessed on September 3, 2012.
14. Tom Scheve, "How the MQ-9 Reaper Works", HowStuffWorks.com, July 22, 2008. See http://science.howstuffworks.com/reaper1.htm, accessed on September 2, 2012.
15. "Weapons: Drones (RPVs)", *Frontline.* See, for more information, http://www.pbs.org/wgbh/pages/frontline/gulf/weapons/drones.html, accessed on September 3, 2012.
16. n. 11.
17. "Top 10 Unmanned Aerial Vehicles Taking Flight", *DiscoveryNews*. See for more information http://news.discovery.com/tech/top-ten-uavs-taking-flight.html, accessed on September 3, 2012.
18. Gary Mortimer, "Boeing Solar Eagle wins $89 Million from DARPA", *Suas News,* September 17, 2010. See http://www.suasnews.com/2010/09/1511/boeing-solar-eagle-wins-89m-from-darpa/, accessed on September 3, 2012.
19. "Drones: What are They and How Do They Work?", *BBC News,* January 31, 2012. See http://www.bbc.co.uk/news/mobile/world-south-asia-10713898, accessed on September 3, 2012.
20. David Axe, "New Armed Stealth Drone Heads to Afghanistan (And Maybe Iran, Too)", *Wired,* December 13, 2011. See http://www.wired.com/dangerroom/2011/12/stealth-drone-afghanistan/, accessed on September 4, 2012.
21. "Predator C Avenger UAS", Aircraft Platforms, *General Atomics Aeronautical*. See for more information http://www.ga-asi.com/products/aircraft/predator_c.php, accessed on September 2, 2012.
22. "IAF's Searcher-II Loss on June 07, 2002," *Vayu Sena,* Vol 3, January 3, 2010. See http://vayu-sena-aux.tripod.com/other-Parakram-IAF-UAV-Wreckage.html, accessed on September 4, 2012.
23. "Indian Navy Commissions Second UAV Squadron at Porbander, Gujarat", *India Defence,* January 17, 2011. See http://www.india-defence.com/reports-4953, accessed on September 3, 2012.
24. "Israel Sells Heron UAVs to India", *Defence Industry Daily,* April 4, 2011. See http://www.defenseindustrydaily.com/israel-sells-heron-uavs-to-india-01476/, accessed on September 2, 2012.
25. Semu Bhatt, "India's Indigenous Drones", *Himal South Asian,* October 2010. See http://www.himalmag.com/component/content/article/379.html, accessed on September 2, 2012.
26. "The Missile Technology Control Regime". See, for more information, http://www.mtcr.info/english/index.html, accessed on September 2, 2012.
27. "Indian Army Approves Nishant UAV", *Aviation* Week. See, for more information, http://www.aviationweek.com/aw/generic/story_channel.jsp?channel=defense&id=news/asd/2011/02/04/04.xml&headline=Indian%20Army%20Approves%20Nishant%20UAV, accessed on September 2, 2012.
28. Bhatt, n. 25.
29. Ibid.
30. Rajat Pandit, "After Combat Drones, India Eyes Solar-Powered UAVs Capable of Flying for a Fortnight", *The Times of India,* April 23, 2011. See http://articles.timesofindia.indiatimes.com/2011-04-23/india/29466001_1_ucavs-combat-drones-spy-drones, accessed on September 1, 2012.
31. "Drone Mission Control hit by Self-Cloning Computer Virus", *New Scientist,* October 10, 2011. See http://www.newscientist.com/blogs/onepercent/2011/10/drone-mission-control-hit-by-s.html, accessed on September 2, 2012.
32. Siobhan Gorman, Yochi J. Dreazen and August Cole, "Insurgents Hack US Drones", *The Wall*

Street Journal, December 17, 2009. See http://online.wsj.com/article/SB126102247889095011.html, accessed on September 4, 2012.

33. Craig Mackenzie and Mark Duell, "'We Hacked US Drone': Iran Claims it Electronically Hijacked Spy Aircraft's GPS and Tricked the Aircraft into Landing on its Soil", *The Daily Mail,* December 19, 2011. See http://www.dailymail.co.uk/news/article-2075157/Iran-claims-hacked-US-spy-planes-GPS-guided-aircraft-ground.html, accessed on September 1, 2012.
34. For more information, see http://www.popularmechanics.com/technology/military/planes-uavs/uavs-overdue-engine-upgrade, accessed on August 31, 2012.
35. Ben Ames, "Power Electronics Drive Next-Generation Vehicles", *Military & Aerospace Electronics*. See http://www.nampet.org/resources/new_4.htm, accessed on September 5, 2012.
36. "Pilotless Fighters Set to Fly Over Britain From 2013", *The Times of India,* July 4, 2012. See http://timesofindia.indiatimes.com/world/uk/Pilotless-fighters-set-to-fly-over-Britain-from-2013/articleshow/14663399.cms, accessed on July 4, 2012.
37. "Next Generation of Military Aircraft will be Unmanned", *Space Daily,* August 24, 2012. See http://www.spacedaily.com/reports/Next_generation_of_military_aircraft_will_be_unmanned_999.html, accessed on September 4, 2012.
38. "Korea to Develop Combat Unmanned Aerial Vehicles", *Unmanned Vehicles,* August 7, 2012. See http://www.unmannedvehicles.co.uk/uav-news/korea-to-develop-combat-unmanned-aerial-vehicles/, accessed on September 5, 2012.
39. Nick Fielding, "US Draws Up Plans for Nuclear Drones", *The Guardian,* April 2, 2012. See http://www.guardian.co.uk/world/2012/apr/02/us-plans-nuclear-drones, accessed on September 4, 2012.

8

India's Next War ?

Nishant Gupta

Know your enemy and know yourself and you can fight a hundred battles without disaster.

— Sun Tzu

When we talk about wars of the future, the first thought that crosses the mind is whether war is a way of life and natural to human beings or not? Will wars continue forever or will the world be able to develop a mechanism to be 'free from wars'? There are two conflicting philosophical opinions about this core issue.

Jean-Jacques Rousseau (1712-78), and other philosophers, argued that man is inherently peaceful and violence is not natural to him—rather, he learned to fight due to societal developments.[1] This philosophy, at least theoretically, suggests that some radical changes in the framework of society may give rise to a new societal architecture which would be totally peaceful and devoid of violence as well as war. While this abstract thought might seem to be nothing more than an overoptimistic, euphoric view, in the foreseeable future, it cannot, nevertheless, be ruled out.

Thomas Hobbes (1588-1679), on the other hand, argued that man is naturally violent and has created organisations to prevent chaos. War is a result of man's individual need to protect himself from the many enemies he faces. Moreover, anthropological evidence also demonstrates that warfare predates civilisation and in the natural state, man was rarely peaceful. Even the Neolithic civilisation has evidence of elaborate fortifications and corpses of people killed in organised battles, and often buried in mass graves. Hence, the argument that humans had learnt to organise themselves to fight their enemies before they even learnt to write, to farm or to construct permanent shelters appears to be more convincing.

Therefore, war has been an integral part of human existence though its aims, nature, character and prosecution have been changing with time. Pre-historic wars were fought for religious reasons, to avenge an insult or for access to commodities. Contemporary wars for control of resources like oil and minerals have parallels in pre-civilised wars which were also waged for control of arable land or access to some precious commodities like fresh water, grazing grounds, etc. [2]

As war has been an integral part of world history, and would continue to be an inseparable feature of society, it would be appropriate to make an attempt to foresee the likely wars of the future and be prepared for them. For the necessary military preparation, it is critical to analyse and understand the likely nature and character of future wars while being conscious of the common mistake of '*preparing for the last war*'. In the attempt to understand future wars, it is imperative to study and understand our own national culture, history and mindset as well as those of probable adversaries. True use of history, as historian Jacob Burckhardt has brought out, is not just to make men clever for the next time—rather, it is to make them wise forever.[3]

What is War?

In general, the term 'war' is used commonly in a variety of contexts like 'war against poverty', 'war against corruption', 'price war' or 'war of words' et al but this paper will keep the focus on the military perspective. Like many other generic terms, it is not easy to define war. General definitions like 'a violent contact of distinct but similar entities' is insufficiently specific and could equally describe a 'gang war'. *Webster's Dictionary* defines war as "a state of usually open and declared armed hostile conflict between states or nations." But in contemporary warfare, non-state actors have also gained prominence and the war spectrum has broadened. At the lower end of the spectrum, there is terrorism and insurgency perpetrated by non-state actors (like Naxalites), while, on the other extreme is 'total war'. Low intensity conflicts and limited wars are in between these extremities. Perhaps the subjective and general definition of Quincy Wright, "War is a conflict among political groups, especially sovereign states, carried on by the armed forces of considerable magnitude, for a considerable period of time," is a more practical way of defining war.[4] Clausewitz's definitions of war as "an act of force intended to compel our opponents to fulfill our will" and "a continuation of political intercourse with a mixture of other means" also describe war well. War essentially has two integral components: violence and political agenda or reason.

Violence: War involves violence but all acts of violence do not necessarily constitute war. Violence is a necessary but not sufficient condition for a conflict to be termed as war. Use of considerable military force, over a considerable period, leading to massive violence is essential. For example, violence in border skirmishes is not a war—it is much below the threshold of war. At the same time, it is difficult to quantify the extent of violence required to term an armed conflict as 'war'. Singer and Small in their influential work *The Wages of War* have specified a figure of 1,000 deaths per year, which cannot be taken as a sacrosanct figure, or the 1982 Falklands War and the 1999 Kargil War would hardly qualify.[5]

Political Agenda/Reason: War is not an end in itself—rather it is an instrument to achieve political objectives. War is a means to an end and not an end in itself. Therefore, it is essentially different from any random violence. In war, an aggressor invariably undertakes cost-benefit analysis and believes that the advantage of winning outweighs the risks involved, while the defender faces the consequences of the war rather than accepting an immediate loss.

Changing Nature of Warfare?

Is the nature of warfare changing? The answer is both yes and no. As per Clausewitz, primarily, war has two natures: objective nature and subjective nature. The objective nature of war comprises essential elements that distinguish war from other activities. War is essentially an instrument of policy and is conducted on a large scale for the purpose of imposing one's will on the enemy by force. It comprises a trinity of violence and hatred, chance and probability, and reason or policy. This objective nature of war is, by and large, universal and does not change with time. Whereas the subjective nature of war, which comprises the methods of force application or the character of war, changes with time and space. It is also important to understand that war is different from warfare. Warfare or conduct of war comes from the society as a whole and changes with time but change in the nature of war is contestable. Thus, one can argue that it is the character of war that depends upon societal, political, social, leadership and technological elements and changes with time while the nature of war is unvarying.[6]

Generations of Warfare: Earlier, the conflicts were, by and large, feudal, inter-religion or inter-clan. With the Peace of Westphalia (1648) emerged the concept of sovereign nation-states and legitimate authority to control and defend their respective territories. Thus, conflicts increasingly became inter-state and the concept of 'conventional wars' was born. Ever since, war has been evolving and presently we are in the era of fourth/fifth generation warfare.[7] First generation warfare (e.g. Napoleonic warfare) was smooth bore musket dominated and was manpower intensive; the second generation warfare (e.g. World War I) was artillery dominated, with fire and movement as key elements, and focus on massed firepower. The third generation warfare (e.g. the German *blitzkrieg* in World War II) was ruled by the quest to restore freedom of operational manoeuvre from the tyranny of attrition from dominant firepower. The fourth and fifth generations of warfare

are debatable. The fourth generation encompasses an evolved form of warfare – with belligerents other than states—that negates the nation's power of conventional military by fighting while being merged amongst the masses (a faceless enemy).[8]

Essentially, evolution has always been a slow process and warfare evolves not just because of technology but because nations prosecute war on the basis of their political, economic, social and technical status and that of the enemy's. Moreover, the evolution of a new generation does not replace the older generation—rather, all generations of war coexist in one form or the other and in various degrees.

Sub-Conventional Wars: While conventional wars are more dangerous, sub-conventional conflicts are more frequent. Post World War II, there has been a proliferation of sub-conventional wars. Since 1945, the total number of armed conflicts worthy of being called "conventional wars" stands at just 20, whereas in the same period, sub-conventional wars – ranging from terrorism, insurgencies, armed violence by non-state actors and armed clashes between militias—number more than 100.[9]

Geo-Political Scenario

The world over, globalisation, democratisation and evolution of technology have greatly impacted international relations as well as war (an instrument of international relations). At least in some parts of the world, the increased globalisation, economic interdependence and democratisation make us believe that war has become obsolete.[10] In most of the post World War II wars, at least one of the nation-states was practically non-democratic. There is a general belief that democracy will lead to peace and a democratic region is more likely to be peaceful than a non-democratic one. However, the possibility of wars due to democracies attempting to overthrow non-democratic regimes to spread the 'democratic zone of peace' cannot be ruled out. In our context, hope for a *'democratic peace'* is still a distant dream.

India, the biggest functional democracy in the world, is virtually the only nation in Southern Asia which has a truly functional democracy. The neighbouring states including China, Pakistan, Bangladesh, Sri Lanka, Nepal, the Maldives and Myanmar have hardly been truly democratic and have had their own share of problems, ranging from civil war, military rule to insurgency.[11] Most of these nations have been swaying from a state of unrest to an uneasy calm, causing anxiety and security issues for India. India's economic growth would be an attraction for these neighbouring states—except for China and Pakistan, that are India's arch rivals—and with careful diplomacy and positive initiatives, a constructive and cooperative relationship can be developed. But the real threat and/or challenge comes from China and Pakistan, the two most significant immediate neighbours that are far from a true democratic set-up. While the former is an opaque Communist state, the latter has an army playing a significant role in national governance and foreign policy; in fact, the Pakistan Army has always been at the political centre-stage.[12]

Moreover, globally, there has been a clear decline in the levels of peace, and the probability of terrorist attacks has increased. As per the 2011 **Global Peace Index,** out of 153 countries, India is 135th, Pakistan 146th and Afghanistan 150th. Overall, South Asia is almost at the bottom of the Index, missing only the last position to sub-Saharan Africa, which remains the least peaceful region in the world.[13] Moreover, the great power rivalry, which emanated in Europe and had engulfed the whole world in the last century, is now shifting to Asia in the 21st century. Thus, India has no choice but to be prepared to secure its national interests and assume a greater role regionally, as well as at the broader level.

China

Until 1800, India and China used to make up half the world's economy.[14] The industrial revolution in Europe and colonial rule in Asia led to the rise of Europe and stripped India and China of their wealth and industry. Nevertheless, history is completing a full circle after three centuries. Economic power is gradually shifting from the West to the East. India and China, the two most populated nations of the world, have become growth engines of the world economy. By 2018, China—India's most powerful neighbour—is slated to be the biggest economy in the world[15], and India would be the third biggest by 2030.[16] Their economic integration is also on the rise and bilateral trade crossed the US $60 billion mark in 2010. **Chindia**—a term once often invoked, expressing optimism over the joint geo-political rise of the two Asian giants—may become a reality and both the nations may develop peacefully.

Though extensive **economic integration** is, indeed, an important factor in reducing the risk of war, it does not essentially prevent war. The example of England and Germany before World War I is a point in case wherein conflicting political aspirations prevailed over economic cooperation.[17] The scope of completely peaceful and cooperative development is getting limited with the countries' growing status and competing interests. The Chinese aspiration to lead the region and play an influential and leading role in the world geo-politics is amply clear from the statement- "...The 19th century belonged to Europe, the 20th century to the United States. The 21st century, as we are coming to realise, can be the Asian century. But with that comes *great responsibility—to lead, to guide, and to take ownership of the collaborative agenda* (emphasis added)...".[18] Thus, competition for economic growth and regional influence would be inevitable and tensions would also rise due to growing internal social pressures and nationalism. This would slowly spill over in a negative way into the realm of high politics of security and diplomacy. The Chinese masses, as it is, consider India as the greatest security threat after the US.[19] Although China claims that it *'will never seek hegemony,'*[20] the denial of a visa to the Army Commander Northern Command, the stapled visas to the residents of Arunachal Pradesh and Kashmir, the attempt to intercept the INS *Airawat* in July 2011 in the South China Sea off the Vietnam coast are some of the Chinese acts which clearly exhibit assertiveness and hegemonic tendencies.

Demography: India's population growth rate is about twice that of China. India's total population will equal China's in 2025—each will have an estimated 1.4 billion people—and is expected to exceed China's population thereafter. In addition, India's prime working-age population will overtake China's in 2028. India's population is projected to continue increasing till 2050, while China's will reach its maximum (about 1.5 billion) in 2032, declining thereafter.[21] However, the broader economy of both nations will be much better than at present and would strongly compete with the military for talent. The income disparity between the military and other 'plum jobs' would be more prominent and would pose a challenge for attracting talent. The global as well domestic economy is likely to recover from the current economic slowdown induced by the 2008-09 global economic crises. Hence, the economic growth of both nations will have an adverse impact on the quality of officers available in the military forces. Being a Communist state, China would be able to address this problem with conscription but maintaining a huge military will definitely be costlier and challenging.[22] Therefore, for both nations, the thrust would be towards a leaner but more effective force structure and air power would be the natural choice because of its unmatchable speed, flexibility, range and being less manpower intensive.

Chinese War Strategy

Since the early days, the Chinese have believed that violence was just a part of warfare, and not necessarily the most important or most useful activity. Sun Tzu was amongst the first war strategists who argued that the purpose of the military was to induce the enemy's compliance, preferably peacefully. Rather than fighting a pitched battle, surprise, deterrence, deception and intelligence were among the more viable options. The powerful Han Dynasty (206 BCE to 220 CE) discredited *'wu'*, the art of warfare in favour of *'wen,'* the art of peace. These beliefs were the stark opposite of the mindset of the contemporary Romans and the Greeks for whom warfare was a central event in civic life. Unlike the Greeks and Romans, the Chinese preferred non-violent means for resolving disputes and believed that war was an admission of failure of all other resorts. Moreover, they preferred defence to offence. The Great Wall of China is an example of the same.

During the Chinese Civil War or 'War of Liberation', the Communist Party of China successfully employed the "passive defence" strategy and preserved their forces by avoiding the strong points of the KMT (Kuomintang or Chinese Nationalist Party) Army. Since 1949, the People's Liberation Army (PLA) has been playing a vital role in national politics[23] and China has shown several examples of military preemption as a strategic defensive act. As per a 2010 Pentagon report, China adopted this strategy in 1950(Korea War), 1962, 1969 (Ussuri river border conflict with the former Soviet Union) and 1979 (Sino-Vietnam conflict). The seizure of Paracel Islands was another example of offensive defence.[24] Historically, to attain its politico-military goals, China has used military power only when certain of victory.

The 1962 Chinese aggression was cleverly planned and timed to coincide with the start of the Cuban missile crisis which heightened tension between the US and the erstwhile Soviet Union. And the day the US initiated steps to end the crisis and lifted its quarantine of Cuba, China ceased its 32-day aggression against India. The war left an indelible historic scar, straining mutual relations, and despite several rounds of talks and confidence building measures, the border issues have not been resolved. It is important to note that in the recent past, China has resolved its border disputes with almost all its neighbours except India.

Doctrine and Technology: The People's Republic of China (PRC) was established in 1949 after an armed struggle under the leadership of Mao Zedong (Mao Tse-Tung) who followed the doctrine of "people's war". This doctrine worked on the principle of defence in-depth by exploiting the enemy's vulnerabilities through mobile and guerrilla warfare after "luring the enemy deep inside". The doctrine was rearticulated to address the deficiencies observed during the Sino-Vietnam War of 1979 as "people's war under modern conditions" wherein reliance on technology was enhanced as compared to reliance on manpower. In 1985, the CMC (Central Military Commision) came up with an entirely new doctrine of **"local border war"**. Since then, the fundamental centrality of 'local border wars' has prevailed though the doctrine has been evolving to keep pace with the new technological developments and concepts of employment of military power. After the Gulf War in 1991, Jiang Zemin created the doctrine of "limited war under high technology conditions," with greater emphasis on aerospace power.

In the last three decades, the PRC has been exhibiting double digit growth which has enabled a 13 percent annual increase in defence expenditure in real terms, at least in the last two decades. Official US estimates of Chinese defence spending are as much as two to three times higher than China's official estimate of its defence expenditures.[25] The SIPRI report states that China has increased its military spending by "170 per cent" in real terms since 2002 and Chinese military spending in 2011 was Yuan Renminbi 923 billion ($143 billion), the second highest in the world.[26]

India, it says, has increased military spending by "66 per cent" since 2002.Several military reforms have also been undertaken across the spectrum, including education, military industry, organisation, manpower policies, weapon systems and technology. Since 1986, the average age of top military leaders has been brought down from 76 to 56 years which is fuelling the transformation and modernisation process.[27]

China is demonstrating significant technological progress in aerospace power capabilities like the 2007 Anti-Satellite (ASAT) missile test, 5th generation twin engine stealth fighter J-20, 4th generation fighter aircraft including the J-10/FC-20, J-11, JF-17, aircraft carrier, Manoeuvrable Advanced Reentry Vehicles (MARVs), Ballistic Missile Defence (BMD) capability and supersonic cruise missiles (conventional as well as nuclear). Greater reliance on air power and the navy has helped in reducing the strength of the army. As per the 2010 Defence White Paper, China aspires to "accomplish mechanization" and "attain major progress in informationization" by 2020 with an integrated civilian-military development model.

The overall military doctrine emphasises on **'active defence'**—a mixture of defence and offence, with greater importance on the former. While the ground war may remain local (strategically defensive but tactically offensive), aerospace power is likely to be an offensive arm (strategically offensive and tactically defensive). The PLA Air Force (PLAAF), following the premise of 'active defence', also believes in 'appropriate offensive activities and long-range strike' operations which implies that the PLAAF would normally not launch a preemptive strike against an enemy, but may resort to offensive action if an attack by the enemy appears imminent.[28]

Next War ?: Another direct open war between the nations is unlikely as China will not attack till it is sure of victory or the stakes are too high. However, initiation of a proxy war or a military action and its escalation into a war cannot be ruled out. China continues to claim about 90,000 sq km of Indian territory in the northeast and occupies 23,000 sq km of Aksai Chin in the north of India, and both nations are in the process of building up their interests in the unstable as well as conflict prone states on their borders, like Nepal and Myanmar (good sources of natural resources).

How would China prosecute a war against India? Air Cmde Jasjit Singh has aptly hypothesised integrated joint campaigns.[29] Land forces, in all probability, would be employed in a strategically defensive and tactically offensive mode to avoid any escalation. Thus, for 'boots on the ground', it would be a local border, localised and limited war along the frontiers which have been marked with a thick nib and are difficult to demarcate. In contrast, the PLAAF would naturally look for air dominance (or control of the air) through neutralisation of the Indian Air Force (IAF) and air warfare. The PLAAF would also be utilised to address the military and civil targets, including artillery sites and lines of communication. Long range offensive capability [IRBMs (Intermediate Range Ballistic Missile) and MARVs] would be employed to address the targets in depth, up to a range of about 1,500 km. China has deployed about 1,300 such mobile missiles against Taiwan,[30] and would be a great challenge for our primitive BMD system if relocated towards Indian frontiers.

Pakistan

Strategic Culture: The strategic culture of Pakistan has three essential ingredients. Firstly, Pakistan inherently looks at India as a security threat and will do everything possible to undo it. In December 1965, President Ayub Khan had told US President Lyndon Johnson, "I know you won't believe it but those Indians are going to gobble us up."[31] Secondly, Islam is the basis for the existence of Pakistan, and Pakistan exploits it for self-protection. Gen Ayub Khan removed the term 'Islam' from the official name of Pakistan but the same was reincluded in 1968 by the political leadership. Thirdly, Pakistan must always be on the right side of the United States, China and Saudi Arabia.[32]

Kashmir essentially has been the cornerstone of Pakistan's foreign policy. Since its birth, Pakistan has been trying to wrest the Kashmir territory from India and the liberation of Indian Kashmir is a central national project. To achieve this motive, Pakistan promotes Kashmiri insurgency and terrorism. Support to the Kashmiri *jihad* has fundamentally shaped its foreign policy. Pakistan seeks to 'bleed India through a thousand cuts' and coerce the Indians into negotiating a diplomatic settlement on Kashmir. Incidentally, Kashmir continues to be the oldest item on the United Nations agenda, which still remains unresolved.[33]

Pak Concept of War: The concept of human inequality and insecurity which led to the birth of Pakistan enabled a significant role for the military in its national politics from the very beginning.[34] Pakistan observes the doctrine of 'offensive defence' and has been the aggressor in all the four Indo-Pak Wars, following more or less a similar pattern. Before initiating the war, non-state actors were employed to make an attempt to achieve the political objective or, at least, weaken India. Thereafter, the level of the conflict was raised (or escalated) to a war. The Kashmir War started with the aggression by Pakistan-led tribals, the 1965 War was preceded by Operation Gibraltar and the Kargil War also involved clandestine incursions by *jihadis*.

Nuclear Weapon and Security Dynamics: Pakistan became a *de facto* nuclear state in the 1980s and India also became nuclear in the same era.[35] Nuclearisation changed the security dynamics of the region and deterred any conventional war on a scale sufficient to inflict catastrophic defeat or significant losses. Prior to the attainment of nuclear capability, there were three wars between India and Pakistan whereas after the 1980s, the Kargil War was the only direct armed conflict between the two states, which was much lower in scale and magnitude as compared to the previous wars.

'Stability/Instability Paradox': As per Glenn Snyder's *'stability/instability paradox'* when nuclear deterrence prevails between two great powers, they get inclined to fight one another indirectly at lower levels of conventional/unconventional warfare.[36] Strategic stability i.e. a small probability of nuclear escalation made aggression in Europe relatively safe for the erstwhile Soviet Union that was conventionally strong and potential revisionist. **High stability encouraged low-level violence during the Cold War era.**

Some scholars believe that the *'stability/instability paradox'* of the Cold War era applies to South Asia in totality, while others believe that the paradox has entirely different connotations, as far as the Indo-Pak equation is concerned, and the situation is, in fact, just the reverse.[37] Pakistan, the revisionist force, is conventionally weaker than India. A high degree of strategic stability will discourage Pakistan from initiating low-level conflict/violence, since a small probability of nuclear escalation increases the odds that a conventionally weak Pakistan will face a befitting retaliation from India. On the contrary, a prevailing significant degree of strategic instability has allowed the ongoing Indo-Pak conflicts. **The danger of escalation and possibility of employment of the nuclear weapon enables Pakistan to engage India in low-level violence while remaining insulated from Indian retaliation.** The strategic instability also helps Pakistan in attracting international attention as the nations which might otherwise be uninterested in an Indo-Pakistan conflict, would seek to mediate to prevent a nuclear confrontation.[38]

Jihad: In 1976, Zulfiqar Ali Bhutto included the term *jihad* in the army's motto. The Pakistan armed forces' motto *'Jihad fi Sabilillah'* i.e. *jihad* in the name of Allah, reflects its acute aggression and fundamentalism, whereas the motto of the Indian armed forces, 'Service before Self', is much more humble and defensive. In the 1980s, the Mujahideen (those who carry out *jihad*) were created by the United States, with Pakistan as its front-line state, to prosecute war in Afghanistan against the erstwhile Soviet Union.[39] Ever since, Pakistan has been using the unaccounted US funds for supporting *jihadis* and waging a proxy war against India[40] under the premise that its nuclear capability deters India from launching a conventional war. Throughout the 1990s, Pakistan continued its involvement and supported Kashmiri and foreign militants fighting against Indian rule.

Kargil: After the 1998 nuclear tests and acquisition of overt nuclear capability, Pakistan crossed the Line of Control (LoC) at Kargil, seized territory and threatened the vital lines of communication to Kashmir. The Pakistani aggression was primarily based on three basic assumptions. First, Pakistan enjoyed a local tactical advantage over India at Kargil. Second, the threat of use of the nuclear weapon would deter India from prosecuting a conventional war. Third, Pakistan would receive international support.[41]

Operation Parakram: After the experience of Kargil, a limited conflict that did not cross the nuclear threshold, India realised a degree of strategic stability. In response to the December 2001 terrorist attack on the Parliament House, India deployed about 500,000 troops along the LoC and the international border, the largest mobilisation in Indian history.[42] Thus, India adopted a '*policy of compellence*'[43] and through Operation Parakram, exhibited its resolve to launch a limited conventional war against Pakistan, if it did not stop sponsoring terrorism/violence in India.

Instability in Pakistan: After Operation Neptune Spear, in which the United States eliminated Osama Bin Laden in May 2011 at his hideout at Abbottabad, next to a Pakistani military base, the US-Pak relations have been significantly strained. But the US still needs Pakistan, at least till the declared withdrawal of its forces and [North Atlantic Treaty Organisation (NATO) forces] from Afghanistan, to be completed in 2014. Complete withdrawal by 2014 is itself debatable, and even if does happen, it is very unlikely that the US would completely abandon Pakistan to its fate.

Due to the ideological radicalism of Pakistan (its leadership as well as population), national and international security is facing a serious threat and Pakistan appears to be at a precarious tipping point from where it may fall into a serious uncontrollable instability and, in the worst case scenario, may even become a 'failed state'. The Pakistani economy is also in shambles and is set to deteriorate further due to the high population growth (3.1 percent) as compared to the lower economic growth at just about 2 percent.[44]

Would Pakistan Attack India?

To divert the domestic and international opinion away from the crisis (which Pakistan has created for itself), in desperation, the Pakistan leadership may resort to the fifth war against India. Right from the start, Pakistan has had an insatiable desire to defeat India and to satisfy this yearning, it may make yet another attempt to seek a military victory over India. Moreover, the Pakistan mindset that Muslims are more martial than the Hindus[45] strengthens their hope of victory, overlooking the ground realities.

Pakistan is showing no signs of abating its terrorism and proxy war against India. Additionally, under the nuclear umbrella and its 'first strike doctrine', Pakistan may initiate a limited war, like Kargil. The land forces are likely to project a strong defensive posture while maintaining the threat of a major armoured offensive, whereas the main thrust would be on long range firepower and employment of ballistic missiles, cruise missiles and Pakistan Air Force (PAF) combat power, with conventional warheads seeking to damage Indian Army targets and IAF bases.

Air Power: The focus of Pakistan on air power is amply discernible from its aggressive rearming since its defeat in Kargil 1999.[46] Since Kargil, Pakistan has focussed on modernisation and strengthening of the PAF and its aerial strike capabilities which include the acquisition of six Swedish Airborne Early Warning and Control (AEWC) aircraft and four Chinese KJ-2000 Airborne Warning and Control Systems (AWACS). Acquisition plans also include aerial refuellers, a large complement of maritime patrol and strike aircraft and supersonic cruise missiles, indicating its desire to develop maritime and long range precision strike capabilities to address high value targets right upto Kanyakumari.[47]

On the other hand, though India undoubtedly has conventional superiority over Pakistan, the dispersed peace-time deployment limits India's ability to bring its forces to bear on Pakistan. Moreover, the IAF has lost its numerical advantage due to the unplanned drop in its combat power from the authorised strength of 39 and a half squadrons to as low as 28 squadrons. It will not be easy for the IAF to meet a potential threat from the PAF as it would also be mandated to deploy its assets for safeguarding the northern frontiers, as done in the past, in 1965 and 1971. Therefore, in all probability, numerically the IAF's deployable strength would be less than that of the PAF, at least till 126 French Rafale fighter aircraft under the Medium Multi-Role Combat Aircraft (MMRCA) deal and indigenous Light Combat Aircraft (LCA) are inducted.

India

India has never been an aggressor and never attacked any sovereign nation. Rather, all five wars (four with Pakistan and one with China) have been thrust upon the country, and there is no development which indicates or hints at any foreseeable change with regards the policy of non-aggression and a resilient mindset. Although national grand strategy is for peaceful coexistence, with a focus on national progress and avoidance of war, the possibility of a war cannot be ruled out. Marxist Leon Trotsky's famous quote that **"you may not be interested in war, but war is interested in you"** is aptly applicable to India.

Indian Doctrine: India follows the doctrine of 'defensive defence'. The Indian national policy is characterised by restraint and preservation of the *status quo*. Aggressive Pakistan has made several bold attempts to revise territorial boundaries while India has always shown matured restraint. Rather, the Indian restraint has progressively increased with each war. During the Kashmir War, the British played a major limiting role as they never wanted an armed conflict between two of their dominions.[48] During the 1965 Pakistani aggression, the Indian political aims were restricted to defend own territory and destruction of the offensive power of the Pakistan military, without any territorial aspirations. Limited enemy territory was permitted to be occupied only to achieve other war objectives (and the same was to be returned after the war). [49] The aims of the Bangladesh War were even more restrained. India just wanted to rehabilitate and send 10 million refugees back to East Pakistan, for which only a part of East Pakistan was to be liberated and in the West, the aim was to remain totally defensive.[50]

While Pakistan depends upon the three As, Allah, Army and America,[51] India depends upon three Ds, Defensive defence, Diplomacy and Deterrence. Interestingly, India's strategic-military restraint gives the national rise an edge (over other nations, including China). Suppliers from across the globe are lining up to supply military hardware to India since they are not afraid that this equipment will be used against them. In contrast, Russia is hesitating to sell advanced weapon systems to China.[52]

Biggest Security Threat to the Nation?: India faces a national security threat from China, Pakistan as well as Naxalism.[53] On several occasions, the Prime Minister of India Shri Manmohan Singh, has termed Naxalism as the biggest security threat to India.[54] On other occasions, he has assuaged the concerns regarding the threat from China by assuring the nation that China will not attack India.

Many analysts differ on both the stands. Naxalism is an internal security problem which highlights a deficit of governance, and systemic deficiencies and inadequacies. Naxalism—an outcome of India's own weaknesses of governance, political institutions and socio-economic structures—is essentially internal and can be overcome by addressing the internal deficiencies and inadequacies.

The threats from China and Pakistan are external in nature, with entirely different dimensions. Cordial relations and avoidance of confrontation through diplomacy are desirable but external threats can only be contained by a strong and credible military force, the ultimate instrument of national defence. The humiliating defeat of 1962 should always remain in the back of our minds and we should not forget that a nation can get peace only if it is able to defend peace and not just by friendly gestures, which were presented by China even before the 1962 War with great acumen. Signing of the Panchsheel Agreement in 1954 and Premier Zhou En-Lai's visit to New Delhi in 1960 during which he exhibited keenness for a border settlement are cases in point.[55]

Some Thoughts About a Future War Scenario

Is Nuclear War a Possibility?: Since China, India and Pakistan are all nuclear states, will the next Indian war be a nuclear war?[56] Though the possibility of a nuclear war cannot be ruled out, its probability is almost negligible. While China maintains the Second Artillery Force for strategic deterrence and India possesses the nuclear triad, both nations have a doctrine of credible deterrence and '*no first use*'.[57] Moreover, use of a nuclear weapon against a nuclear state would certainly invite a nuclear counter-strike, thus, no wise nuclear state would use a nuclear weapon against a nuclear state, though many observers do not consider Pakistan a 'wise state'.[58]

Localised, Limited Border Wars: Since war is a means to an end and not an end in itself, no wise state would endeavour to destabilise and shock a nuclear weapon adversary in such a manner that it may feel compelled to use the nuclear weapon, in the absence of any other viable option. Hence, amongst the nuclear states, the scope of a conventional war would be limited in space; type and quantum of force employed; objectives and targets; levels of casualties inflicted; collateral damage; and duration of war. Rather, the scope of a conventional conflict would be contained and moderated to only coerce, irritate, punish and/or weaken the enemy while carefully avoiding the insurmountable extreme threat, jolt, humiliation or actual loss. In localised, limited border wars, land forces would normally restrict their operations close to border areas and would not attempt deep penetration strike. The recent Cold Start doctrine of the Indian Army reportedly follows the same principle.[59] The Kargil War in 1999 is a classic example of inter-state war under the nuclear threat. But both nations observed well calculated restraint, and employment of air power was not an exception. While the IAF was mandated to not to cross the LoC, Pakistan did not employ combat air power at all.

Two-Front War: China has a patronising relationship with Pakistan and has been supporting Pakistan in various ways, including supply of military equipment and technology.[60] Is it possible that Pakistan and China would open well coordinated simultaneous war fronts against India? The possibility appears to be bleak as China does not exhibit any such tendencies. Moreover, seeing the past trend, in case Pakistan initiates a war against India, China may continue to support Pakistan diplomatically as well as in terms of supply of military equipment, but it is highly unlikely that

China would also open a front and try to take leverage out of the situation, though China may intervene seeing Pakistan losing the war, the way it responded in 1965. However, under the nuclear overhang, such a possibility may not arise since a losing Pakistan would resort to a nuclear attack (or at least threaten to do so), and change the war dynamics.

On the contrary, in case competition and tensions (like the ongoing border issues) with China deteriorate and lead to a war, the possibility of Pakistan opening a front – to take mileage out of the situation and settle scores with India or wrest Kashmir from India – cannot be ruled out. The 1962 War had certainly boosted Pakistan's confidence against India and had Pakistan started a war immediately after the Chinese aggression and not waited till September 1965, the results could have been different and less favourable to India. Thus, undoubtedly, India needs to be prepared to face a two-front war.

Imperatives of Future Wars

Ascendancy of Air Power: There are obvious reasons for increasing dependence on air power.

- While **air dominance** would be a prerequisite for the operational freedom of the army and navy, air power would be a natural choice due to its elements of unmatched **speed, flexibility and range**.
- It is the only instrument of violence which can neutralise targets (military as well as civil) deep in the enemy territory without the need of defeating fielded ground forces.
- **Increasing Sensitivity to Casualties:** During World War I, 2,500 casualties per day were acceptable to the coalition forces as "ordinary wastage"[61] whereas, today the sensitivity towards casualties is very high. In 1991, the US led coalition forces significantly reduced own casualties by prosecuting 42 days of military action exclusively through air power till the last 100 hours when the ground forces experienced combat. In Kosovo and Libya, the war was fought by coalition forces exclusively through air power and ground troops were not employed at all.
- **Technological Advancements:** Development of space capabilities, MARVs, cruise missiles, Unmanned Aerial Vehicles (UAVs), Unmanned Combat Aerial Vehicles (UCAVs) has increased the precision and offensive range while reducing the collateral damage and vulnerability of own airmen.

Justifiability: Justifiability of war is increasingly gaining importance. Use of force to achieve a political objective needs to be justified to the international community as well as the domestic population. The longer the war, the more difficult it would be for the greater power to avoid international criticism and maintain domestic support. Therefore, all bigger nations would aspire for an early culmination of war.

Legality: Future conflicts would impose increasing restrictions on the commanders and their actions would be more and more constrained. Martin van Creveld has aptly expanded Low Intensity Conflict Operations (LICO) as lawyer infested conflicts. The commander would be required to be cautious about the legality of his actions as a small mistake (especially in front of the wrong camera) may antagonise public opinion, and affect the legality and justifiability of the war. Additionally, the commanders' actions are more likely to be challenged in the courts of law.

Political Constraints: Various factors, including the nuclear overhang, increased globalisation, economic interdependence, democratisation, transparency, human rights, sensitivity to collateral damage and casualties, and social media explosion have increased the political constraints against the initiation and prosecution of war. In the ongoing Iran conflict, the United States is exhibiting much greater self-control as compared to what was observed earlier—before initiating the Iraq War or Afghanistan War. A study of the Indian wars also reflects increasing restraint in political aim as well as force employment.

Politico-Military Paradox: The obvious fallout of a limited war is limited effects, thus, no nation should expect a "decisive military victory" from its military. Rather it is expected to lead to a stalemate. Furthermore, a smaller nation's ability to delay or deny achievement of the adversary's political aim is likely to be projected as a victory. Thus, enforcement of the political will on the adversary would be a significant challenge. The most probable solution to this politico-military paradox of achieving the political aim without the risk of escalation to the nuclear level would be to undertake selective punitive/coercive strikes through employment of aerospace power. Thus, the land forces would be strategically defensive and tactically offensive while air power would be strategically offensive and tactically defensive.

Conclusion

Strengthening of internal economic capabilities and emergence as a great power must continue to be India's top priority.[62] But essential balance between economic growth and national defence cannot be overlooked as national defence and sovereignty are a function of the nation's capability to handle the security challenges and threats (internal as well as external).

Escalation of a proxy war or a sub-conventional war to a conventional war cannot be overruled. There might be several situations wherein both the adversaries are tempted to use conventional weapons and forces. The 'perpetrator' may get tempted to escalate the proxy war and employ conventional forces to achieve the desired political aims, as happened in 1947-48, 1962, 1965, and again in the Kargil War in 1999. On the other hand, the 'victim' nation may use its conventional forces to bring the proxy war into the open when pushed to the wall rather than fighting with all the limitations of a 'no war no peace situation'. Pakistan did so in 1971, and India was prepared to do so in 2001 after the terrorist attack on its Parliament on December 13, 2001.[63] Nevertheless, limited local border wars appear to be most plausible future possibility.

In any case, aerospace power would be the national instrument of choice for its advantages and proven track record in recent wars.[64] Therefore, India must enhance its aerospace capabilities through indigenous development as well as acquisition from external sources and appropriate employment through effective leadership, doctrine and befitting training.

This should not be construed as war alarmism or war mongering. Rather it would be unwise and dangerous for the national planners (and the IAF) of a growing power to entirely depend upon diplomacy, overlooking the war preparation and the worst case scenarios.

Notes

1. Michael S. Neiberg, *Warfare in World History* (London: Routledge, 2001), p. 6.
2. More often than not, *history repeats itself* and the possibility of future wars for water are being widely talked about and cannot be ruled out.
3. John Andreas Olsen, ed., *A History of Air Warfare* (New Delhi: Vij Books, 2010).
4. Michael Sheehan, "The Changing Character of War", in John Baylis, Steve Smith, Patricia Owens, eds., *The Globalization of World Politics: An Introduction to International Relations* (London: Oxford University Press, 2011), p. 212.
5. Ibid., p. 214.
6. Colin S. Gray, *Another Bloody Century: Future Warfare* (London: Weidenfeld and Nicoloson, 2005) and Prakash Menon, "Sub-conventional Conflicts", in Gurmeet Kanwal and Samarjit Ghosh, eds., *Future Wars Changing Nature of Conflict* (Delhi: Matrix Publishers, 2011), pp. 123-125.
7. Although generations of the war model is not an absolute model, it helps in understanding the evolution of warfare over the centuries. Prof Lawrence Freedman and Prof Antulio Echevarria, in particular, do not find anything new in the concept.
8. Gray, n. 6, pp. 141-142.
9. A.K. Singh, "Conventional Wars, Emerging Perspectives" in Kanwal and Ghosh, eds., n.7, p. 60.
10. Sheehan, n. 4, p. 212. The North Atlantic region has been described as a security community; a group of states for which war has disappeared as a means of resolving disputes amongst themselves, though they may continue to use war against opponents outside the security community.
11. The recent *'coup'* against President Mohamed Nasheed in Maldives on February 07, 2012, is a case in point.
12. Both the major Indo-Pak Wars were initiated by Pakistan under military rulers—Gen Ayub Khan in 1965 and Gen Yahya Khan in 1971.
13. Prahlad Shekhawat's article in *The Times of India (Crest Edition)*, Delhi, January 8, 2012.
14. "China and India Contest of the Century," *The Economist*, August 19, 2010, accessed at http://www.economist.com/node/16846256, on January 10, 2012.

15. In August 2010, China had already become the world's second biggest economy after overtaking Japan.
16. "National Sovereignty no More Absolute", *The Hindu* (Delhi), January 8, 2012.
17. Ralph N. Clough, "Conflicting Tendencies: Economic Integration Vs Political Impasse" in Andrew Scobell, ed., *The Cost of Conflict: The Impact on China of a Future War (*Pennsylvania: Army War College (US), Strategic Studies Institute, 2001), p. 29.
18. "Asia at the Helm", *Beijing Review*, Vol. 53, No. 44, November 4, 2010, reproduced in Dr Pushpa Adhikari, "China's Neighbourhood Policy and South Asia," *USI Journal*, Vol. CXLI No. 586, p. 515.
19. *Indian Express*, "Many Chinese Think India Greatest Security Threat After US: New Poll" (New Delhi: Express News Service, December 02, 2009) http://www.indianexpress.com/news/many-chinese-think-india-greatest-security-t/548808/ accessed on January 15, 2012.
20. *China's National Defense in 2010, Chapter II*. Chinese White Paper on National Defense, accessed on February 16, 2012 at Chinese government official website http://english.gov.cn/official/2011-03/31/content_1835499.htm .
21. *China and India, 2025 : A Comparative Assessment* (Santa Monica: RAND Corporation, 2011),p. 104.
22. Ibid., p. 30.
23. Prof Parris H. Chang (former Deputy National Security Advisor, Taiwan), "China's Emerging Military Leadership". A presentation during the 4th "Jumbo" Majumdar International Seminar in Delhi on February 4, 2012.
24. Brahma Chellaney, "Lasting Lesson of 1962: Don't be Caught Off-Guard Again," *The Times of India*, (Delhi), January 22, 2012.
25. n. 21, p. 79.
26. Aditya Kaul, "China Gets Stronger As We Cut Arms Spending", *Daily News & Analysis*, http://www.dnaindia.com/india/report_china-gets-stronger-as-we-cut-arms-spending_1677384
27. Jasjit Singh, "Some Aspects of Our Wars in Future," *Air Power Journal*, Vol 6 No.3, Monsoon 2011.
28. Air Cmde Ramesh V. Phadke, *People's Liberation Army Air Force (PLAAF): Shifting Airpower Balance and Challenges to India's Security* (Stanford University: Centre for International Security and Cooperation, 2002), p. 11.
29. Kaul, n. 26, pp. 18-19.
30. Ian Jeffries, *Political Developments in Contemporary China: A Guide* (London: Routledge, 2010).
31. Dennis Kux, *India-Pakistan Negotiations* (Washington: United States Institute of Peace,2006), p. 17.
32. Ijaz Khan, *Pakistan's Strategic Culture and Foreign Policy Making* (New York: Nova Science Publishers, 2007), p. xiv.
33. S. Paul Kapur, "India and Pakistan's Unstable Peace," *International Security*, Vol. 30, No. 2, Fall 2005, p. 143.
34. Sumit Ganguly, "Pak Polity and Its Throne of Bayonets", *Asian Age* (Delhi), January 03, 2012.
35. In 1974, India carried out its first nuclear test and in 1998, both India and Pakistan showed their nuclear capability to each other as well as to the world.
36. T. V. Paul, James J. Wirtz, Michel Fortmann, *Balance of Power: Theory and Practice in the 21st Century* (California: Stanford University Press: 2004), p. 324.
37. Kapur, n. 33, pp. 127-152, describe the stability/instability paradox in detail.
38. Ashley J. Tellis, *Stability in South Asia* (Santa Monica: RAND Corporation, 1997).
39. To dislodge the Mujahideen from Kabul, the Taliban, an even more radical entity, was created in 1996. It was dethroned by the US war against terrorism and Al Qaeda.
40. Gen V.P. Malik, " Indo-Pak Security Relations in the Coming Decade: Lessons from Kargil for the Future," accessed at http://www.satp.org/satporgtp/publication/idr/vol_17(1)/VPMalik.htm on February 11, 2012
41. Kapur, n. 33, pp. 127-152.
42. Ibid., pp. 148-149.
43. *Compellence* is similar to deterrence and is yet conceptually distinct. Like deterrence, compellence seeks to manipulate the incentives of the opponent in order to affect his behaviour. Unlike deterrence, which is concerned with persuading the opponent not to take some action, compellence is an effort

to persuade him to change his action.

44. Singh, n. 27, p. 19.
45. Altaf Guhar, "Four Wars and One Assumption," *The Nation*, September 1999. A series of four articles was published soon after Kargil.
46. In Kargil, the combat power of the PAF was not employed due to various reasons, including its stark inadequacy.
47. Singh, n. 27, p. 22.
48. Dasgupta, *War and Diplomacy in Kashmir* (Delhi: Sage Publications, 2002) p. 53, and Larry Collins and Dominique Lapierre, *Mountbatten and Independent India* (Delhi: Vikas Publishing House, 1984).
49. R.D. Pradhan, *Debacle to Revival: YB Chavan as Defence Minister 1962-1965*(New Delhi: Orient Longman, 1998), p. 262.
50. S.N. Prasad, *History of Indo-Pak War, 1971*(New Delhi: History Division, Ministry of Defence, Government of India, unpublished), p. 279. The professional execution of the war and extremely favourable circumstances led to an early culmination of the war with 93,000 Prisoners of War (POWs) and the liberation of the whole of Bangladesh. Till date, the 1971 War is the only Indian war which resulted in an unambiguous victory and unconditional surrender of enemy forces.
51. Hassan Abbas, *Pakistan's Drift into Extremism: Allah, the Army, and America's War on Terror* (New York: East Gate Book, 2005).
52. Sunil Dasgupta, "On a Wing and a Prayer", *The Times of India*, Crest Edition (New Delhi), February 18, 2012.
53. The USA has different parameters and approach towards national security. US Defence Secretary Leon Panetta has cited cyber warfare as the biggest security threat. "Defence Secretary Dubs 'Cyber Warfare' US' Biggest Security Threat", January 7, 2012, Washington, DC, ANI http://www.dnaindia.com/world/report_defence-secretary-dubs-cyber-warfare-us-biggest-security-threat_1634513, accessed on January 15, 2012.
54. Althea Carbon, *Naxalism the Biggest Security Threat to India* (New Zealand: University of Canterbury) accessed at http://www.indiafutureofchange.com/featureEssay_D0012.htm on January 15, 2012.
55. Chellaney, n. 24.
56. Out of about 200 countries, only eight are believed to have nuclear weapons and three (Iran, North Korea and Syria) are states of immediate proliferation concern.
57. *China's National Defense in 2008*, Chapter VII. Chinese White Paper on National Defense, accessed at Chinese governmentt official website http://english.gov.cn/official/2009-01/20/content_1210227.htm on February 16, 2012.
58. Bharat Varma in a panel discussion on Pakistan at *Star News* on January 12, 2012.
59. Walter C. Ladwig, "A Cold Start for Hot Wars? The Indian Army's New Limited War Doctrine", *International Security*, Vol. 32, No. 3, Winter 2007/08, pp. 158–190.
60. More than 60 percent of Pakistan's conventional weapons have either been supplied by China or manufactured under licence in Pakistan.
61. Walter J. Boyne, *The Influence of Air Power Upon History* (New York: Pelican Publishing Company, 2003), pp. 48-49.
62. Paul, et. al., n. 36.
63. Malik, n. 40.
64. John Andreas Olsen, ed., *A History of Air Warfare* (New Delhi: Vij Books, 2010).

9

Emerging Missile Threat

Debalina Chatterjee

The end of the Cold War has made such a strategy [MAD] largely irrelevant. Barely plausible when there was only one strategic opponent, the theory makes no sense in a multipolar world of proliferating nuclear powers. Mutual destruction is not likely to work against religious fanatics; desperate leaders may blackmail with nuclear weapons; blackmail or accidents could run out of control. And when these dangers materialise, the refusal to have made timely provisions will shake confidence in all institutions of government. At a minimum, the rudiments of a defense system capable of rapid expansion should be put into place.

— Henry Kissinger, March 9, 1995.[1]

Weapon procurement is an integral part of military modelling. It involves the selection of one weapon system from other competing weapon systems. The concepts of defence, deterrence, disarmament, arms race and arms control directly emanate from the concept of technology. Once a country has acquired nuclear weapons or sophisticated conventional weapons, it is only a matter of time before it develops credible delivery mechanisms. Missiles are viewed by many countries as "cost-effective weapons" and "symbols of national power"[2] and comprise one of the most dynamic innovations of firepower. In fact, delivery systems like the inter-continental missiles have enhanced the raw firepower and have become a threat to aircraft, tanks, etc. From the long range Inter-Continental Ballistic Missiles (ICBMs) to the smaller unguided anti-tank guided weapons and unguided light anti-tank weapons, countries portray their might in myriad types of missiles. Missiles have several components like the airframe, a propulsion system, guidance system, control surfaces, and a warhead which could be either conventional or nuclear. Increasing the thrust of the missile could improve its range which would reduce the cost and also enable the missile to carry more weapons.

World War II had seen the use of missiles like the V-1 and the V-2 (*Vergelungswaffe* which means a weapons which can be used for retaliation) though the real use of missiles could be dated back to the Vedic times wherein there is mention of the use of missiles like the Brahmastra and Pasupatastra and even anti-missiles like the Upasamhara. Post World War II, the world got exposed to a new kind of lethal weapon called the nuclear weapon. The dropping of the atomic bombs, Fat Man and Little Boy, in Japan in 1945, revealed the cataclysmic effects that could be caused by these nuclear weapons. By 1959, the USA had developed ICBMs like the Titan and Atlas which were liquid fuelled.

The era of the Cold War witnessed the development of missiles with increased range like the Intermediate Range Ballistic Missiles (IRBMs) and ICBMs, and cruise missiles, capable of causing grievous, catastrophic effects. The Cuban Missile Crisis or the Jupiter Missiles Crisis in 1962 when both the superpowers were on the verge of nuclear brinkmanship with each other has still not been forgotten. Stationing of the US Jupiter missile in Turkey, pointing directly towards Moscow, posed a threat to the security of the erstwhile Soviet Union. The Soviets, in return, stationed missiles like the Frog missiles in Cuba, pointing towards important American cities. This was a step taken by the Soviets to make the US aware of what it feels to have a missile pointed at one. By the 1980s, countries were able to target nuclear weapon systems at the enemy's command centres, thereby making the command and control of a country vulnerable to an attack. For instance, the US Pershing II missiles were stationed in Europe, with the Soviet Yankee class submarines near the Atlantic coast, thereby enabling attacks to take only a few minutes from launch to impact. Guided weapons like long range strategic rockets, the dogfight missiles which were carried by aircraft, the short range anti-tank missiles, and the surface-to-air anti-aircraft defence systems became decisive factors in wars. With both the superpowers possessing around 70,000 nuclear weapons, with some fitted on ballistic missiles like Battlefield Short Range Ballistic Missiles (BSRBMs), Short Range Ballistic Missiles (SRBMs), Medium Range Ballistic Missiles (MRBMs) and IRBMs, missiles became more cataclysmic.

With the Revolution in Military Affairs (RMA), the age of missiles has become more dangerous and poses greater threats to mankind as warfare has meliorated in both qualitative and quantitative terms. Weapons of mass destruction bring about amelioration in a country's power "vastly exceeding what could be achieved by any considerable territorial acquisition".[3] High-tech systems are usually made to flirt with these missiles, thereby, enhancing their ability to produce cataclysmic effects. Technological advancements have coerced states to shift from atomic weapons to thermonuclear weapons and from single warheads to Multiple Independently Targeted Reentry Vehicles (MIRVs).

Today, several countries have developed missiles for security and deterrence. Countries may develop indigenous missile technology, acquire missiles from another country or build them in collaboration with another country or simply be under the umbrella of another country. National Defence under Article 51 of the United Nations Charter has given the opportunity to states to develop weapons of mass destruction and their delivery vehicles under this excuse. For example, India has indigenously developed its missile technology under the Integrated Guided Missile Development Programme with the Prithvi, Agni, Aakash, and many more. China, for instance, had proliferated the M-11and M-9, and North Korea, the Taepo Dong categories of ballistic missiles to Pakistan. Argentina's Condor missile was developed with contributions from German technology. Russia and India jointly developed the BrahMos supersonic cruise missile, while Brazil and South Africa jointly developed the A-Darter fifth generation short range infrared homing air-to-air missile. Germany's HOT is a Franco-German anti-tank missile.

Missile Threats Come from Both Ballistic and Cruise Missiles.

A ballistic missile may be a short range ballistic missile with a range of less than 1,000 km, a medium range ballistic missile with 1,000 to 3,000 km range, an intermediate range ballistic missile with range from 3,000 to 5,500 km, while for the above 5,500 km range, inter-continental ballistic missiles are used. Every ballistic missile has three flight phases: boost phase, mid-course phase and terminal phase. In the mid-course and terminal phases, a ballistic missile can possess greater destructive capabilities. In the coming years, the Department of Defence would invest over $100 billion in nuclear delivery systems which could sustain existing capabilities and modernise some strategic systems.[4] The United States possesses short range ballistic missiles like the MGM-52 (Lance), M39, M39A, ICBMs like the MIRV-ed Minuteman III, Trident D-5 with 8 MIRVs. Russia possesses short range ballistic missiles like the Frog-7B, SS-1B, SS-1C, SS-26,ICBMs like the RS-24 with 6 MIRVs, SS-18s with 10 MIRVs, SS-19s with 6MIRVs, SS-25, Submarine Launched Ballistic Missiles (SLBMs) like the SS-N-18 with 3 MIRVs, 10 MIRV-ed SS-N-20, and 4 MIRV-ed SS-N-23. Israel has also made considerable progress in ballistic missiles like the Jericho-2 MRBMs. Libya possesses Scud-B missiles and Frog-7 rockets. Ballistic missiles are one of the best mediums to carry conventional and nuclear weapons. Ballistic missiles may or may not pose a threat; however, the existential threat cannot be neglected. Due to their higher circular error probable and longer ranges, they have the ability to cause severe destruction, especially while delivering nuclear weapons and, hence, could form the best deterrent. In fact, it is not just the possession of nuclear weapons which provides the best deterrence—possession of an effective delivery system is necessary to provide deterrence as a nuclear weapon would not pose much of threat without an effective delivery system. However, missiles have now been developed with precision guided weapons which would reduce collateral damage and would only pinpoint the desired target, thereby reducing casualties. Surface-to-air ballistic missiles are smaller in size and easier to transport and, hence, can be an option for guerrilla warfare and terrorist activities. For instance, the Stinger surface-to-air missiles were provided to the Mujahideen by the USA during the Soviet invasion of Russia in 1979. The Sri Lankan Liberation Tigers of Tamil Eelam (LTTE) were reported to have tried to buy surface-to-air missiles from the Federal Bureau of Investigation (FBI) agents.[5]Russian missiles are always feared to fall into the hands of terrorist organisations or rebel groups like the Chechens.

While the F-16s are an option for Pakistan for delivery of nuclear weapons, the M-11 ballistic missiles seem to be the best option for it. Iraq used the Scud missiles in 1991 during the Gulf War. In 1998, former Secretary of Defence, Donald Rumsfeld, had said, "Ballistic missiles are attractive, and they're attractive for several reasons. There are no defences against them. They tend to arrive at their targets."[6]Theatre missiles like SRBMs and MRBMs with 'state of the art guidance technologies' give countries a unique credibility as they enhance the ability of a country to attack multinational forces, lines of control, logistic sites, and cities.

Missile development by a country may not only scare neighbouring and enemy countries, but provoke them too. Acquisition of missiles could be the result of threat perceptions and also a reason for doing so. Saudi Arabia faces threats from Iraq, Yemen and Syria. Yemen possesses surface-to-surface missiles like the FROG-7s, Scud-Bs and SS-21s for delivering conventional warheads. Even though their operational level is not clear, the existential threat cannot be eschewed. Missile threats from Iran cannot be neglected as Iran could use surface-to-surface missiles to not only deliver conventional weapons but also nuclear weapons. Iran possesses Scud-B missiles, longer range Scud-C missiles and the Shahab missiles based on the No Dongs. Due to lack of efficient air power and modernised surface vessels, anti-ship missiles are an option. The Seersucker, CS-801, CS-802, CS-801K are the anti-ship missiles of Iran. Turkey's quest for nuclear weapons, and its growing friendship with Iran and China, could result in Turkey trying to establish defence ties with China and Iran. In case that happens, Turkey could acquire missiles from China, which could completely alter the geo-strategic and geo-political equations in the Eurasian zone.

Even North Korea has developed ballistic missiles and, according to BBC reports, the state possesses more than 800 ballistic missiles. In 2002, North Korea had stated that it had the right to "counter the US nuclear threat" with a credible deterrent. [7] North Korea possesses short range ballistic missiles like the KN-02s, and acquired the Scud-B ballistic missiles from Egypt in return for its support to Egypt against Israel during the Yom Kippur War. However, by 1984, North Korea started to develop its own Scud-B missiles and also developed the Scud-C missile, also known as the No Dong. Later, North Korea also developed the Taepo Dong missiles. Today, cruise missiles have become a favourite of the military due to their versatility: stealth, accuracy and ability to be guided even after the missile has been launched. The evolution of cruise missiles may be traced back to World War II with the V-1 missiles in Germany. However, the second generation cruise missiles lost their importance against the ballistic missiles and bombers. The cruise missiles were no match for the ICBMs. Ballistic missiles proved to be more accurate and reliable than cruise missiles and could evade missile defences while bombers were also far more destructible than ballistic missiles. Those were the times when cruise missiles would follow a steady path and could not carry any active or passive defences along with them. Moreover, an ICBM could reach its target in a few minutes, thereby enhancing its accuracy, while it would take a cruise missile hours to reach the target. However, with time, cruise missiles became more sophisticated. The Tomahawk cruise missiles found greater use during Operations Desert Storm in 1991, Deliberate Force in 1995, and Allied Force in 1999, and many other wars. India's BrahMos supersonic cruise missiles can evade any defence system in the world, thereby posing a great threat to Pakistan and China. In case Pakistan develops a Ballistic Missile Defence (BMD), the BrahMos could be used to destroy its command and control systems and nullify the BMD.[8]

The new missile threats emerging from China comprise not just the threat from ballistic or cruise missiles, but the threat of these ballistic or cruise missiles being developed with counter-measures against ballistic missile defences. With China's new "three attacks three defends" strategy, it has become important to develop stealth aircraft, long range cruise missiles and attack helicopters which would enhance its attacking capability. It also needs to defend from precision strike, electronic warfare, and reconnaissance and surveillance. [9]Chinese missiles pose a threat not only to India, but also to countries in the Asia-Pacific region, especially Taiwan. The Pentagon has been worried about garrisoning of Chinese missiles like the DF-15 and the DF-11 opposite Taiwan in the Nanjing Military Region which includes Jiangsu, Zhejiang, Anhui, Fujian, and Jiangxi provinces.[10] Solid propelled ballistic missiles like the DF-21s and DF-15s could help China evade any ballistic missile defences in the boost phase as they would have a shorter boost phase than liquid propelled missiles. Chinese inter-continental ballistic missiles are less likely to be a threat in the South Asian periphery but a big threat to the US.

Fig 1: Missile Threat Modelling[11]

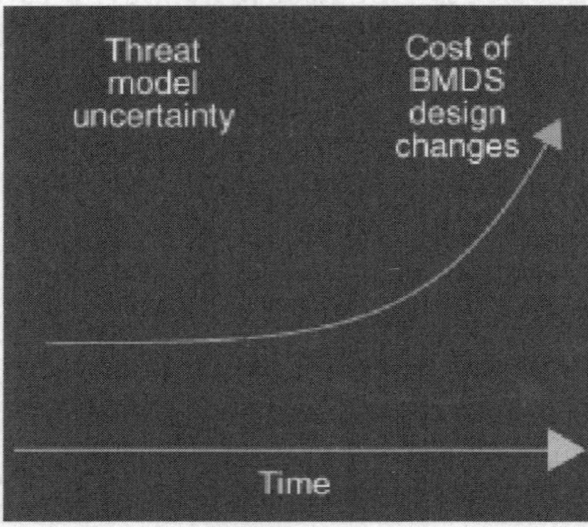

Both missile threats and the missile defence system should sychronise well with the timeline and this remains the biggest threat for missile threat modelling. Sometimes, a missile defence system is developed to counter a threat which has not been developed, tested or deployed. Certain characteristics of missiles could easily be changed and, hence, missile defences have to be built in such a way as to accommodate a range of alternatives in the systems.

Fig 2: Theatre Ballistic Missiles Threat[12]

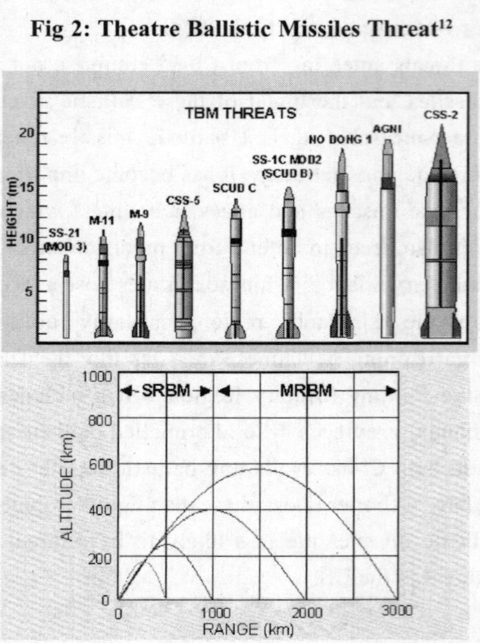

Fig 3: Features Which Make Theatre Ballistic Missiles Threatening[13]

MULTIPLE LAUNCH ROCKETS		
TARGETS	*CAPABILITIES*	*WARHEADS*
• Assembly areas	• High rates of fire	• Ideal for massive ordnance delivery
• Missile defense/artillery locations	• Highly mobile ("shoot and scoot")	• Chemical
• Defensive positions	• Rapid reload	• High explosives
• Troops in the offense	• Area denial	• Bomblets
• Chokepoints/routes of advance	• Low signature/flight trajectory	• Mines

Counter-Measures on Missiles Make Them More Dangerous

Today, there is growing concern about missile defences. These missile defences may be both ballistic missile defences and cruise missile defences. Gen Ronald Kadish, Director of the Ballistic Missile Defence Organisation (BMDO) had warned in the year 2000 that ballistic missile threats emerging from states which pose a threat to international security would increase with their ability to acquire and launch longer range missiles with just simple counter-measures.

While deterrence by denial appears to be a good option, this process can face severe challenges against counter-measures. Counter-measures are designed by ballistic missiles to overwhelm the missile defence and reach its assigned targets. In other words, while there are defensive measures against offence, there are further defensive measures against these defences. Hence, defensive defence has actually become more expensive than offensive defence; rather, 'deterrence by denial' is more of an exorbitant burden on the defence budget than 'deterrence by punishment'. Deterrence by punishment means to inflict punishment on a country in response to an attack. The development of missiles like IRBMs and ICBMs to deliver conventional and nuclear weapons is a clear example of deterrence by punishment. Deterrence by denial means to provide resistance against any attack. States, in their attempt to provide better defence against missile threats, have enabled these missiles, both ballistic or cruise, to pose a greater threat to a territory. Any country which is capable of developing long range ballistic missiles would surely develop counter-measures to make these ballistic missiles more credible.

Biological and chemical warheads could be made into sub-munitions which could be released after the boost phase and make the missile defence more effective. China, for instance, uses biological and chemical warhead sub-munitions. In case nuclear weapons are used, they could be deployed into balloons and then several empty balloons could be released simultaneously. These are called 'anti-simulation balloon decoys'. Liquid fuelled ballistic missiles are now being replaced by solid propelled ballistic missiles in order to overwhelm a ballistic missile defence effectively. Ballistic missiles are now being fitted with decoys to cause confusion between a missile and a decoy. The Agni-I could be fitted with decoys. Missiles could be fitted with electro-magnetic pulse bombs to cause severe destruction. Cruise missiles could be fitted with such bombs and since cruise missiles have the ability to stay unintercepted, these bombs may be used to damage the command and control systems of a country. [14]

Ballistic missiles, like the inter-continental ballistic missiles, have now become more destructive than earlier. With time, the delivery accuracy of these missiles was improved by increasing the values of the ballistic coefficient[15] by using "slightly blunted slender sphere cone geometrics, thus, increasing the impact velocity so that the final descent was less affected by winds."[16]

Multiple Independently Targeted Reentry Vehicles (MIRVs) and Manoeuvrable Advanced Reentry Vehicles (MARVs) on ballistic missiles further make them cataclysmic due to their increased warheads. For instance, the Chinese DF-21s are equipped with MIRVs. The Indian Agni-V is expected to be fitted with MIRVs. Stealth technologies on missiles could help them evade a ballistic missile defence as is the case with the Indian Agni-I. Sometimes, a ballistic missile's trajectory could be depressed in order to enable it to evade a ballistic missile defence as could be the case with Chinese DF-31s. MARVs with global positioning systems could make ballistic missiles more devastating. The Chinese short range ballistic missile, the CSS-5, and the US intermediate range ballistic missiles like the Pershing II, are some examples.

Pakistan's Missile Arsenal: A Case Study

The development of missiles is viewed from a **realist** paradigm in any country, and Pakistan is no exception. In realism, the state is the most important actor, and securing the state becomes the most important task, hence, hard power prowess is necessary to protect the state. Pakistan had always been a realist state, and its foreign policy against India is based on **real politik**—it would not compromise on military modernisation even at the cost of keeping its people hungry.

Robert Jervis has described the **security dilemma** as a situation in which "the means by which a state tries to increase its security, decrease the security of others".[17]In Pakistan's case, India's growing missile technology programme is a direct threat to Pakistan's security. The region of South Asia is anarchic and Jervis states that the "heart of the security dilemma" emanates from the "anarchic contexts of international relations". The security dilemma has another aspect linked with it—the **action-reaction** model. This means that if India acts by enhancing its missile technology capability, Pakistan would react by enhancing its missile capability too. This would lead to an arms race.

However, to maintain the stability-instability equation in the region, it would be best if Pakistan has the same missile capability as India's. This means **missile proliferation** as the state does not have adequate technological knowhow to build up its indigenous missile arsenal. Pakistan was provided the M-11 category surface-to-surface missiles by China. Pakistan is not only acquiring missiles but is exporting some of the versions like the Hong Qings to countries like Sri Lanka and Bangladesh so as to deter India from all sides of the South Asian periphery. Pakistan's strategists have adopted the doctrine of **'offensive defence'** and their missile technology is developed depending on this strategy. It is less likely that Pakistan would be able to build a ballistic missile defence. It is also less likely that it would want to be under the BMD umbrella of any other country. With an offensive defence strategy, Pakistan would want to enhance its offensive capabilities rather than adopt a defensive defence strategy. This could be done by developing counter-measures on its missiles which could negate the credibility of the Indian ballistic missile defence.

Pakistan conducted its nuclear tests immediately after India's nuclear tests in 1998. Its attempt at nuclear capability is to deter aggression and also for the 'defence of sovereignty', but it has announced that its force would follow the principle of 'minimum deterrence'. However, nuclear weapons need delivery systems and missiles are often the best mode for this. Delivery of nuclear weapons and conventional high explosives munitions, with the help of ballistic missiles, is a cost-effective option. Pakistan needed missiles to deliver the nuclear weapons, as aircraft have certain limitations. They cannot deliver nuclear weapons to a greater range and also cannot easily penetrate India's air defence. Hence, it was important for Pakistan to hasten its missile build-up process. The M-11 missile can carry both nuclear and conventional high explosives munitions. Pakistan has also bought No Dong missiles from North Korea which was confirmed by the DCI Nonproliferation Centre in 2000. Pakistan also received the Harpoon missiles from the USA. Imported missiles would be in semi-knocked down or completely knocked down state. The imported missiles, which would be in semi or completely knocked down state, would enable the Pakistanis to enhance their indigenous missile production expertise as it would help them analyse the technical aspects of the missile. It would also help them act rationally in times of conflict.

Pakistan is a state comparatively smaller and weaker than India and suffers from the **small state syndrome**. Therefore, there have always been apprehensions of it being dominated by India at any time. Pakistan has developed ballistic and cruise missiles—it has developed three categories of missile: short range ballistic missiles, medium range ballistic missiles, and intermediate range ballistic missiles. Short and intermediate range ballistic missiles were termed "tactical" and "battlefield" by the Cold War superpowers. Pakistan wants to match up to India's level at any cost. This might be reflected as the **power transition effect,** whereby smaller states want to become powerful like the bigger state around them. Pakistan is a **revisionist state** and, hence, dissatisfied with its small state status and wanting to compete with India in its hard power potency. Pakistan's missile technology would enable it to improve its **composite index of national power** against that of India, though it would adversely affect its **comprehensive national power equation** against India.

Pakistan's quest for missile technology reveals a **domino effect** in the South Asian region. Many might conclude that Pakistan is developing missiles as deterrence against India, which is, on the other hand, developing missiles as **deterrence** against China and Pakistan. However, it could also be concluded that Pakistan now sees Iran as a potential threat as Iran is nuclearising, with assistance from China. This has led Pakistan to develop a sophisticated missile programme to deter Iran and the Central Asian countries. The missiles could also be developed to prevent Afghanistan from influencing the Pashtuns in the region of Pakistan to demand a new Pashtunistan. Thus, there is a **reversed domino effect** in the region, which means that India has to develop its missile technology as it has no other option but to keep up with the pace of Pakistan's missile technology, thereby resulting in an arms race in the region.

Both India and Pakistan could choose to limit the arms race by not increasing their missile arsenals. This could have stopped the arms race and thereby made the region of South Asia less volatile to threats. However, because both the countries are suspicious of each other, they preferred to arm themselves rather than disarm in order to bring stability in the region. This reveals a situation of the **prisoner's dilemma** in the region. One aspect that might be taken into consideration is that since India and Pakistan are both developing countries, the **Pareto efficiency** of building missiles in one country does not make the other worse off to a greater extent.

Third World countries often consider missiles to be the **best option** against conventional weapons. This is because, due to lack of adequate resources to modernise, and the opportunity cost of modernisation, the conventional weapons, especially in India and Pakistan, are of very poor quality. As a result, Pakistan has to defend its forward areas with missiles. 'Missile posturing' in Pakistan is the 'best' way to deter Indian conventional attacks.

Pakistan sees nuclear weapons delivered by missiles as a "vital deterrent to India's much larger conventional forces, and as a necessary counter to India's nuclear program".[18] Pakistan's battlefield short range ballistic missiles include the Hatf-1, Hatf-2, Hatf-2A, Hatf-3 and Hatf-4 missiles. The Hatf-2 or the Abdali poses threats to the Indian military's airfields. The Hatf-1 could be used as an unguided artillery rocket. This could be catastrophic as the Hatf-1 could be nuclear tipped. The Hatf-3 or the Ghaznavi is a threat to airfields, military bases and cities. The warhead could be high explosives, nuclear or sub-munitions. Sub-munitions could act as counter-measures against ballistic missile defences and could also be effective against a military column. The Hatf series could be used for both offensive and defensive purposes. The Hatf-4 or the Shaheen-I can carry both conventional and nuclear warheads and Pakistan is also developing MIRVs thereby nullifying an Indian BMD at the terminal phase. Pakistan's Ghauri-1, Ghauri-2 and Shaheen-2 are capable of providing effective deterrent credibility to Pakistan against India. The Ghauri could be a threat to India's armoured tanks as it has the capability to carry anti-tank warheads. In 1999, in a flight test of the Ghauri-II, "the missile reached the target distance of 1,165 km in 12 minutes".[19] However, Pakistan's ballistic missiles are in a semi-knocked down or completely knocked down state, thereby reducing the chances of an accidental attack on India in times of peace. Pakistan's missile proliferation, for example, proliferation of the Bakhtar Shikan or Hong Ying missile defence systems to Sri Lanka and Bangaldesh further escalates the concerns for India.

Multi-Launch Rocket Systems: The Threat Overlooked?

Today, even artillery has undergone a complete revamp with missiles replacing guns, sometimes for combat. The Multi-Launch Rocket System (MLRS) fires surface-to-surface rockets and the Army Tactical Missile System (ATacMS).[20] These MLRS could be used as ballistic missiles with extended range. These systems can deliver high volumes of fire and a variety of warheads and the high mobile launchers can support effectively forward artillery missions. Due to the mobility and the short burn time of the rocket, it results in "little warning for manoeuvre forces" and the short range "precludes engagement" by the present missile defence systems.[21]MLRS have multiple warhead capabilities, thereby making even limited warfare catastrophic. MLRS are equipped with dual purpose, improved conventional munitions bomblets which further enhance their efficiency. The original MLRS launcher is the M-270 or the self-propelled loader. There are also the M-142 HIMARS (High Mobility Artillery Rocket Systems). These can fire either six rockets or one ATacMS. The unguided M-26 was the first MLRS rocket and is armed with dual purpose improved conventional munitions and was used during Operation Desert Storm in 1991. The Chinese AR3 MLRS is able to fire guided and unguided 300 mm rockets. Low cost autonomous attack sub- munitions have been pursued by the US Army as payloads for the MLRS.[22]

Fig 4: M26, M26A1, M28A1 MLRS Rockets [23]

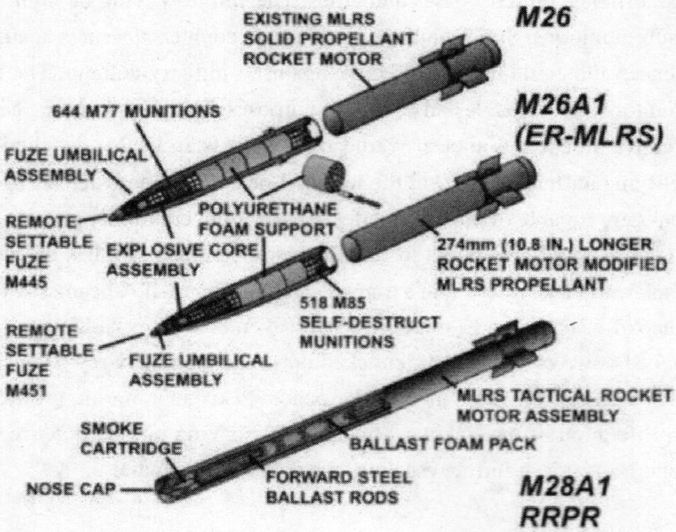

Fig 5: Features Which Make MLRS Threatening[24]

MULTIPLE LAUNCH ROCKETS		
TARGETS	*CAPABILITIES*	*WARHEADS*
• Assembly areas	• High rates of fire	• Ideal for massive ordnance delivery
• Missile defense/artillery locations	• Highly mobile ("shoot and scoot")	• Chemical
• Defensive positions	• Rapid reload	• High explosives
• Troops in the offense	• Area denial	• Bomblets
• Chokepoints/routes of advance	• Low signature/flight trajectory	• Mines

Do Indian Missile Systems Pose a Threat to the World?

India's Prithvi missiles are nuclear tipped short range ballistic missiles. Hence, limited conflicts against Pakistan, for instance, could result in severe destruction. If the Agni-V is inducted and proves to be credible, it would be a serious threat to Pakistan and also China to some extent. With MIRVs fitted on the Agni-V, the devastation caused would be much worse than that caused by a single warhead. India is also making progress in cruise missiles. The BrahMos supersonic cruise missile is the fastest cruise missile in the world. India is also planning to develop this missile. In case the Surya ICBM project becomes a success, it would have serious implications. Any range within 8,000 km would not pose much threat to the West, but a range more than that could make the West suspicious of India's motives. India's PINAKA multi-barrel rocket launcher enabled India to win the Kargil War. India has also concentrated on the Prahar missile which has enabled India to bridge the gap between MLRS and SRBMs.

Conclusion

With emerging security threats to states from non-state asymmetric powers, the big question is: does the Westphalian system formed in 1648 after the Thirty Years of War (1618-48) still exist or is now a 'Westfailure system'? Today, states have crossed the boundaries of their territories to develop relations with other states in order to acquire sophisticated weapon systems. Today, the security dilemma plays a vital role in that sometimes states prefer to befriend even enemy countries in order to be able to acquire credible weapon systems. For example, during the Cold War, the world witnessed a Sino-Soviet split. However, post Cold War, the Sino-Russian relations started to develop again and China acquired technologies and equipment for missiles, nuclear weapons and anti-missiles from Russia. This was one of the factors which enabled Russia to sustain itself economically after the Soviet collapse. Even though Russia kept denying it, it was reported to have sold S-300 surface-to-air missiles to China.

Often states have to depend on other states for missile and nuclear technology due to the comparative cost advantages. This happens mostly in the developing countries where the cost of acquiring these technologies is prohibitive. For instance, Pakistan developed strong ties with China and acquired some of the sophisticated missile systems like the M-9s and the M-11s.

It is a strange phenomenon that in spite of terrorist organisations having easy access to missiles due to their ties with friendly countries, they have never posed a missile threat to any country. It leads us to believe that terrorist organisations do not want to cause collateral damage but wish to create mayhem in the area they choose to attack in order to jeopardise the stability and tranquillity of the area for some time. However, with surface-to-air missiles escaping from military depots in Libya, the threat that these missile could come into the hands of terrorists cannot be negated.

Missiles, whether ballistic or cruise missiles, would pose a threat, and any country could be a threat for that matter. At the same time, every country has the sovereign right to protect itself and enhance its security. If states are referrent objects, its security is the utmost priority for every state.

If analysed carefully, both ballistic and cruise missiles tipped with nuclear weapons could form a credible deterrent and prevent states from entering into a war. South Asia could be the best example for this. Both India and Pakistan have not indulged in any war, not even limited conflicts since the Kargil episode. This is because both countries have acquired nuclear weapons and are enhancing their missile arsenals with sophisticated missile technologies.

The best way to deal with the threat is to keep enhancing arsenals in order to enhance deterrence. This is because it is a known fact, that disarmament would not be an option. Arms control could be an option to reduce missile threats, but not many countries would be willing to go for it. Today, possessing missile and nuclear capabilities enhances a state's hard power prowess and helps it to earn honour in the forum of world politics. However, parity has to be maintained in the missile arms race in order to maintain the stability-instability paradox. In case India acquires the ICBMs. Pakistan too will need to acquire these or else, due to the security dilemma, Pakistan could indulge in a 'first strike'.

Notes

1. Cited in "The Threat", MISSILETHREAT.com.
2. "Ballistic and Cruise Missile Threat", http://www.fas.org/irp/threat/missile/naic/NASIC2009.pdf
3. Henry A. Kissinger mentioned it in an article, "The Rules on Preventive Force: Nuclear Weapons, Terrorism Require Rethinking a Time-Honoured Approach", *The Washington Post,* April 9, 2006.
4. US Senate, Committee on Foreign Relations, The New START Treaty, Treaty doc. III-5 (US Government Printing Office: Washington DC, December 2010),p.87.
5. Amy Zalman, "Surface-to-Air-Missiles", http://terrorism.about.com/od/tacticsandweapons/g/SAMs.htm
6. "Unveiling the Ballistic Missile Threat: The Ramification of the Rumsfeld Report", *National Security Report,* Vol 2, Issue 4, August 1998.
7. "North Korea's Nuclear and Missile Programs", *International Crisis Group,* Asia Report, N 168, June 18, 2009.
8. The author had given similar suggestions in "Counter Measures", *Force,* November, 2011.
9. Dean Cheng, "China's Active Defense Strategy and Its Regional Impact", *The Heritage Foundation,* February 1, 2011.
10. n. 1.
11. Figure taken from John S. McLaughlin, "Ballistic Missile Threat Modelling", http://www.aero.org/publications/crosslink/spring2008/06.html
12. "FM 100-12 Army Theatre Missile Defense Operations", http://www.fas.org/spp/starwars/docops/fm100-12/chap2.htm
13. Ibid.

14. A similar notion was given by me in n. 8.
15. Ballistic Coefficient= Vehicle Weight/ Drag Coefficient^Reference Area Used.
16. John C. Adams, Jr, "Atmospheric Re-entry", 2003, http://exoaviation.webs.com/pdf_files/Atmospheric%20Re-Entry.pdf
17. Robert Jervis, "Cooperation Under the Security Dilemma", *World Politics, 30,* January 4, 1978, pp.167-214.
18. "Foreign Missile Developments and Ballistic Missile Threats Through 2015", *Unclassified Summary of National Intelligence Estimate,* December 2001, http://www.dni.gov/nic/PDF_GIF_otherprod/missilethreat2001.pdf
19. "Pakistan Test Fires Ghauri-II", *The News* (Pakistan), 1999.
20. "MLRS", http://www.army-technology.com/projects/mlrs/
21. "FM 100-12 Army Theatre Missile Defense Operations", http://www.fas.org/spp/starwars/docops/fm100-12/chap2.htm
22. William C.Corkle, Jr., "Future Missile System Trends (US) and Their Impact on Aerodynamic Technology", Paper presented at the RTO AVT Symposium on "Missile Aerodynamics", held in Sorrento, Italy, May 11-14, 1998.
23. "Lockheed Martin (Vought) MLRS Rockets (M26/ M30/ M31)", *Directory of US Military Rockets and Missiles",* http://www.designation-systems.net/dusrm/app4/mlrs.html
24. Ibid.

10

West Asia Today

M. R. Khan

The West Asian region lies at the crossroads of three continents. The Red Sea and the Persian Gulf are the two East-West channels known to mankind since the dawn of history. Historians regard this region as the cradle of civilisation. Three of the world's oldest civilisations, the Mesopotamian, Egyptian and Persian flourished in the region and the fourth one, Indian, was adjacent to it. It is the birthplace of the three Semitic religions practised by more than half of humanity. According to legend, Abraham, the great patriarch of Judaism, Christianity and Islam, was born in the city of Ur in Mesopotamia and later migrated to Palestine. The world's first empires were established here by the Pharaohs of the old Kingdom and by Sargon I of Mesopotamia. It was a vital part of the ancient Silk Route. Because of its geo-political importance, the region was always contested between the great powers of the day since ancient times. The Persians dominated it under the Achaemenids, followed by the Greeks under Alexander the Great. Before the coming of Islam, the Roman and Persian Empires fought for centuries for dominance in the region. The great Arab Empires of the Umayyads and Abbasids of the 8th and 9th centuries, covering nearly 11,000,000 sq km, were established in Damascus and Baghdad. During the Middle Ages, it was the battle ground of the Crusades, and during the colonial period, the European powers like the British, Portuguese, French, Dutch, and Russians jostled with each other and Ottoman Turkey as well as the local powers, to control the area. The British, who came to dominate the Gulf during the 19th and the better part of the 20th century, considered it the key to the security of their South Asian and Southeast Asian possessions and it became a part of the Great Game in their competition with the Russians.

Discovery of oil in the region progressively added to its strategic importance. Oil was first discovered in the Gulf in commercial quantities at Masjid Sulaiman in Iran in 1908, and the following the year, the Anglo-Persian Oil Company was formed to exploit it. Subsequently, oil was discovered in commercial quantities in Iraq in 1927 followed by Saudi Arabia, Bahrain and Kuwait. Though oil was an important issue, in all probability its strategic value was not sufficiently appreciated prior to World War II. The British oil companies felt that they had sufficient oil for their needs, and although they wished to reserve possible deposits for the future, they were unwilling to invest the money needed to develop them. As a result, they surrendered the Saudi Arabian concession to the US in 1933. By the time World War II broke out, aviation had also come of age. Marshal of the Royal Air Force (RAF) Sir Hugh Trenchard, known as the father of the RAF, firmly believed that air power would be the primary policing force in the Middle East. Hence, during the war, there was much better appreciation of the Gulf's significance as an aerial route to India as well as of the role of oil as a strategic commodity.

The post-war years saw the British withdrawal from the subcontinent and the partition of India into two separate countries. But the withdrawal was not seen as reduction in the British interests because London continued to hold possessions in Southeast Asia as well as the Far East, and oil interests in Iraq and Iran, besides its close ally Washington's deep involvement in the Saudi oil. By 1949-50, more than 80 percent of Britain's crude imports came from the Gulf area. A third general motive for the continued British presence in the region was the perceived threat from the southward thrust of the USSR, not only to the British interests but to the well-being of the Western Alliance throughout the world. The defensive concept of the northern tier, the Baghdad Pact and the Central Treaty Organisation (CENTO) could be seen in parts providing a screen for the defence of these interests.

When the British left the Gulf in 1969 after a colonial involvement of nearly 400 years, it was a relatively tranquil place. The newly independent states of Bahrain, Qatar and UAE, along with the older states of Kuwait, Saudi Arabia and Oman, were looking at a bright future thanks to their growing oil revenues. Though it was felt that the British departure may create a geo-political vacuum, London and Washington assessed that the two major powers of the Gulf, the Kingdom of Saudi Arabia and Iran, were close Western allies, and along with Israel, could be depended upon to look after Western interests. The Shah of Iran particularly felt obliged to the Western powers because he had recovered his throne in 1953 through a military coup engineered by the British and American intelligence agencies which overthrew a democratically elected government led by Prime Minister Mohammed Mosadegh and converted a constitutional monarchy into an authoritarian one.

The Cold War Years

The starting point of US interests in the Gulf were the concessions it won from the British for oil extraction in Saudi Arabia with the founding of the Arab-American Oil Company in 1933. The emergence of the state of Israel in 1948 was an addition to these interests, as Washington was committed to its security, albeit the decision was taken after some deliberations. Till the time the British were there, Washington was dependent on them for safeguarding its interests and had only a token presence in the Gulf. By 1970, the oil producing states of the region were providing nearly half the requirements of the Western Alliance and 70 percent those of Japan. The US too had become increasingly dependent on imported oil, particularly from the Gulf. It received its first jolt during the 1973 oil crisis but was powerless to consider any precipitate action due to the lack of tangible military assets in the area and the Vietnam backlash. During the period following the crisis, Washington's dependence on the Gulf oil rose sharply to 25 percent of its total requirement in 1977. Therefore, the primary US interest became maintaining the unimpeded flow of oil from the Gulf to the West and Japan. Any disruption in this flow could have disastrous consequences for the economies of the industrialised nations. The other long-term interest of Washington in the West Asian region as a whole was containment of Communism and restricting the Soviet access to the region.

In 1973, President Nixon signed an agreement with the Shah of Iran under a policy known as the Nixon Doctrine. The doctrine simply stated that in view of the US experience in Vietnam, Washington would now refrain from any direct intervention and would manage its interests through empowerment of its regional allies. Under this agreement, the Shah of Iran was to look after the Western interests in the region whereas Washington would provide the Shah the most sophisticated weapons in its arsenal, other than nuclear. Accordingly, between 1972 and 1978, Tehran ordered arms worth $ 19.5 billion from the US. Also, following the quadrupling of the oil prices in the post 1973 period, the Gulf states acquired great wealth and their imports from the US grew from $3.5 billion in 1973 to $12.5 billion in 1977. While the US accounted for roughly 50 percent of the world's arms exports during this period, the Gulf states accounted for nearly 60 percent of these orders. Therefore, trade with the region, including the lucrative arms trade, became another major US interest which had further significance as it helped Washington balance the huge outgo due to oil imports. As stated earlier, the other close ally of Washington in the region during this period was Saudi Arabia; hence, the policy was also called the "Twin Pillars" policy. The Soviet expulsion from Egypt and the close ally Israel's victory in the Yom Kippur War further helped place the foreign policy mandarins in Washington in a comfort zone.

The Twin Pillars policy served Washington's interests in the region satisfactorily throughout the decade of the Seventies. However, a succession of events towards the end of the decade altered the picture considerably. The first of these events was the Iranian revolution which resulted not only in the loss of a major pillar of the US policy, but also its takeover by a regime implacably hostile to US interests. The hostage crisis and the botched attempt to rescue them further aggravated matters. This was followed by the Soviet invasion of Afghanistan, the invasion of North Yemen by the pro-Soviet South Yemen, and the signing of the Soviet-Ethiopia treaty of friendship. These events created a belief among the US foreign policy planners that Washington's interests in the Gulf and West Asia were being seriously threatened. The thought further gained currency with the increasing presence of the Soviet Navy in the Indian Ocean.

The perception that US interests in the Gulf were threatened led to President Carter stating in his State of the Union address of January 23, 1980, "An attempt by any outside force to gain control of the Persian Gulf region will be regarded as on assault on vital interests of the United States of America, and such an assault will be repelled by any means necessary, including military force."The declaration later came to be referred to as the "Carter Doctrine." At that juncture, Washington had limited military capabilities in the region to translate the doctrine into reality. The same year, a rapid deployment force was created at Tampa, Florida. The hardcore realist Administration of President Reagan happily adopted the doctrine, and by 1983, it had evolved into the US Central Command with earmarked forces totalling 230,000 military personnel drawn from the four Services. The Iran-Iraq War broke out in September 1980. Iraq was backed by all the Arab states of the region, whose rulers were deeply disconcerted by Ayatollah Khomeini's rhetoric of accusing them of being agents of the Western imperialism and anti-Islamic, with an appeal to their citizens to overthrow them. Washington, which was in the process of building up its military capabilities in the region, decided to rely on maintaining a balance of power policy in the region and preventing either of the two warring countries from emerging as a hegemonic power towards the end of the war. The US would do many flip-flops during the destructive eight-year war to fulfill this objective, ultimately intervening actively against Iran towards the closing stages of the war and forcing it to sue for peace.

During the Cold War era, the primary Soviet interest in the region was the security of its Central Asian domain. The Soviets also used the Gulf as a strategic pressure point, in view of its importance to the West, to balance any weakness against the North Atlantic Treaty Organisation (NATO) in Western Europe. After the invasion of Afghanistan in 1979, pacification and maintenance of its pro-Soviet socialist regime became another important Soviet interest, besides its other long-term objectives of spread of

Communism, reduction of Washington's influence in the region, and outlets to the Indian Ocean. Therefore, the USSR had a strong interest in maintaining in power governments in the region which were friendly to Moscow. In addition to the leftist regimes allied to Moscow in Afghanistan, Syria and South Yemen, the Soviets were also interested in preserving the friendly Baathist regime in Iraq. The US failure to resolve the Palestinian problem helped Moscow in achieving its goals, since many Arab states saw Israel as their main enemy and Washington as their closest ally, and Moscow could keep them engaged and dependent on its military hardware and opposed to American foreign policy.

The First Gulf War and the Aftermath

The collapse of the Soviet Union and the emergence of the United States of America as the sole superpower brought to an end the superpower rivalry in West Asia and eased the pressure on American foreign policy in the region despite no solution of the Palestinian problem being in sight. West Asia looked somewhat peaceful and inter-Arab relations seemed to have reached a level of equilibrium. Egypt was back in the Arab fold after a brief period of isolation following its contractual peace with Israel. Iraq, which was instrumental in isolating Cairo in 1978-79, had made up with it, and the two had come together to form a loosely structured Arab bloc against Iran. The bloc also included Saudi Arabia, Jordan, Morocco and the smaller Gulf countries. Egypt was fully reinstated to its former pivotal position in the Arab affairs at the 1989 Casablanca Arab Summit. Syria was the only major country standing apart from Arab blocs such as the Arab Cooperation Council (ACC) and Arab Maghreb Union (AMU), because of its hostility to Iraq due to the split in the Baath Party ruling the two countries and the personal antipathy between the two dictators. This tranquillity was to change with the suddenness typical of the region

Iraq's claim on Kuwait had been an old one, going back to the 1930s when King Ghazi first proffered it. Every successive government in Baghdad had maintained it. The claim was based on the fact that during the Ottoman rule, Kuwait was administered as a district of the *Vilayat* of Basra. A beleaguered Saddam saw annexation of Kuwait as a one-stop solution to all his problems arising out of his futile eight-year war with Iran, and started preparing the ground for it. He demanded that Kuwait repay its \$12billion debt to Iraq. He accused Kuwait of treachery and stealing oil from the Rumailah oil field and demanded a compensation of \$2.4 billion besides immediate lease of the islands of Warbah and Bubian and an enormous unspecified sum as the nucleus of an Arab Marshall Plan to benefit Iraq for all its sacrifices in protecting the Arab nation from the marauding Persians. Kuwait had no option but to reject these egregious demands. The Iraqi President warned Kuwait of dire consequences if it failed to change its treacherous behaviour. He summoned US Ambassador April Glaspie for a controversial meeting and discussed his disagreements with Kuwait and inferred, erroneously, as later events would prove, from that meeting, that if he annexed Kuwait but oil continued to flow, Washington's reaction would be muted. His preparations were now complete.

Kuwait was invaded by Iraq on August 2, 1990. The reaction of the Gulf states was one of shock and disbelief. They were accustomed to the sabre rattling of the Iraqi President but did not believe that he would dare occupy a sovereign fellow Arab state. After several attempts at mediation by Arab states failed, it became clear that Baghdad had no intention of vacating Kuwait. The Arab world split down the middle on the issue. Yemen, the Palestine Liberation Organisation (PLO), Tunisia, Mauritania and Sudan sided with Iraq, Algeria was neutral but closer to the Iraqi position, and the rest of the Arab nations sided with Kuwait and condemned the Iraqi aggression. The Western nations were equally surprised and despite the advance surveillance systems and intensive intelligence network, none of the leaders had definite warning of the invasion. The United States, terming it a serious threat to world peace, called for an emergency meeting of the Security Council within hours of the invasion. The Council rejected the Iraqi contention that it was invited by a group of revolutionaries who had staged a successful *coup d' etat*, and it passed Resolution 660, with the support of 14 members, with only Yemen abstaining, condemning the invasion and demanding Iraq's unconditional and immediate withdrawal.

Washington and the other Western countries saw the invasion as a serious threat to their interests in the region. Control of nearly 20 percent of the world's oil reserves by a mercurial dictator was nothing short of alarming. President Bush I had been active in the oil industry of Texas prior to entering politics and fully appreciated the strategic dimensions of the invasion. He launched a strong diplomatic offensive to rally world opinion against Iraq. The UN Security Council (UNSC) Resolution 661 imposing sanctions, was followed by Resolution 678 under Chapter VII of the UN Charter on November 29, 1990, clearing the way for use of force. Baghdad was given the ultimatum to implement all the Security Council resolutions and vacate Kuwait by January 15, 1991. Washington, having amassed enormous war material and nearly half a million troops, could not afford to give the beleaguered Saddam an escape route and manoeuvred cleverly to ensure that. The war, when it came, was short and decisive. The technological superiority of the Coalition was overwhelming and despite trying every trick in his bag, Saddam's army, prepared for World War II-like encounters was no match for an army equipped for modern war. However, he escaped, with a large part of his military intact, to fight another day.

Despite winning the Gulf War, President Bush I lost the election. The Clinton Administration felt that with Russia marginalised as was evident during the Gulf War, and the United States emerging as the sole superpower, adhering to the balance of power equation in the Gulf was no longer the optimum policy. It was appreciated that both the Gulf powers, Iran as well as Iraq, with their attitude, should be construed as threats to Washington's interests in the region and the US was capable of containing both of them. Accordingly, the new policy unveiled by Martin Indyk was termed "Dual Containment" at the strategic level. The objectives of the policy were spelt out as bringing down the regime in Baghdad and changing the behaviour of the government in Tehran, as at that juncture, bringing down the regime in Tehran was not considered a realistic aim.[1]

The dual containment in respect of Iraq was partially successful in the sense that the UN sponsored sanctions as the foundation, and the US imposition of northern and southern no fly zones over the Iraqi air space, kept the Iraqi President effectively within a box, allowing him little space for manoeuvre. Nevertheless, the objective of toppling the regime, despite several covert attempts and a couple of large scale missile attacks to punish Baghdad, could not be achieved. As regards Iran, the policy was specifically aimed at changing Iran's attitude towards the Arab-Israeli peace process, nuclear proliferation and terrorism. In the absence of UN sponsored sanctions, pressure on Iran was envisaged through engineering an international agreement on constraining trade with Iran. The policy was even less successful in the case of Iran as the American allies in Asia and Europe did not tow the American line, arguing that there was a sizeable reformist lobby within Iran, hence, *détente* and providing Tehran an opportunity to integrate in the international system was likely to be more successful in mellowing Iran's outlook on the aforementioned issues. The negative aspects of the "Dual Containment" were, firstly, that it required a large scale, direct injection of US forces in the region, thereby, increasing the anti-American feeling and giving a flip to extremism in the region; secondly, the drastic reduction in Iraq's and its leader's stature, the disturbed power equilibrium in the region, and, lastly, the imposition of indiscriminate sanctions had resulted in a humanitarian crisis and a great loss of innocent lives.

Another important development in the Gulf during the post Gulf War years was a thaw in Saudi-Iran relations with the restoration of diplomatic ties. In April 1991, Ali Akbar Velayati, the Iranian Foreign Minister, during a visit to Riyadh, met King Fahd and proposed a Gulf Cooperation Council (GCC)-Iran security alliance for peace and amity in the region and pointed out that lack of such an arrangement was the main cause of the Gulf War and the heavy presence of foreign forces in the region, and received some assurance of consideration. The Saudi King, as a gesture of goodwill, agreed to increase the quota of Haj pilgrims from Iran to 115,000 compared to the quota of 40,000 fixed in 1988. The Saudis also agreed to allow 5,000 relatives of those martyred in1987 to visit Mecca. The Iranians, on their part, agreed that their pilgrims now onwards would refrain from any demonstration during the Haj. Velayati's visit was followed by the historic visit of the Saudi Foreign Minister Saud al Faysal to Tehran towards the end of 1991.

The United States Administration looked at these ties with some concern. The main cause of concern was that with the two Gulf rivals coming closer, and Iran under Rafsanjani also improving its relations with the other southern Gulf Kingdoms, the legitimacy of America's heavy military footprint in the region could come into question. Washington, accordingly, made its counter move by offering and concluding bilateral defence cooperation agreements with all the GCC countries in a short time. These agreements included basing facilities, prepositioned material, milcon, interoperability, the legal status of the US forces stationed in the region and an assurance of the US defence umbrella. The aforementioned developments and certain other political events such as Iran's and its allied tribe Hazara's exclusion from the Saudi-US sponsored Afghan power sharing accord in1992-93, and Iran's support to Qatar and offer of troops during a border incident with Saudi Arabia, put the rapprochement process on hold[2]. The rise of sagacious Crown Prince Abdullah as virtual King in 1995 during King Fahd's illness, once again gave an impetus to *détente*. Abdullah appreciated that Rafsanjani needed support to keep the hardliners within Iran at bay. The two countries also cooperated in countering the Al Qaeda, reckoning it to be a common threat. Under the Presidency of Khattami, relations between the two countries warmed further, resulting in the historic visit of the Iranian President to Jeddah and the holy places, followed by the signing of a number of regional and security arrangements on terrorism, money laundering, drug trafficking, and illegal immigration in 2001-02. Overall, relations between Iran and Saudi Arabia throughout this period were marked by a pragmatic approach of accommodation and cooperation, when the interests of the two sides clashed.

Invasion of Iraq and the Change in the Gulf's Balance of Power

When President Bush II took office, the new Administration's foreign policy focus was on evolving a strategy to maintain American global dominance and prevent competition from a future rival such as China, whereas in West Asia, the Clinton Administration's policy of dual containment was continued. The events of 9/11 changed the picture entirely, bringing the West Asian region once again into focus. The Bush II Administration also consisted of a group of foreign policy exponents, prominent among them Donald Rumsfeld, Paul Wolfowitz, John Bolton, I. Lewis (Sooter) Libby, Douglas Feith and Richard Perle, collectively known as "neoconservatives". The Vice President was also an active member of the group. Some of them came from Jewish think-tanks and were strongly pro-Israel, with emphasis on the Middle East. They advocated use of overwhelming US hard power to shape the world security environment to America's advantage and talked of a change of regime in Iraq as an imperative for a stable West Asia.[3] Rattled by 9/11, Bush was now prepared to shift priority as the neoconservatives envisaged and, accordingly, the 2002 National Security Strategy document called for "full spectrum dominance" and the strategy of dealing with resistance to American hegemony by preventive wars[4] and unilateralism, with the maxim that those not with us in the war on terrorism are against us, instead of the traditional method of containment.

The neoconservative ideas found further currency in the press and media through the writings and talks of such scribes as Robert Kagan, William Kristol, Charles Krauthammer and some others. A case against Iraq's possession of Weapons of Mass Destruction (WMD) was built up with the help of the Central Intelligence Agency (CIA) and the other intelligence agencies feeding some manipulated intelligence, despite overwhelming evidence to the contrary to a neutral observer, and the public opinion mobilised within the US in favour of an invasion of Iraq. Iraq was invaded in March 2003, in the face of heavy international opposition and despite a frightened Saddam repeatedly offering unhindered and complete access to the suspected sites of WMD. The Iraqi Army, crippled by years of sanctions, and along with it the Baathist regime, collapsed quickly.

Swayed by the neoconservative ideas, Washington's planners, when deciding to invade Iraq, ignored many other long-held strategic considerations, such as Saudi apprehensions about the rise of Shia power and Turkish concerns about the emergence of the virtually autonomous Kurdish north Iraq, adjacent to their own restive Kurdish region. It was appreciated that while the removal of the only strategic counter-weight to Iranian primacy might disturb the balance of power in the Gulf, it was reasoned that the awesome demonstration of the US military power and the swift end of Saddam would frighten Iran into accepting Washington's hegemony and stop resisting its policies. The assumption proved right for a while as Iran cooperated on Afghanistan, abandoned its quest for nuclear weapons in 2003, according to the US intelligence estimates, and, in the same year, sent a number of signals through track-two channels for a comprehensive settlement of all outstanding problems with Washington. But it quickly changed its stance when it perceived that the American occupation forces were losing control and it observed the mayhem and chaos prevailing in Iraq. Tehran now saw the Iraqi situation as a god sent opportunity to consolidate its position by backing anti-US Shiite groups.

The rise of Shia power in Iraq awakened and inspired a Shia revival throughout the region, but more specifically in countries with a sizeable Shia population like Bahrain, Kuwait, Saudi Arabia, Yemen and Lebanon. The enhancement of the Shia aspirations in the GCC countries added to their domestic problems and their ruling elite's sense of insecurity, forcing them to back the militant Sunni groups, and, according to some reports, even Al Qaida in Iraq, ostensibly to balance Tehran's support to the Shia groups. Iran's close relations with Syria where a minority Shia faction, the Alawites, are in control, and its considerable influence with the Lebanese Shia group, the Hezbollah, have further added to the Iranian aura and talk of a Shia crescent running across the region, much to the discomfiture of the Saudi regime.

In the final analysis, Iran, no doubt, has benefited the most in strategic terms from the invasion of Iraq and its profile in the region has been greatly enhanced. Virtually every Shia leader in Iraq has an Iranian connection, as is evident from Baghdad's support to the Iranian policy in Syria, Lebanon, and, to some extent, even in Bahrain and Palestine. This should have been apparent to Washington as the Shia Islamic sect, known as believers in the twelve imams (*Asna Ashris*) has many cult-like features and the hierarchic structure and jurisdiction of its clergy extends beyond national boundaries which makes religious ties more important than even ethnic considerations. The other beneficiary of the destruction of Iraqi military power is Israel, as was intended by the neoconservatives, since Tel Aviv's most implacable and militarily powerful Arab foe and a constant source of contiguous threat, has been liquidated, at least for the foreseeable future.

The Arab Spring and its Impact

The Arab Spring has been compared to an internal catharsis of the Islamic countries, long victims of political oppression, rampant corruption, cronyism and bad governance. For the last several decades, many of these countries in North Africa and West Asia have been ruled by the strongmen and dictators who elicited support from the Western countries on the pretext that they were the only ones with secular credentials and their weakening or fall would inevitably result in the adherents of political Islam, fundamentally hostile to Western interests, taking over and usurping political power. The ruse had worked and they had continued to stay in power through money, strong-arm tactics and political repression through their secret police, collectively known as *Mokhberat*, sometimes holding, and rigging, elections to satisfy the call for democracy in some Western capitals.

The example of the Iranian revolution further frightened even liberals in the West in favour of the status quo despite the lip-service often paid to the cause of democracy. The incident in the Tunisian town of Side Bouzid provided the spark for the simmering discontent of years to explode. Modern media and communications made mobilisation, especially among the media savvy, frustrated large young population of educated unemployed, a product of the demographic explosion of the last several decades, easy. Egypt followed Tunisia, and within days, the unrest had spread to Morocco, Yemen, Bahrain, Libya, Jordan and Syria. Even Saudi Arabia did not appear entirely safe, especially with the rumblings in the oil rich, Shia dominated, restive east. It was only with massive largesse and political concessions that King Abdullah could ward off the trouble for the time being. Similarly, the rulers of the other GCC countries, sensing that the long standing demands of their people for greater freedom and participation in national decision-making could surface with irrepressible force, hastily announced unprecedented concessions and entitlements and pacified the discontent, once again, it appears, for the time being.

Bahrain, however, could not be pacified because of the fundamental problem of a Sunni minority ruling a Shia majority, that has been virtually excluded from the political and military echelons of power. Despite the use of force by King Hamad bin Isa Al Khalifa, supported by the heavy influx of forces from the neighbouring monarchy of Saudi Arabia and considerable casualties, Bahrain continues to simmer. The response of the Western bloc that actively intervened in Libya and is openly supporting rebels in Syria, has been muted in the case of Bahrain in a similar situation, and for obvious reasons. Nevertheless, it appears, that the situation in Bahrain will continue to be unstable unless better sense prevails and long overdue reforms, correcting the widespread discrimination against the Shias, are implemented. Diversionary tactics of putting the blame on Tehran are unlikely to work.

The revolutionary changes of the Arab Spring were not so much inspired by the Islamist as they took advantage of the fact that they were the only organised opposition in many of these countries, overt or covert, since the secular opposition was not allowed to develop and prosper, whereas the Islamists, driven by ideological zeal, were prepared to brave the club. Therefore, in virtually every Arab country where a regime change has taken place, or is in the process, the trend is towards Islamism. In Tunis, the *Ennahda* is the majority faction, in Egypt, the *Ikhwan* and the *Salafis* are in complete control, in Libya, the situation is still fluid but in the interim General National Congress elected in August 2012, the Islamist group, the Justice and Construction Party, is evenly matched with the nationalist group and the general opinion appears to be in favour of anchoring the new Constitution in the principles of the *Sharia*. In Yemen, the Islamic Islah Party is the dominant political force, and even in relatively modern Syria, the main opposition to Bashar-al-Assad's regime, the Syrian National Council, is led by the Syrian Muslim

Brotherhood. Also, in monarchies like Jordan and Morocco, where the rulers have been forced to introduce political reforms towards constitutional monarchies, the leading parties in the Parliaments forming the coalition governments are Islamic.

These developments are causing some nervousness among the Western powers as well as secular liberals in the Arab world itself. The apprehension is that the Islamists, once entrenched, may dispense with democratic process and put in place quasi-fascistic regimes perpetually antagonistic to the Western interests. These fears seem to be exaggerated. The mainstream Islamic parties in each and every country affected by the Arab Spring have vowed to continue with democracy and are increasingly modelling themselves on the Turkish pattern and these include *Ennahda*, as well as the Muslim Brotherhood, the parties which were once seen as *Salafist.* Time and again, the recent polls, in virtually every Muslim country, have shown that an overwhelming majority favours moderate Islamic practices, with emphasis on economic progress and material well-being—a phenomenon also referred to as "Post Islamism." This kind of public opinion pressure for development and economic gains would leave no choice for even Islamist regimes but to seek accommodation in international institutions and the existing world order, and that can only be achieved by adhering to the accepted norms and the rules of business. The mainstream Islamists also emphasise that they would uphold women's rights within a liberal interpretation of Islamic tenets, as well as the rights of religious and ethnic minorities.

But, perhaps, it is in strategic terms that the greatest impact of Islam leaning regimes coming to power in the aftermath of the Arab Spring is likely to be felt. The new democratically elected governments in all these countries are likely to be far more responsive in their foreign policy to public opinion, which is often anti-American and invariably anti-Israel. Washington may no longer be able to pursue with ease its traditional security concerns of peace with Israel on uneven terms or of isolating Iran. The Iran-Egypt relations are already warming despite some glitches such as Egypt's dependence on Washington's financial assistance, conflicting views on the Syrian crisis and the *Salafists'* attitude to the Shias. The restoration of diplomatic ties appears only a matter of time. Similarly, the new incoming regimes in Syria and Yemen may be far more strident in their anti-Israel stance and covert assistance to the militant factions of Palestine, than the existing one. Though the post Assad regime in Syria will certainly be a Sunni dominated one, Tehran may not be as much of a loser as is being assumed. That is because its proxy, the Hezbollah, despite the generally prevailing anti-Shia sentiments, evokes great sympathy in the Arab street due to its good showing in the Lebanon War against Israel, which restored some Arab pride, after successive routs in the earlier wars.

Thus, the incoming regime may still make common cause with Tehran as far as support to the Hezbollah is concerned.

The Washington-Riyadh partnership of several decades has also come under strain due to developments in the wake of the Arab Spring. The Saudis were greatly upset by Washington's attitude to uprisings in Egypt and Bahrain and perceived it as an unreliable partner. For a short while, they thought of hitching their bandwagon with the Russians and the Chinese. However, developments in Syria, where the Russians and Saudis found themselves on opposite sides, have resulted in strained relations, though the long-term interests of the two have a fair measure of convergence. With the US consumption of oil flattening and its domestic production on an upward curve, with predictions of self-sufficiency in a few years, the Saudis are increasingly looking at China and, to some extent, India, as their premier customers. Particularly important is the fact that the new refineries coming up in China as well as India can easily accept the Saudi heavy crude which otherwise has few takers in the developed world. The Saudis, rattled by the events of the Arab Spring, are, increasingly, more comfortable in forging relations with Beijing or even Moscow, as unlike Washington, democracy, human right issues and gender equality, etc. which make the autocratic Saudi Royals extremely uncomfortable, are not on the Chinese agenda.

All in all, Islamist regimes are likely to have their own foreign policy agenda which will be based far more on Islamic solidarity to cater to their constituency, though for economic reasons, the United States would continue to have leverage in the region but ties are likely to be more formal, and US military and political influence would wane considerably. Another reason why Washington has lost ground in West Asia is an increasing perception among the Arab countries that its ability to influence the Israeli-Palestinian peace process, the most important issue of the region, has virtually become zero, due to the intransigence of the present Israeli regime. The United States would increasingly rely on its soft power, such as the craze for fluency in English and the internet, the proclivity of the youth to ape American culture even in the Islamic countries, and education and technology, to maintain a semblance of its earlier influence. Another tool Washington is likely to use to maintain political leverage is military assistance and the sale of military hardware, especially in the GCC countries.[5]

Iran and the Nuclear Issue

Iran is the 17th largest country in the world and the 16th most populous. Its area of 1,648,000 sq km is second only to Saudi Arabia, but its population is two and a half times that of the desert Kingdom. Its southern border is formed by the 1,770-km coastline virtually covering the entire Persian Gulf northern littoral and of the Gulf of Oman. Iran is also one of the great ancient civilisations and through much of recorded history, it has been a dominant power of West and Central Asia, as well as its cultural hub. It has considerable influence in the Central Asian countries and western Afghanistan as much of this region was a part of the Saffavid Empire, in the not too distant past, and Persian is a widely spoken language in the area. It is a centre of Shia learning, and the influence of its clergy, which is now also its ruling elite, extends to every part of the Muslim world with a sizeable Shia population. In the modern era, its hydrocarbon proven reserves, that is, oil and gas taken together, in Barrels of Oil Equivalent (BOE), are only second to Saudi Arabia's. Iran's strategic importance is further enhanced by the fact that the only seaward access to the Central Asian region, considered an important hub of strategic minerals and industrial raw materials, is through its territory. Hence, it is not surprising that its national aspirations are to become the prime regional power. The invasion of Iraq and the elimination of Tehran's only possible rival for primacy in the region have further strengthened these aspirations.

This primacy was easily conceded to it by the Western powers and more specifically the United States during the Shah's regime, after the British departure in 1969, as mentioned earlier. The situation changed completely after the 1979 revolution. The genesis of the present poor US-Iran relations and the resultant instability lies in Washington's support to the erstwhile oppressive regime of the Shah and its subversion of the secular democratic regime of Prime Minister Mosadegh in 1953 to bring back the ousted Shah through a CIA and British intelligence engineered coup. Ayatullah Roohullah Khomeini, the leader of the Iranian revolution, was an implacable foe of America and branded it as the Great Satan and the cause of all ills in the world. President Bush II returned the compliment, calling Iran a member of the Axis of Evil. Despite sporadic attempts at thaw, under, by Iranian standards, the liberal regimes of Rafsanjani and Khattami, the relations have remained strained mainly due to the Iranian hostility towards Israel and the mutual distrust.

The US stand is that Iran is a threat to the stability of the region because of its alleged quest of nuclear weapons, its support to the terrorist outfit Hezbollah in Lebanon, and the Hamas and Islamic Jehad in Palestine, and its opposition to the US sponsored Arab-Israel peace process as well as its threatening attitude towards Israel. However, in the last decades or so, Iran's alleged quest for nuclear weapons has become the main bone of contention between the two nations. Several rounds of US and European sponsored UN sanctions have been imposed on Iran, asking it to stop all uranium enrichment and open up its entire nuclear establishment to more intrusive inspections by the UN watchdog

International Atomic Energy Agency (IAEA). Particularly crippling have been unilateral sanctions by the Obama Administration in 2011, later endorsed by the European Union.

Ali Khamenei, Iran's supreme leader and the real power centre of the clerical regime, who further consolidated his position when his group captured a majority of seats in the Iranian Parliamentary elections of March 2012, is convinced that Washington's real aim is to bring down the regime, and the nuclear issue is an excuse to humiliate Iran and deny it its rightful place in the comity of nations by preventing it progressing in peaceful use of nuclear energy. This view is further strengthened by the IAEA being unable to furnish any conclusive proof of Iran's intentions of making a nuclear weapon, except pointing out some technical violations of the Nuclear Non-Proliferation Treaty (NPT) of which Iran is a signatory, and pointing a finger of suspicion at Tehran due to its acquisition of some dual use technologies. Washington ignores even its own National Intelligence Estimate's reports which have consistently maintained that they have found no evidence to assume that Iran has resumed its quest for atomic weapons after abandoning it in 2003.

Israel's strident and aggressive attitude which it partly attributes to Iran's conservative President Ahmedinejad's bellicose pronouncements, has further complicated the geo-political situation. Israel insists that Iran's uranium enrichment of 20 percent, which Iran maintains is for its medical purposes Tehran reactor, is an existential threat since it brings Iran a step closer to the highly enriched weapon grade uranium. Tel Aviv is threatening unilateral military action if Iran is not stopped, especially the activities in its Furdow plant which is located deep in the mountains and is considered relatively secure, as it is difficult to access. As of November 2012, several rounds of talks between Iran and the P5+1 (the five permanent members of the UNSC and Germany) have taken place without any tangible results. The Western powers insist that Iran must stop all enrichment, ship out uranium enriched to 20 percent, a stockpile estimated at 200 kg, to a safe country, and shut down the Furdow plant. In return, they promise to supply fuel for its medical purposes reactor, help in nuclear safety, and provide spare parts for its civilian airliner currently under sanctions. Tehran, on its part, has demanded that all sanctions be lifted first and then it will stop further enrichment to 20 percent except as required for the medical reactor.

Apparently the talks have been futile because both sides have refused to come down from the maximum. But the sanctions are biting, and as a result, Iran's economy, which has not been in good shape for a long time, has deteriorated dramatically over the last year. Its currency has lost two-third of its value, causing demonstrations in the bazaars and raid on money changers. Despite the pressure from Israel, Washington has desisted from resorting to military action to prevent Iran from achieving suspected nuclear weapon capability, fearing a larger conflict, huge escalation in oil prices and certain disruption of its supplies, as well as further adverse effects on the world economy, which is already in the throes of stagnation. President Obama , who has been reelected, knows that the public opinion has no stomach for military intervention after the Iraq experience and the endless war in Afghanistan. Israeli Prime Minister Netanyahu has often threatened unilateral military action, but in September 2012, he relented saying that the latest intelligence reports indicate that till the spring of 2013, Iran is unlikely to have weapon grade uranium even for a single bomb and, hence, Israel can wait for the issue to be resolved diplomatically. But he continues to maintain that Israel would do everything in its power to prevent Iran reaching the break-out stage, including unilateral action to destroy its nuclear establishment.

One adverse effect of tension in the Gulf region is the prevailing high prices of oil despite the slowdown in the world economy, including that of the two Asian giants, China and India. Experts opine that 15-20 percent of this may be risk premium because of the prevailing conditions, and the fear of a flare-up at short notice or unexpectedly. At the time of writing of this article, a ray of hope is that during the last phase of the Presidential debate, President Obama expressed willingness to engage in direct talks with Iran to resolve the nuclear issue. On the other hand, Iran as well as the six global powers, have also indicated that the two sides are prepared to come down from the maximum positions they have taken in all the previous talks, to reach a settlement.[6] A reformulated proposal from the six powers will offer relief from the existing sanctions and some other incentives in a gradual manner, as Iran would concede to the key Western demands in a step by step manner, as a way out to overcome the mutual distrust which has ruined the previous talks. However, much will depend on how the supreme leader perceives the internal situation in Iran and the emerging equations in its domestic politics and makes concessions, as well as on Washington's willingness to gradually lift sanctions while Iran complies with the demands of the Western powers. The clerical regime is well entrenched in Iran by virtue of its grassroots support, especially in rural Iran, and a strong grip over the religiously inspired military cadres of the Iranian Revolutionary Guards Corps (IRGC) and the large quasi-military Basij militia. Hence, there appears to be little chance of an 'Arab Spring' like development in Iran in the immediate future.

Situation in Syria

Syria is extremely diverse in its religious and ethnic composition. Though a vast majority of its habitants are Muslim Arabs of the Sunni and Shia Alawite faith, it is also home to Kurds, Armenians, Assyrians, Christians and Druze. During the post World War II period, the main political movement, after independence from the French colonial rule, was pan-Arab nationalism. In 1963, the quasi-fascist party, Al Baath, based on the same ideology, took over power and has ruled Syria ever since. However, after a period of instability and some quick regime changes, Hafiz Al-Assad took firm control through a military coup in 1970 and ruled the country over three decades with an iron hand. His rule was one the most oppressive and brutal even by Arab standards. Tens of thousands are estimated to have been killed by him in suppressing a rebellion by the Muslim Brotherhood in the city of Hama in 1982. He also took advantage of the civil war in neighbouring Lebanon to extend Syrian political control over that country. Syria left Lebanon only in 2005 under international pressure.

When Hafiz died in 2000, his son Bashar al-Assad took over as the President in a smooth transition and has remained so since, through several sham elections. His rule too has been equally oppressive except for some cosmetic changes. The ruling elite and the military forces cadres are dominated by the Alawite Shias who comprise only 10-11 percent, while nearly 72 percent of the population is Sunni and is poorly represented in the echelons of power. In that sense, it is an unnatural and unjust regime. The father and son managed to remain in power through a complex web of concessions, incentives tied to loyalty, and brutal suppression of opposition. However, this equilibrium was disturbed in the wake of the Arab Spring and after peaceful demonstrations demanding democratic changes were violently dealt with, a widespread rebellion broke out in March 2011. A civil war has raged since then and more than 30,000 people are estimated to have died in the confrontation. The main opposition, consisting of several groups, is the Syrian National Council (SNC), led by the Syrian Muslim Brotherhood whose leadership is located in neighbouring Turkey. The armed group fighting the government forces is the Free Syrian Army which mainly consists of army deserters, volunteers of the Muslim Brotherhood, and a host of Sunni extremist factions, including Al Qaeda.

Oblivious of the human suffering, Syria has become a chessboard of geo-political competition for a number of powers whose interests are involved. Turkey, Saudi Arabia, Qatar, and members of the Arab League, including Egypt, are supporting the rebel groups primarily because these countries together form a Sunni club with a strong influence of Islamism. The Syrian regime is dominated by the Alawites who are an extreme faction of the Shias. Hence, not only is public opinion in these countries against the regime and sympathetic to the mainly Sunni rebels, but in view of the fact that the present regime is a close ally of Iran, the main Shia power, its fall would be considered by these governments as the key to containing Iran and with it, the increasing Shia influence in the region. Erdogan, the Prime Minister of Turkey and the leader of its ruling party, not only knows that his constituency of Anatolia strongly supports the rebels, but also calculates that the fall of the Assad regime will be a geo-political gain for Turkey because the next regime is bound to be strongly pro-Turkey, and might even prove a help in resolving its long standing Kurdish problem as well as cutting to size the troublesome Alawite minority of Turkey. Therefore, Ankara has provided the rebels every conceivable help except heavy weapons, that also because doing so may bring about a direct confrontation with the Syrian Army, which the Turkish armed forces are opposed to.

Iran, on the other hand, is hell-bent on supporting the Bashar regime because Syria, besides being a Shia dominated regime, has been Tehran's closest ally for decades and the main conduit in supplying arms to its proxy, the Hezbollah, in Lebanon, and other extremist groups in Palestine. Washington and its European allies and increasingly even Israel, which in the early part of the civil war was ambivalent, calculating that a known devil is better than an unknown one (a regime possibly led by the Muslim Brotherhood), are backing the rebels on the calculus that the fall of Assad will be a severe blow to Iran and would strangulate the Hezbollah, both considered prime threats to Western interests in the region. Washington believes that even if the Muslim Brotherhood comes to power in Syria, it would be easier to manage, from their experience in Lebanon and now in Egypt, compared to the Assad regime. Russia, along with China, strongly supports the Assad regime because its only Mediterranean naval base at Tartus is on the Syrian coast, besides it has been the major supplier of arms to Syria throughout the regime's life. Russia also has large commercial interest in Syria running into billions of dollars, and thousands of Russians were working in the country prior to the outbreak of the civil war. Russia and China also fear that the Islamists and the Western powers, emboldened by the success in the Levant, may attempt to destabilise the Central Asian region next door, where similar unpopular and oppressive regimes, but friendly towards Russia and China, are in power.

The current situation in Syria, at the time of writing of this article, is that after nearly 20 months of fighting, neither side appears likely to win in the near future. Rebels control roughly half the country's area and are especially strong in rural areas. There are daily reports of massacres, including those of women and children which the two sides blame on each other. Government forces have been brutal in their use of heavy weapons and air power against civilian targets, claiming that the rebels are sheltering there. The international clamour for intervention, or imposition of 'no fly zones', safe havens and safety corridors to restrain the government forces, or at least imposing crippling and compelling sanctions, is growing louder as the Arab and Western media are constantly highlighting the humanitarian dimension of the problem in a tendentious manner.

Washington and the European powers, plagued by economic woes and intervention fatigue, are wary of any deeper military involvement, and have insisted that they are providing only non-lethal aid. Russia and China, on the other hand, are determined to veto any meaningful measures by the UNSC to put pressure on the Assad regime. The two UN envoys, Kofi Annan earlier and now Lakhdar Brahimi, have failed in mediating between the two sides or even enforcing a meaningful ceasefire. The Syrian opposition, mainly consisting of the Syrian National Council (SNC) is a house divided and its leadership primarily consists of exiles who have not been in Syria for years and, therefore, there has been a disconnect between them and the fighters on the ground.[7] The opposition is also criticised for not being representative enough as it has failed to attract minorities like the Alawites, Kurds and Christians in adequate numbers.

The United States has maintained that their red line in the Syrian conflict is if the risk of Damascus' supposedly large stockpile of chemical weapons falling into the extremist hands, or its use by the regime, becomes imminent. However, in the long run, survival of the present regime in Damascus or its regaining the lost ground appears extremely suspect but the key figures of the regime, as and when it is toppled, retiring into safe hilly havens along the Mediterranean coast of Syria, which is largely inhabited by the Alawite minority to which Bashar belongs, and a prolonged civil war, is a possibility. Similarly, the longer the conflict goes on, the greater is the possibility of it spilling over to the neighbouring Lebanon and Turkey, or even Iraq, and the bloody retribution between the parties involved in the aftermath.

Libya and Yemen

The countries affected by the Arab Spring broadly fall under two categories. Those where political institutions were well established but were subverted by the authoritarian rulers to maintain themselves in power, and those where the very first regime after the power transfer from a monarchy or the colonial rulers happened to be an authoritarian one and did not allow them to be developed. Libya and Yemen fall under the latter category. Col. Gaddafi ruled Libya over four decades and ensured that no political institutions were allowed to develop. When his regime fell in October 2011, the country was left in a political and security vacuum. Hundreds of armed groups, which were formed during the uprising, continue to function in the form of militias even today and are a cause of near anarchy prevailing in the country.

The good news coming from Libya is that the results of the election to its National Congress held in July 2012 have broken the pattern of an Islamic wave and the centrist National Forces Alliance led by an American educated political scientist Mahmoud Jibril, has won 40 seats out of the 80 available for party affiliations. Another 120 seats were open only to independent candidates, many of whom have joined the coalition government led by an associate of Mr. Jibril, Mohammed al Magarief, as according to an agreement signed when he held the reins of the interim government, Jibril cannot hold any office in the present one. Jibril comes from the most populous Libyan tribe, the Warfalla, and besides the ideology, this may also have contributed to his victory, as loyalty to the tribe still runs high in Libyan society. This government has been formed for a limited period of 18 months during which it will supervise preparation of a Constitution. At the end of 18 months, another election is scheduled to be held to form a government for a tenure which would be prescribed in the Constitution itself.

The interim government of Magarief coopted many of the militias ostensibly under the Ministry of Defence to maintain law and order as Gaddafi's army and the police had been disbanded, but the ministry has found it difficult to exercise jurisdiction over them and enforce discipline. Their leaders whimsically obey or disobey the ministerial directives, in accordance with their own interests. Matters came to a head when one of them, the Islamist Ansar al Sharia, in association with Al Qaeda, was suspected of a hand in the assassination of the American envoy and the attack on the American Consulate in Benghazi in September 2012. In the aftermath of the Benghazi attack, the people, already fed up with the arbitrary and high-handed ways of the militias, came out on the streets and started attacking them, and several died in the clashes. Magarief has ordered disbanding and disarming of all the militias, authorised as well as unauthorised, and asked them to vacate the government buildings that most of them have been occupying. It remains to be seen if this can be accomplished as the previous interim government had failed in its several attempts to rein in the militias. Concomitantly, the government is also using the militias to fight forces loyal to the previous regime in pockets such as Bani Walid, Gaddafi's home town. All in all, the situation in Libya continues to be unstable but despite that, the Western countries appear to be satisfied as a friendly regime is in place, oil continues to flow, and the Western oil companies are busy digging new oil wells to meet the target of the two million barrels per day (mbpd) production by 2013, to compensate for the Iranian oil.

Yemen, located at the southwest end of the Arabian Peninsula, is an ancient civilisation with a special place in Semitic folklore. To the early Europeans, it was the land of spices and frankincense and acted as a connecting link with the markets of India and Somalia. The ancient Arabs believed that it was the place of their origin. In modern times, British occupied its southern part and the port of Aden, because of its importance as a choke point of the Indian Ocean located at the Bab al Mandab. With the opening of the Suez Canal, its importance was further enhanced. Despite its meagre oil reserves, it remains an important country because of its location at the crossroads of the oil trade. South Yemen turned Communist in1970 after the British departure, while the North had a republican structure. The two parts formally merged together in 1990 to form one united country. However, a civil war broke out in 1994 between the two which was won by the North. Yemen's social structure continues to be tribal in nature and loyalty to the tribe takes precedence. The unequal treatment in allocation of resources to the southern part by the Sana'a based government has encouraged fissiparous tendencies and separatist movements, keeping the South in constant turmoil.

Another constant problem in Yemen is the conflict between the Zaidi Shia insurgent Houthi tribes inhabiting the North and the majority Sunnis controlling the central government. The autocratic government of President Ali Abdullah Saleh ruled Yemen for three decades through strong-arm tactics and manipulation of tribal equations. In the wake of the Arab Spring, a widespread rebellion broke out in 2011 against his rule, plagued by cronyism, widespread corruption, and political oppression. The rebellion initially started as a protest against unemployment and economic hardships but soon turned into a unanimous demand for Saleh to step down. Hundreds died in street fighting between the security forces and the demonstrators. After several times going back on his promises, Saleh finally stepped down in February 2012, after he was severely injured in a bomb attack, under an agreement mediated by the GCC heads of states. His Vice President Abdrabbuh Mansour Hadi, has taken over as President.

Though Abdullah Saleh has left, his close family continues to remain in powerful positions in the government and the security forces, constraining Hadi's freedom of action. Taking advantage of the chaotic conditions prevailing in the country, the Al Qaeda affiliates, Al Qaeda in Arabian Peninsula (AQAP) and Ansar al Sharia have entrenched themselves in the country and continue to remain active despite large scale Saudi operations against them and the frequent drone attacks by the Americans which have eliminated their prominent leaders. The weak central government has allowed many tribal leaders to run parts of the country as their fiefdom and the society is so highly weaponised that establishing any kind of order is difficult. These conditions are aggravated by the widespread poverty and very gloomy economic situation, making the outlook in Yemen highly unstable.

Palestinian Problem

No essay on West Asia can be complete without touching upon its most destabilising factor, the perennial "Palestinian Problem." The injustice done to the Palestinians by the colonial powers and an almost irrational and strategically imprudent US support to even the most oppressive Israeli policies in the occupied territories, is the most emotive issue not only among the Arabs but across the Muslim world. It is a major cause of Muslim extremism and the anti-American feeling among the Muslim masses. Mr. Netanyahu's rightist government has further aggravated the situation with its refusal to stop the building activity in the West Bank as well as East Jerusalem, scuttling any chances of a peace process and encouraging the belief in some quarters that the real Israeli objective is a greater Israel by converting the West Bank into Bantustan, leaving virtually no contiguous territory to the Palestinians for a separate state.

The original Palestine was a small territory of 26,890 sq km. When the state of Israel declared its independence in 1948, its area consisted of 20,770 sq km carved out of the original Palestine, which was nearly 80 percent of the land, leaving a small area of 6,120 sq km for the Palestinians. After the first Arab-Israeli War, Israel occupied the West Bank of the river Jordan, the entire Jerusalem and the Gaza Strip and started building settlements on the occupied territory despite strong objections from the Arabs as well as the international community. Israel found the settlements on the Gaza Strip unsustainable and vacated these in 2005. But it continues to build Jewish settlements on the West Bank and in East Jerusalem, further squeezing the meagre land left for 3.5 million Palestinians[8], and that also not contiguous and littered with numerous barriers manned by the Israeli security forces, severely restricting the freedom of movement for the Palestinians. In the light of Israel's stubborn refusal to halt the building of new settlements, ignoring even Washington's pleas to do so, and strong public sentiments on the issue, it has become impossible for the Palestine Liberation Organisation (PLO) to proceed with any meaningful peace process. The prevailing sense of despondency among the Palestinians on the futility of the peace process which cannot prevent relentless encroachment of their already congested and barrier ridden habitat, and excesses by the Israeli security forces, are encouraging support for the extremist factions like the Hamas and Islamic Jehad.

Washington's ability to influence the peace process has virtually become nil due to the compulsions of its domestic politics and the emboldened intransigence of Netanyahu. Not only that, the Americans have failed to put pressure on Netanyahu to stop expansion of settlements in the occupied territories; they made a mockery of their own policy when they vetoed a UNSC resolution passed with a strong majority in 2011, condemning Israel on the settlement issue. Mehmood Abbas, the PLO President, has been making backdoor attempts for membership of the UN which have been backed by the international community but are opposed by Israel and the US. Washington and Israel are also imprudently trying to block efforts at reconciliation between Al Fatah and Hamas, when, in reality, a negotiated settlement is much more likely to succeed if both factions agree.

The contours of a two-state solution of the Palestinian problem have been visible for some time and have garnered wide international support. These include Israel's return to the 1967 borders with any exceptions being compensated by the exchange of territory, a token right of return for the Palestinians, preservation of a status quo on the control of holy places, and a formula to share the city of Jerusalem. In return, the Arab nations should recognise Israel's right to exist and declare an end to hostilities. King Abdullah of Saudi Arabia had also proposed a solution more or less on similar lines. The European nations as well as Russia support a solution based on these principles. The US and Israel would certainly oppose any right of return and insist on complete demilitarisation of the created Palestinian state, but these issues would have to be negotiated. Hopefully President Obama, who once described the Palestinian-Israel conflict as a festering wound which poisons everything in the region, in his second term, can bring some pressure on the two adversaries for a negotiated settlement. This would go a long way in the quest for peace in the troubled region.

Indian Options

India's high stakes in the region are well known. Nearly 80 percent of our energy imports are from the region, and together, the GCC is our largest trading partner, with trade in excess of $120 billion. Numbering six million, the Indians comprise the largest expatriate community in the Gulf, remitting nearly $50 billion annually to the mother country. The potential of trade with the GCC countries is immense as they virtually import everything and the landed cost of goods from India is very low due to the region's proximity with the subcontinent as well as other factors. As India's manufacturing sector further develops in quality and quantity, we could run a trade surplus with the region despite the heavy import of energy. Similarly, the Foreign Direct Investment (FDI) coming from these countries to India is paltry compared to what they have been investing in the US and Europe, and could see a sizeable increase as the reforms gather momentum, factors relating to the ease of doing business improve (NIB, etc.), the regulatory mechanism strengthens, and India's bourses mature, attaining the standards of the developed countries. A free trade agreement with the GCC countries has also been in the pipeline for some time and is expected to be concluded shortly.

Iran too is geo-politically an important country for us, not only as a supplier of energy but also as a gateway to Afghanistan and the nations of the Central Asian region, where we have significant interests, not to mention ambitious joint projects like the development of Chabahar port, the gas pipeline and the North-South Transport Corridor. In the last decade and a half, our relations with Israel have also assumed importance as a major supplier of the state-of-the-art arms and other technologies. Hence, the United Progressive Alliance (UPA) government rightly initiated the Look West policy in 2005. A major challenge of our foreign policy has been to balance our relations with the three parties whose mutual relationship has been at best adversarial, and at worst, outright hostile. The Iran-Washington conflict has further compounded the problem as we seek close relations with both.

The 'Arab Spring' brought a further set of dilemmas to our foreign policy planners as we were required to choose sides, especially as a member of the UNSC, bringing to the fore the need for a carefully calibrated foreign policy for the region. We not only need to take into account the changing strategic factors such as the loss of equilibrium in the regional balance of power, widespread political awakening, and reduction in Washington's influence and prestige as a result of the Arab Spring and in its own shift of focus towards East Asia, but also the internal fault lines of West Asia and the Arab world. Therefore, a strong embrace of the so-called strategic autonomy which would serve our interests and principles becomes important. Thus far, our outlook, in accordance with our strategic culture of caution and circumspection, has served our interests well, with a few exceptions, Syria being one of them. We must appreciate that in the present environment of widespread political awakening in the Arab world, an authoritarian and brutal regime so completely dominated by a small religious minority, is unnatural and therefore, unstable, and its survival is highly unlikely over a period of time. We must back the SNC not only because we would be backing the winner, but because the vast majority of the Syrian people, including certain faction of Alawites are backing it, it is in line with our principles, and it has widespread support among the Arab nations as well as the international community. Our ambivalence on Syria could have repercussions on our relations with the GCC which is strongly backing the SNC, and the wide ranging interests therein.

We also need not fear the Islamist who have come to power or are a majority faction in most of the new governments formed in the wake of the Arab Spring as they are very keen to put up a moderate face and are desperate to be a part of the international system to improve their economic lot. Undoubtedly, there were economic factors like inequality, unemployment, widespread corruption, cronyism and the lack of meritocracy combined with political repression, and not Islamism, which brought about the revolutionary change. The Islamists had been around for decades but had not made much headway till the deteriorating economic factors provided them an opportunity to gain power because of their better grassroots support structure. They not only have to behave responsibly as the incumbents of authority but also have to improve the economic conditions of their people to survive, which is not possible without being responsible members of the international order. Whatever one has seen of them so far, it is evident that they have no intention of going the Taliban way. Therefore, India must extend a hand of friendship and continue business as usual with them, without any apprehensions of export of extremism.

The ever increasing profile of Turkey in the Islamic world has not been discussed in detail due to the paucity of space. The mildly Islamic regime of AKP led by the charismatic Tayyip Erdogan has won three elections on the trot in secular Turkey. The amazing turnaround in the Turkish economy and the revival of Islamic practices under Erdogan's stewardship, a phenomenon sometimes also referred to as post Islamism, has made Ankara a model to be emulated in the eyes of most of the newly emerging Islamist regimes. Turkey's deeper involvement in the affairs of West Asia and the Muslim world at large, including Iran and Afghanistan, its strongly pro-Palestinian stand, close relations with other Sunni Muslim powers, notably Pakistan and Saudi Arabia, and strong military profile have made it the most influential player in the region. India must cultivate closer political and economic relations with Ankara.

Another factor that India's policy-makers have to consider is the changing world energy scene. The US production of gas and oil has improved dramatically in the last few years through a large scale exploitation of the shale oil and gas deposits by the use of an old technology in a new, much improved garb, called 'fracking.' Though oil prices are holding, gas prices in the US have plummeted. Some experts are predicting that America is expected to become self-sufficient in energy by 2020. There are other countries outside the Middle East which have vast deposits of shale oil and gas like Australia, Poland and Argentina to name a few. The Australian deposits are so large that it could become the largest exporter of gas by 2030. These developments mean that the US is likely to gradually reduce its footprint in the Gulf over a period, though the Israel factor may still determine the size of its eventual presence and the speed of withdrawal. Though geo-political changes take time to implement, India must prepare to fill this vacuum to ensure its energy security by expediting development of its maritime forces, specially a reckonable blue water navy.

And, lastly, India must put in more vigour in its quest for an observer status in the Organisation of Islamic Cooperation. India is home to the second largest Muslim population in the world and as a pluralistic society, it is entitled to it. New Delhi's presence there would serve its interests well and will short circuit the efforts to malign its role in Kashmir. Saudi Arabia, as well as Iran, appears amenable to India's candidature as an observer and it may be an opportune moment to put in a little extra diplomatic effort to push our case.

Notes

1. Sakolsky, ed., *The United States and the Persian Gulf: Reshaping Security Strategy for the Post Containment Era* (Washington DC: NDU 2003), p. 35.
2. Shahram Chubin and Charles Tripp, "Iran-Saudi Arabia Relations and the Regional Order," *Adelphi Papers,* Vol.20 (IISS, Oxford University Press 1996), p.199.
3. James Mann, *The Rise of the Vulcans: The History of Bush's War Cabinet* (New York: Viking, 2004) describes them and their agenda in detail.
4. The word preventive was later replaced by preemptive due to the considerations of International Law.
5. "The Arab Spring: Implications for US Policy and Interests," p.9, Middle East Institute November 2011, www.mei.edu
6. See, "Global Powers Launch New Push to End Iran Nuclear Crisis," *The Guardian*, October 11, 2012.
7. See "As Fighting Rages , Clinton Seeks New Syrian Opposition," in *International Herald Tribune,* October 31, 2012.
8. Today, 2.5 million Palestinians live on 40 percent land of the West Bank, whereas Israeli settlers numbering only .350 million occupy nearly 60 percent of the land. The situation in East Jerusalem is becoming equally grim. Israel allows only 15 percent water to the nearly seven times population of the Palestinians.

11

Nuclear Forensics: An Overview

Stuti Banerjee

When one talks of nuclear material, the most common image that comes to mind is of material that is used in a nuclear power plant or in weapons. However, it is wrongly assumed that nuclear material is confined to just these two uses. Today, nuclear material can be found in hospitals where it is used in a number of medical procedures. It is also found in laboratories around the world and in industry, both medical and research. These materials can be lost, abandoned or stolen and they present a similar threat as when nuclear material from a secure government facility is unaccounted for. They present a more lucrative target for profit than secure government facilities due to the lack of security.

Nuclear or radioactive material has always to be under regulatory control, even when it is not being used or is being discarded. The first priority is always to determine its exact location at all times and ensure that it remains secure. A second, equally important task is identifying where these materials originated, both to address nuclear security vulnerabilities and support enforcement of national laws that prohibit acts of transfer of material without proper procedures established. A detailed record also helps the regulatory authorities to maintain accurate data of nuclear material that has been mined, used and how much waste has been generated, so as to make sure that it is disposed of responsibly. In all these actions, nuclear forensics plays a contributory role.

Nuclear Forensics

Nuclear forensics as a broad term can be used to explain the methods through which useful information is extracted from any nuclear or radioactive material. However, it is mostly used to describe the methods through which nuclear material, whether intercepted intact or retrieved through post explosion debris, is characterised (as to composition, physical condition, age, provenance, history) and interpreted (as to provenance, industrial history and implications) for a nuclear device design. This characterisation and interpretation results from field work to obtain representative samples of the device materials, laboratory analyses, computer modelling, and comparison with databases that contain empirical data from previous analyses of materials/ samples or that may be the result of numerical simulations of device performance or both.[1] It is the analysis of intercepted illicit nuclear or radioactive material and any associated material to provide evidence for nuclear attribution.

The key questions that nuclear forensics answers include are: What is the material? Does it pose a threat? Who is responsible for the loss? Where did the material originate? Have any national laws have been broken? As Klaus Mayer, head of the nuclear forensics programme at the European Commission's Institute for Transuranium Elements has stated, "We try to get the material to talk to us, to tell us how it was produced, when it was produced, for what purpose it was produced."[2] The goal of nuclear analysis is to identify forensic indicators in intercepted nuclear and radiological samples or the surrounding environment, for example, in containers or transport vehicles. It is the analysis of such samples to garner associated information that provides the evidence needed for determining the history of the sample material. Thus, nuclear forensics is both characterisation of the sample as well as interpretation of the data collected from the sample and its surroundings, as also reconstruction of a particular event involving the sample.[3] It requires a combination of technical data, relevant databases, and specialised skills and knowledge to retrieve, analyse, and interpret the data collected. As with any product, nuclear material also incorporates the attributes of the environment through which it passes. It carries with it the 'signatures' of the various processes that it has been through in the process of its refinement and use. These signatures deliver vital clues to the forensic experts for investigation. Features such as the isotopic content, chemical constituents, and physical shape tell the story of the material's origin, manufacture, use and age.

Nuclear forensics, when combined with law enforcement and intelligence data, can suggest or exclude the origin of materials and of a nuclear device or device designs, and thereby contribute to attribution of the material or device to its source. As part of the overall attribution process, it may be more or less helpful, depending on the circumstances. Recognition of the role and limitations of nuclear forensics and nuclear attribution is necessary if errors in both understanding and expectations are to be avoided.

During the first 50 years of the nuclear weapons era, radiochemistry techniques were developed and used to determine the characteristics (such as yield, materials used, and design details) of nuclear explosions carried out by the United States and by other countries. That application can still come into play if a nuclear explosion is detonated and debris recovered. Generally, however, the current principal emphasis is on applying nuclear forensic techniques to help attribute either intercepted materials or an actual explosion to its originators. This emphasis places different and new requirements on the technical analysis. In particular, it makes the availability of databases and libraries that include samples from various countries much more important than was the case when the principal application was diagnosing an explosion from a known source.

Nuclear forensics can come into play in several different scenarios. The first scenario is interception of contraband nuclear material or an intact device. A second scenario involves a "dirty bomb" or a Radiological Dispersal Device (RDD). Several possible scenarios could play out with RDDs. A third scenario involves a fizzle or primitive device, in which a nuclear explosion takes place but the yield is so low that destruction and contamination are limited to a few blocks. Such an event could cause hundreds to thousands of casualties well within the range of destruction of prior terrorist incidents. It would cause the death and destruction of thousands of lives and would require a major response. The fourth scenario is a nuclear explosion with yield in the kiloton range. Such an event would be a major disaster, unparalleled outside of war, with tens to hundreds of thousands of casualties and large-scale destruction if the explosion occurs in a city. Nuclear forensics could also be used for verification of nuclear stockpiles and states can seek its help to locate the source of an unidentified sample material.

The role of nuclear forensics, as every other branch of nuclear security, is to prevent the use of nuclear and radioactive material in a clandestine manner. However, if such an operation is successful, then the role of nuclear forensics changes too. It now has to use the vast army of trained personnel to collect samples from the site for analysis to establish a chain of custody. The samples have to be tested and examined so as to establish the people behind such attacks. Nuclear forensics is to also help establish if any further such detonations by rogue/splinter/terrorist organisations and groups or individuals would follow and how best to prevent them.

While answers may not be available immediately as to how such a device was made, transported and detonated at a particular place, nuclear forensics would, over a period of time, be able to give law enforcement officers and intelligence officials' valuable information and significant insights. However, it should be pointed out that information from a forensics examination is a continuous flow. Thus, investigators have to be prepared to get information gradually.

Nuclear forensics investigates not just high level threat scenarios but also those that seem to be of relatively low level such as trafficking in lower grade uranium. It is possible that such low level threats may lead to a more serious threat.

The Methodology of Nuclear Forensics

Any investigation by nuclear forensics starts from the moment the radioactive or nuclear material is found or apprehended by law enforcement officers or is unaccounted for, and unclaimed. The first step taken by the experts after securing the material is to draw up a list of questions. It is these questions of what, when, where, and who, that, when answered, provide them with the complete picture of the nature of the material, its origin and intended use. The answers would also tell the experts where the material was mined from, why it was mined, the plant where it was processed and who sold the material, who was the buyer and what was the end use for which it was bought. All these questions are asked to establish the source from where the material was diverted and how.

Like any other forensics investigation, nuclear forensics also involves the use of conventional testing methods on the samples collected. The investigators gather the maximum amount of information imbedded in the material seized. For example, they may be able to determine the morphology of the material, the structure of the material's components, the composition of traces in the material and its packing, the isotopic composition of the nuclear material itself and of minor constituents.[4] Finding the fingerprint of a nuclear material or a material that is related to it is the goal of nuclear forensics. This fingerprint is available because the nuclear material is able to attach and carry with it elements from its production process. The investigators also have to look at the various other substances that may have come in contact with the nuclear material. It is important to have cooperation between the two branches of forensics as the answering of questions about the immediate history of the device or material calls for traditional and modern skills such as fingerprinting, DNA profiling and electronic and digital decoding, not to mention close cooperation with law enforcement agencies and intelligence services. It is imperative for them to start working immediately.

The International Atomic Energy Agency (IAEA) has established such a plan which is the accepted norm. The plan provides information to frontline officers and first responders on how best to respond to events leading to the detection of unauthorised acts involving nuclear and radioactive material. The agency accepts the fact that most first responders would be law enforcement officers who would not have the required expertise to use the information effectively. While not addressing this issue in much detail apart from stating that they need to call for assistance, the agency has a detailed plan of action for the experts as well as the laboratories.

According to the IAEA action plan, for the inherent characteristics of nuclear material which define a certain fingerprint of the nuclear material, and for every sample, an analytical procedure has to be developed comprising the seizure, the nature of the material and of its packing, and other evidence. The analytical strategy includes a model action plan with several analytical techniques that reveal the characteristics of nuclear material and makes the investigated information comparable to reference data. The plan calls on the investigators to conduct their investigation according to the plan, which calls on them to:

A. *Secure the Site*

The goal of this step is to secure the incident site and to minimise the risks and hazards associated with radiological and nuclear leaks. It calls on the investigators to take control of the site as well as of the material. This is done with the view of making sure that the material is not further contaminated nor poses a hazard. It is also to minimise the number of people who come in contact with the material. The goal of this first step is to make sure that all the evidence is gathered and properly marked and preserved.

According to the IAEA action plan, the team that is deployed to any such site has within it a team leader or incident commander. It is the duty of the incident commander to make decisions regarding the team's methods of collecting evidence while keeping in mind the issues concerning public safety, environmental protection, the safety of the response personnel, and preservation and collection of evidence. Apart from the incident commander, the team ideally should comprise on-scene control personnel, a radiological assessment team, and an incident investigating officer who would head both, a conventional forensics team as well as a nuclear forensics team.

It is acknowledged that such a site would also yield evidence for conventional investigators. Thus, cooperation between the two is essential. The collection of traditional forensic evidence might interfere with the collection or analysis of radioactive/toxic evidence. Therefore, it is essential that appropriate thought be given to the relative timing of the collection of radioactive evidence versus traditional forensics evidence.

Collection of evidence is the first step in the forensics investigation. This evidence needs to be catgorised to judge which laws have been broken as well as how best to proceed with any further investigation. Thus, portable equipment such as gamma ray detectors are an essential part of any nuclear forensics team.

B. *Laboratory Analysis*

Further investigation is carried out at specialised national nuclear forensics laboratories. Here, the samples are once again to be checked thoroughly for hidden explosives before unpacking. The laboratories have to perform a detailed investigation on the evidence gathered, which would include visually gathering data from the evidence as well as processing it with the assistance of equipment. The data gathered is then interpreted to provide the information related to the evidence, in terms of the processes used to create or manufacture the material. This data is checked with the records available with the IAEA, which could help investigators to find out the source of the leak of the material, which could lead to, possibly, further investigations.

Once the investigation is over and the evidence presented to the concerned authorities for further action to be taken, the competent authority is put in charge of disposing of the material in the most appropriate and safe manner. [5]

Areas of Cooperation

A nuclear forensics investigation requires international cooperation to succeed. Any investigation, whether carried out on intercepted nuclear and radiological materials or on debris collected from a nuclear detonation, has an international dimension. For example, the uranium could have been mined in a country that has not necessarily processed the raw material and a third country could be the end recipient, whereas the theft could have occurred during transportation in the territory of another state. In such a situation, the investigators following the step-by-step journey of the uranium from the mine to the end destination would have to travel through all these countries to arrive at a conclusion, backed by evidence.

Nuclear forensics, as with the field of forensics in general, requires it to gather the evidence as quickly as possible. It is to make sure that the evidence is not contaminated or lost. To be able to achieve this goal, it needs equipment and trained people who are able to respond promptly and able to process the data accurately. It is based on their findings that decision-makers would be able to act and formulate a plan of action. Current techniques of gathering data derive largely from the nuclear weapons test programmes of the Cold War. Leveraging the Cold War infrastructure enabled a baseline forensics capability to be established very quickly, but it has the disadvantage of having developed a capability that relies largely on the science and technology that was developed during the nuclear testing era, with timelines and priorities sometimes very distinct from those of nuclear forensics. Current analysis methods need to keep pace with the developments and goals of nuclear forensics for the coming century.

To achieve optimum results, research and development has to be undertaken in certain key areas.

- **Equipment:** Advanced, automated nuclear forensics equipment should be developed to speed up the process of collection of data and analysis process. Significant research and development has to be carried out in the field to help nuclear forensics achieve results as quickly as possible so that the violators are brought to justice. Within this area, what requires the urgent attention of governments is the development of automated field deployable instruments that could provide an accurate analysis of the evidence in a shorter time span. The need is to develop an all-weather, rapid response, capable of meeting the requirements of all types of scenarios.

- **International and Up-to-date Database:** The requirement for cooperation in this field is beyond doubt and acknowledged by the states. They have to systematically provide information on all aspects of the nuclear cycle that they are processing to the IAEA. This would greatly help nuclear forensics teams to investigate theft. As of today, various groups and organisations in individual states hold information. However, consolidation of this information into one accessible nuclear forensics database and the development of tools to utilise it, needs cooperation between governments. The comparison of data from a particular intercept or terrorist event with data from databases supports three different objectives. One is to try to identify one or a few possible matches between the intercepted sample(s) or collected debris and entries in the database. Another is to rule out other possibilities as potential matches. A third objective is to enhance the preventive effect of nuclear forensics by making clear ahead of time the existence of internationally agreed methods of analysing and identifying nuclear materials to assist in the overall attribution process.
- **Sample Archives:** While a database would help in investigations, a sample archives with physical samples of nuclear material catalogued in the database would be of enormous help to the nuclear forensics investigators. The sample could contain more information than may have been analysed and incorporated into the database and would prove to be very useful in investigation under any circumstances. Sample archives consist of analysed samples, that is, small (grams or less) amounts of plutonium, uranium, and possibly other fissile materials from identified sources; corresponding databases contain an analysis of the history and composition of the sample from its originating source as well as indexed records of nuclear material properties, production locations, and use histories. Access to the physical samples is needed to validate the database, and to allow more detailed analyses, as needed. For maximum credibility and deterrent effect, it is important that the methods of analysis that correlate samples to their sources be internationally vetted and accepted.
- **Nuclear Device Modelling:** Cooperation among states should also extend to reverse engineered nuclear devices, based on the information available within the database.

- **Training of Personnel:** As has been pointed out above, nuclear forensics is a specialised subject. Today, there is an urgent need for states to bring together their scientific expertise and skills to increase the number of appropriately trained scientists. This can be achieved by strengthening the university programmes in the field and increasing interactions between students and laboratories and investigators.[6]

While there is no doubt that cooperation is the need of the hour, there are a few hindrances on the path that cannot be overlooked. This global database could take the form of a network of national nuclear "libraries" that could help in tracing the origins of materials seized in transit or used in an attack. Supporters of the effort are of the view that it would lead investigators to maintain tighter global control over sensitive substances and technologies, keeping them out of the hands of rogue nations or terrorist organisations. However, those who oppose such open disclosures are of the view that information such as the nature and composition of the uranium or plutonium used as nuclear fuel, how it is processed, all comprises commercial information closely guarded by nuclear power plant corporations for commercial reasons. They also feel that the information could be used by other states to perfect their weapon designs as well as nuclear weapon grade material. Thus, a system has to be agreed upon by all states that any information that is added to the database would be used only for the purposes of investigation.

States have to be encouraged to disclose their nuclear material. Material that is unaccounted for would, most likely, be of interest to terrorist groups and individuals. The primary motivation for disclosure of information and samples to this proposed database and for participation in the associated forensic analysis would be assurance of access to, or participation in, attribution assessments and the consequent political or military steps. Participation, cooperation, and transparency could greatly reduce the probability that one's own country would be mistakenly identified as the source of the material used in the attack.[7] While it is acknowledged that international cooperation will require time and effort, steps could be taken to develop bilateral arrangements that would benefit nuclear forensics investigators.

A good beginning has been made by the United States and Russia, the two largest nuclear weapon states and, perhaps, the two that have the largest number of nuclear weapons and largest amounts of nuclear weapons material in the world. The two states have taken the initiative to combat the problems of nuclear terrorism together. They can further expand this initiative by working closely with other nuclear weapons states to promote high standards of safety and propose a standard set of rules for liability and accountability from all states that have nuclear and radiological material. It has to be kept in mind that this accountability is to be confined not just to the physical safety of the material but would also extend to the personnel who would be guarding it. This would be done in such a way that they are not under any threat. It would also deter the experts in the area, including nuclear forensics scientists, from believing that they are above detection.

Cooperation in the field is, however, not restricted to those states that have nuclear weapons or nuclear weapon material. Cooperation would also be sought from those states that are part of the non-proliferation regime, in an effort to deter nuclear terrorism activities. Disclosure could be made a part of the various nuclear non-proliferation and disarmament treaties to further cooperation.

International Agreements Relevant to Nuclear Forensics

- **International Convention for the Suppression of Acts of Nuclear Terrorism (2005):** The convention provides for a definition of acts of nuclear terrorism and covers a broad range of possible targets, including those against nuclear power plants and nuclear reactors. Under its provisions, the alleged offenders must be either extradited or prosecuted. It also encourages states to cooperate in preventing terrorist attacks by sharing information and assisting each other in connection with criminal investigations and extradition proceedings. The treaty requires that any seized nuclear or radiological material is held in accordance with IAEA safeguards, and handled according to the IAEA´s health, safety and physical protection standards. The innovative provisions of the convention, which address the special nature of the problems that are likely to arise in post-crisis situations involving the unlawful use of nuclear or radioactive material, are set out within it. It addresses the issue of the modalities of return and storage upon the completion of any proceedings connected with an offence under the convention. Thus, a state party is required to return any radioactive material, device or nuclear facility, after consultations with the state parties concerned, in particular regarding modalities of return and storage, to the state party to which it belongs, or to the state party of which the national or legal person owning such radioactive material or device or facility is a national or resident or to the state party from whose territory it was stolen or otherwise unlawfully obtained. The Article also addresses the special regimes that apply with regard to the possession of radioactive or nuclear material.[8]
- **United Nations Security Council Resolution 1540 (2004):** On April 28, 2004, the United Nations Security Council unanimously adopted Resolution 1540 (2004) under Chapter VII of the United Nations Charter which affirms that the proliferation of nuclear, chemical and biological weapons and their means of delivery constitutes

a threat to international peace and security. The resolution obliges states, *inter alia*, to refrain from supporting, by any means, non-state actors from developing, acquiring, manufacturing, possessing, transporting, transferring or using nuclear, chemical or biological weapons and their delivery systems.

- Resolution 1540 imposes binding obligations on all states to adopt legislation to prevent the proliferation of nuclear, chemical and biological weapons, and their means of delivery, and establish appropriate domestic controls over related materials to prevent their illicit trafficking. It also encourages enhanced international cooperation on such efforts. On April 20, 2011, the Security Council adopted Resolution 1977, which reaffirms that the proliferation of nuclear, chemical and biological weapons and their means of delivery constitutes a threat to international peace and security, and extends the mandate of the 1540 Committee for a period of ten years to 2021. The Security Council, thus, recognises that full implementation of Resolution 1540 (2004) by all states is a long-term task that will require continuous efforts at national, regional and international levels.[9]
- **UN Security Council Resolution 1373 (2001):** Reacting to the event of September 11, 2001, the Security Council adopted this resolution, approving a wide-ranging, comprehensive resolution with steps and strategies to combat international terrorism. The council noted with concern the close connection among international terrorism and transnational organised crime, illicit drugs, money laundering and illegal movement of nuclear, chemical, biological and other deadly materials. In that regard, it emphasised the need to enhance the coordination of national, sub-regional, regional and international efforts to strengthen a global response to a threat to international security.[10]
- **Convention on the Physical Protection of Nuclear Material (CPPNM) (1987):** The convention is the only legally binding international instrument in the area of physical protection of nuclear material and one of the 13 international counter-terrorism instruments. It establishes measures related to the prevention, detection and punishment of offences related to nuclear material. It calls upon states to identify and make known to each other directly or through the IAEA, their central authority and point of contact, having responsibility for physical protection of nuclear material and for coordinating recovery and response operations in the event of any unauthorised removal, use or alteration of nuclear material or in the event of a credible threat thereof. States shall also cooperate and consult as appropriate, with each other directly or through international organisations, with a view to obtaining guidance on the design, maintenance and improvement of systems of physical protection of nuclear material in international transport.[11]

In 2005, an amendment to the convention was adopted. While the original convention had called on states to provide physical protection to nuclear material during transportation, the amendment called on states to protect nuclear facilities and material in peaceful domestic use, storage and transport. It also provides for an expansion in cooperation among states regarding measures that could be used to apprehend criminals and locate and recover nuclear and radiological material. (The amendment is pending till two-thirds of the states party to the convention ratify it.)

Nuclear Forensics as Deterrence

Such thorough investigation is also hoped to deter states from nuclear materials trafficking and coveted use.

The term nuclear forensics came into importance in the 1990s with the rise in the number of incidents that involved the smuggling of nuclear and radioactive materials. However, that is not to say that the methods as used by nuclear forensics teams across the world are also new. It is well documented that similar methods, as applied today by nuclear forensics experts, were used by the Allies to continuously check the contamination level of soil and water bodies and the atmosphere as a result of the German military's experimentation with nuclear and radiological materials during World War II. It would be safe to say that methods that were developed then, have formed the bases for modern-day nuclear forensics techniques, albeit with major developments.

With terrorism gaining prominence during the decade of the Nineties, a need was felt for developing expertise in the field of nuclear forensics. Since 1995, the IAEA has maintained a database of cases that involve the illegal transfer, unauthorised use, and procession of nuclear and radioactive material. It is an official record of all incidents that have been reported by member states or have been detected to be cases of illegal trafficking. Since illicit trafficking and theft of nuclear material can lead to nuclear proliferation and the possible construction of improvised nuclear devices or radiological dispersal and exposure devices, measures to detect and respond to such acts are essential components of a comprehensive nuclear security programme.[12] Since its inception, the IAEA has been able to confirm 2,200 cases that have been reported to it.

The other problem that is currently being faced by the states is the problem of '*orphaned sources*'. According to the United States Nuclear Regulatory Commission, orphaned sources are those that have been abandoned or are being ignored by their legitimate owners. Security for them cannot be assured or is at the minimum, as required by law. They can pose a hazard to the health and safety of the general population. These sources are also called orphaned sources that are in the possession of individuals who are not authorised to have them. These sources can easily be diverted for malicious use.

The need for nuclear forensics is now being explored in the field of deterrence. It has always been said that prevention is better than cure. Applying a similar principle, it is being acknowledged that nuclear forensics could be better utilised as a preventive measure rather than be restricted for use in the aftermath of a situation. To be able to preempt a situation, to be able to control its outcome or to prevent it from happening at all, especially with regard to nuclear or radioactive material, would be a major achievement. It has been recognised that 'nuclear leakage' would be one of the biggest threats to the non-proliferation movement and to the security of states. Widespread knowledge of techniques to make a crude bomb and easy availability of this knowledge has meant that it is well within the reach of a terrorist organisation to make such a device if they are able to acquire the raw materials for it. While knowledge cannot be controlled, states have to take all available steps to make procurement of raw materials as difficult as possible.

Deterrence has been a means through which nation-states have ensured their security. Deterrence means that one adversary is well aware that the consequences of its actions would be countered by a response that would be 'credible'. The theory explores the conditions under which states can deter another opponent from taking an action that is contrary to that state's interests. Most often, deterrence involves the threat to use force in response to such action. In the case of nuclear deterrence, this action is compounded by a devastating outcome. It has also been questioned if a state can take devastating counter nuclear attacks against another state that is perceived to be responsible, especially when the evidence against the adversary might be less than unequivocal. Terrorists do not belong to one particular country or control any territory and are more often than not willing to die for their cause. The traditional deterrence concepts of states would prove to be inadequate to deal with them.

Thus, states have to look beyond and come up with new strategies. For example, when states have to involve themselves with intercepting nuclear materials at an earlier stage, the response against a supplier could be more acceptable as it would be backed with evidence. It would also not court controversy and, thereby, would be viewed as more credible. Earlier intervention allows decision-makers more time to craft a broader and more measured response. However, a new deterrent strategy would be effective for some situations only. What would further strengthen the deterrent regime would be cooperation between the nations.

While there are more nuclear scientists across the world and still more learning the art, there are very few who would be able to counter the emergency situation that arises out of the detonation of a nuclear bomb in the heart of a major city. Thus, to be able to respond quickly and to know what procedures need to be followed, nuclear forensics experts have to be trained. They have to be provided with the equipment and laboratories that would aid in processing the various elements to present the complete data for further action. Today, terrorists have the option of procuring nuclear and radioactive material from close to 40 countries that have these in one form or the other. While it is the responsibility of the states to ensure the security of such materials, in a worst case scenario, they can be used by a terror group to make a crude bomb. In such a situation, it would be the responsibility of nuclear forensics to provide the clues on which the authorities would act.

It is the aim of the nuclear forensics teams to encourage nations to ensure the security of their nuclear and radiological materials or weapons to prevent unwanted transfer to a third party through loss of control. It is also to help trace the source of the illicit material and identify smuggling networks. A major aspect of nuclear forensics is to discourage states from providing nuclear material to terrorists.

Nuclear material can be divided into five general categories:

- **Unirradiated Direct Use Material:** This is the best material to build nuclear weapons. It is the most widely desired material for states and unlawful organisations that would like to acquire a nuclear weapon.
- **Irradiated Direct Use Material:** This is found usually in spent fuel. It requires more processing time than the unirradiated direct use material.
- **Alternative Material:** This includes sources such as research reactors which are different from commercial reactors. They can be located at universities, institutions and private companies and they do not have the same level of security as is provided to a commercial reactor. When such reactors shut down, the fuel that remains as well as the waste has to be accounted for and secured.
- **Indirect Use Material:** All nuclear material except direct use material. It includes: depleted, natural and low enriched uranium, and thorium, all of which must be further processed in order to produce direct use material.
- **Commercial Radioactive Sources:** These are more widely available. They are of use in such things as smoke detectors, and in radiotherapy. Till now, governments had not paid much attention to the safety of such sources. However, it is increasingly becoming clear that such sources also need to be secured. They might or might now be used for the purposes of building a crude bomb or a device, but can pose a health hazard to the general population. A case in point was the health hazard created by the wrongful disposal of equipment that had radioactive material held by Delhi University.

It has to be kept in mind that a nuclear forensics investigation involving the interdiction of nuclear or radiological material prior to a detonation differs from the post-detonation situation in two important respects. First, the samples available for laboratory analysis retain their original chemical and physical structure, and, second, for intercepts of small quantities such as most of the ones that have occurred, the speed of analysis leading to attribution is generally not a critical issue.

It is unfortunate but nuclear material lawfully gained is very poorly accounted for. It is for this reason that nuclear forensics has gained such an important status. The teams have to not only help prevent the theft of radioactive and nuclear material but also to help fit the jigsaw puzzle together in the event of any incident, be it a detonation of a crude nuclear bomb or theft of material.

The Goal of Nuclear Forensics

Nuclear forensics does not have rules that can be applied to all situations and all evidence. While the broad outlines of working remain the same, it is, largely, an interactive method through which the results of one analysis are added to the guiding principles of the future analysis.

Nuclear forensics and nuclear forensics interpretation have become increasingly important tools in the fight against illicit trafficking in nuclear and radiological material. However, nuclear forensics is a method of investigation that is restricted to not just the field of nuclear trafficking. It is also used in the field of collection of data for environmental sampling for various agencies, and verification of nuclear arms treaties. It is also immensely useful in helping implement various arms control treaties. It can be used for detecting if nuclear tests have been conducted by states, when monitoring compliance with the 1963 Partial Test Ban Treaty. Similarly, within the context of the 1996 Comprehensive Test Ban Treaty (CTBT), forensics can help determine a test through the potential origins of particles and gases in the air. The IAEA can also apply these techniques for the process of verification of the age of samples and the production process for their database or to collaborate if the information given on the sample by a particular state is authentic or not. Its helps in the commitment to hold fully accountable any state, terror group or non-state actor that supports or enables terrorist efforts to obtain or use weapons of mass destruction, whether by facilitating, financing or providing expertise or safe haven for such efforts. Thus, nuclear forensics is part of nuclear accountability also.

Owing to the significant capital costs of the equipment and the specialised expertise of the personnel, work in the field of nuclear forensics has been restricted so far to a handful of national and international laboratories. In fact, there is only a limited number of specialists who have experience working with nuclear material and affiliated evidence. Most of the laboratories that have the requisite equipment, personnel and experience to perform nuclear forensics analysis are participants in the Nuclear Smuggling International Technical Working Group (ITWG). Their good offices can be used by all members of the IAEA. Consequently, there is a need to disseminate information on an appropriate response to incidents of illicit trafficking of nuclear and other radioactive material, including a comprehensive approach to gathering evidence that meets the appropriate legal standards and to developing insights into the sources and routes of contraband nuclear and radioactive material.[13]

States can help the IAEA in its efforts to put roadblocks on the path of individuals and groups that sell and buy nuclear material through illegal sources. The law enforcement agencies of the various states have to identify smuggling routes, and block them. This would have to be a continuous process and one in which the enforcement agencies have to always try to stay ahead of the smugglers.

Governments have to take a number of steps to strengthen the institutions of nuclear forensics in their countries as well as take an active part in the initiatives as launched by the IAEA. All governments have to commit to pursuing and using the full force of the law to stop such illegal acts. Cooperation is necessary as most cases of illegal trafficking involve at least two nations or more. In such a scenario, national and international laws have to be streamlined so that it is possible to prosecute criminals to the full extent of the law. States have to be determined to pursue the investigation. Doing so would also help in detecting future instances of terrorism and would also act as deterrence for nuclear terrorist activity.

The need for cooperation among nation-states is not limited to just the judicial sphere but extends to cooperation in developing the field of study as well. There is a limited number of experts in the field; the equipment for detection and analysis as well as setting up of laboratories is an expensive task. In such a situation, for the subject to develop, states have to come together to help each other. There is need for more bilateral as well as multilateral initiatives to develop sound research and development facilities, establish norms for working on cases which span boundaries, advancing best practices in conducting the investigations, along with establishing a global database.

States have to accept that issues related to nuclear security and safety are not confined to a territory but have a universal impact. The best way to combat nuclear trafficking, nuclear terrorism and proliferation is through a robust system that is able to prevent such acts through detection, and respond and deter them through prosecution. All of these are aspects of nuclear forensics.

Notes

1. "Nuclear Forensics, Role, State of the Art and Program Needs: Report of Joint Working Group of the American Physical Society and the American Association for the Advancement of Science", URL_ https://cstsp.aaas.org/files/complete.pdf, Accessed on October 23, 2012.
2. IAEA, "Nuclear Forensics: Key to Ensuring Nuclear Security", URL-http://www.iaea.org/newscenter/news/2012/nuclearforensics.html. Accessed on October 23, 2012.
3. IAEA, "Nuclear Forensics Support: Reference Manual", IAEA Nuclear Security Series#2, Technical Guidance, Vienna, 2006, URL-hhtp://www-pub.iaea.org/MTCD/publications/pdf/pub1241_web.pdf. Accessed on October 21, 2012.
4. Klaus Mayer, Maria Wallenius and Ian Ray, "Nuclear Forensics—A Methodology Providing Clues on the Origin of Illicitly Trafficked Nuclear Materials", URL http://radchem.nevada.edu/classes/nfss/readings/kristo/Nuclear%20Forensics%20-%20Methodology%20Providing%20Clues.pdf. Accessed on October 29, 2012.
5. The points have been referred from IAEA, *Nuclear Forensic Support: Technical Guide Reference Manual* (Vienna: IAEA, 2006), pp. 11-23
6. The points have been referred from n. 1.
7. Ibid.
8. IAEA, "New Convention Against Nuclear Terrorism Bolsters Global Framework", URL- http://www.iaea.org/newscenter/news/2005/conv_nuclterror.html and United Nations, "International Convention for the Suppression of Acts of Nuclear Terrorism", URL- http://untreaty.un.org/cod/avl/ha/icsant/icsant.html. Accessed on November 10, 2012.
9. United Nations, 1540 Committee "United Nations Security Council Resolution 1540 (2004)" URL- http://www.un.org/en/sc/1540/. Accessed on November 10, 2012.
10. United Nations Security Council, "Security Council Unanimously Adopts Wide-Ranging Anti-Terrorism Resolution; Calls For Suppressing Financing, Improving International Cooperation, Resolution 1373 (2001) Also Creates Committee to Monitor Implementation", Press Release, URL- http://www.un.org/News/Press/docs/2001/sc7158.doc.htm. Accessed on November 10, 2012.
11. IAEA, "Convention on Physical Protection of Nuclear Material (CPPNM) and Amendment Thereto," URL- http://www-ns.iaea.org/conventions/physical-protection.asp?s=6&l=42 and IAEA, "The Convention on the Physical Protection of Nuclear Material", URL- http://www.iaea.org/Publications/Documents/Infcircs/Others/inf274r1.shtml. Accessed on November 10, 2012.
12. IAEA, *Combating Illicit Trafficking in Nuclear and other Radioactive Material* (Vienna: IAEA, 2007), p. 01.
13. IAEA, *Nuclear Forensic Support: Technical Guide Reference Manual* (Vienna: IAEA, 2006), pp. 01-02.